MW01630550

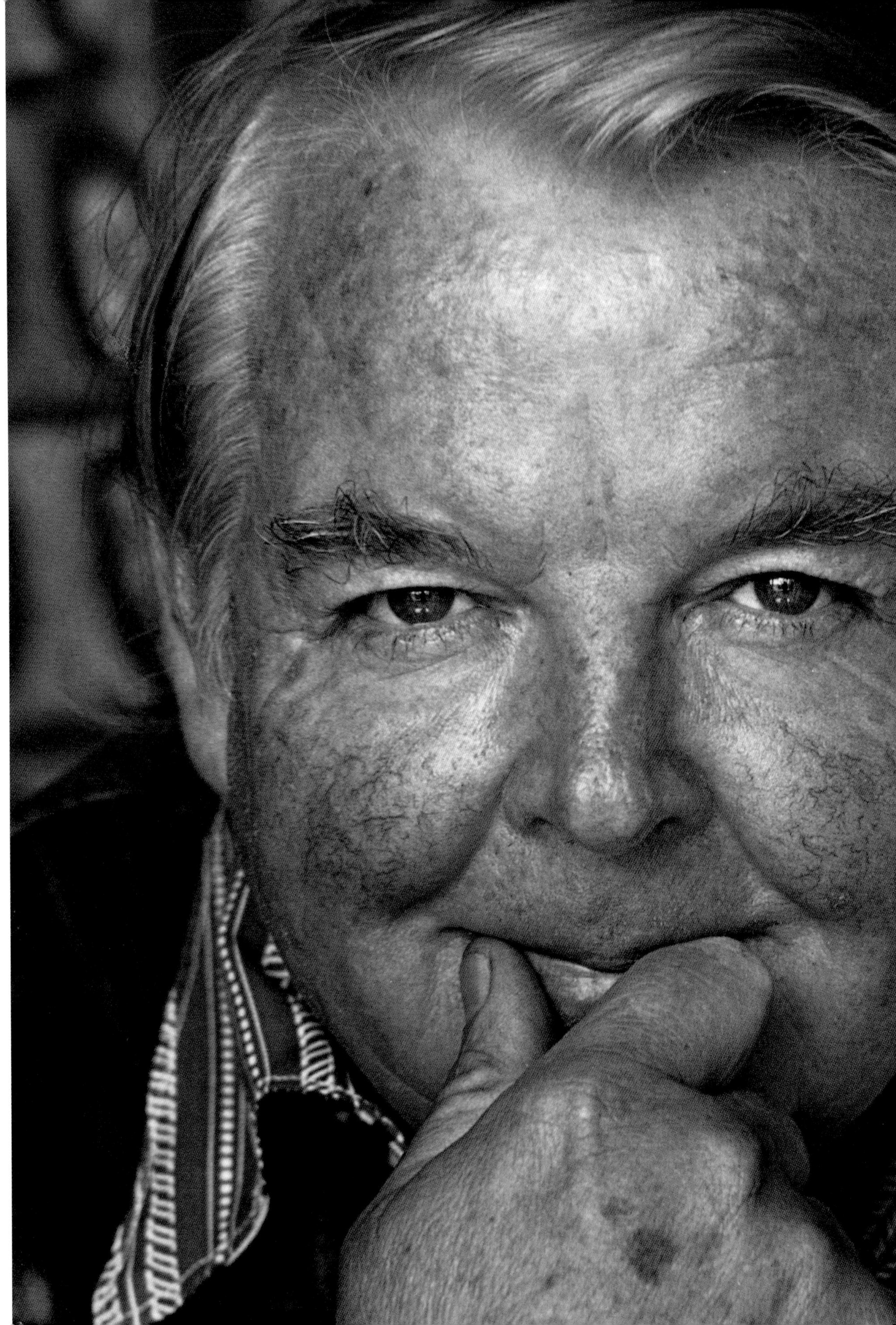

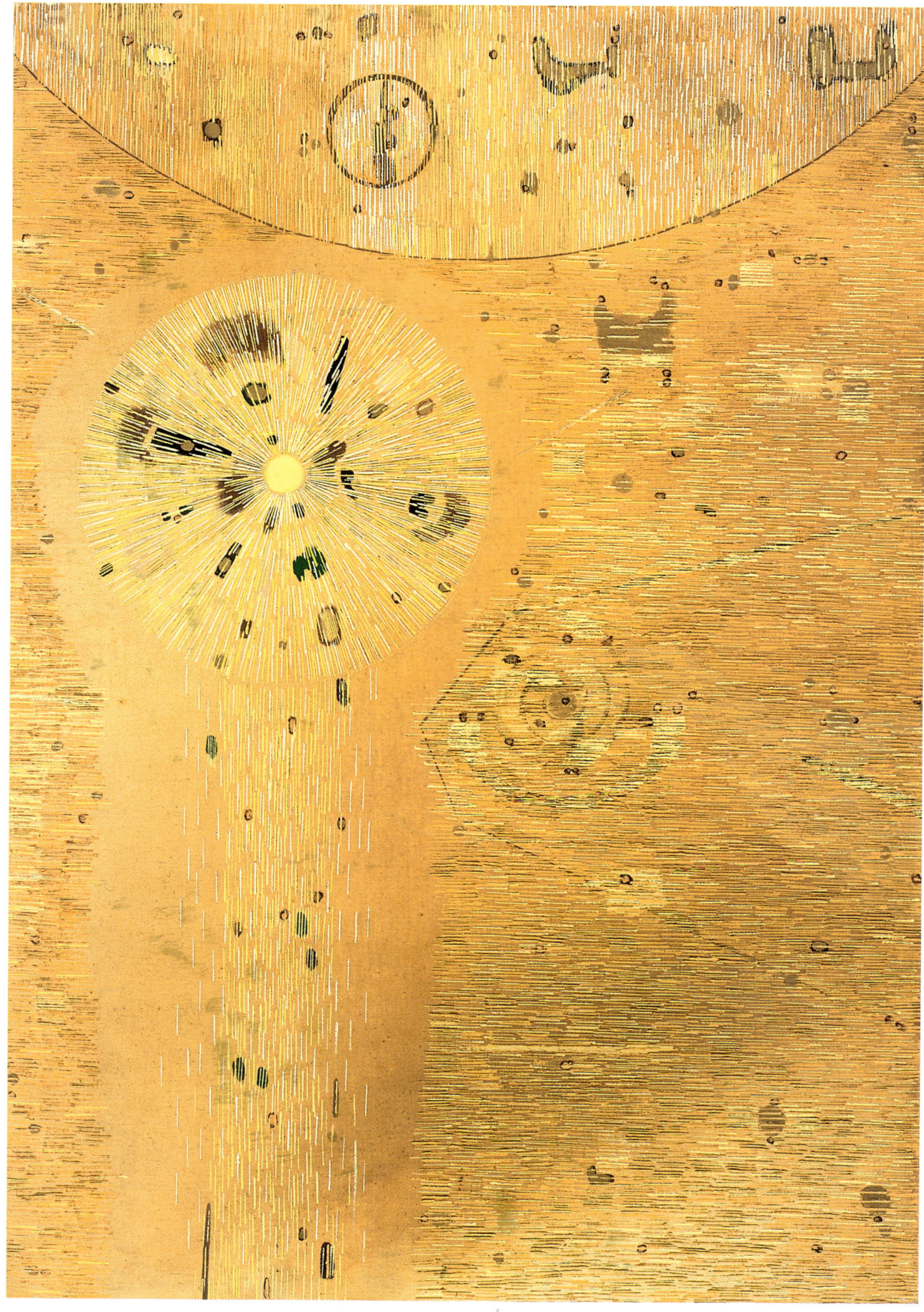

# Lee Mullican
## An Abundant Harvest of Sun

Carol S. Eliel

*with contributions by*
Amy Gerstler
Lari Pittman

Los Angeles County Museum of Art

This catalogue was published in conjunction with the exhibition *Lee Mullican: An Abundant Harvest of Sun*. The exhibition was organized by the Los Angeles County Museum of Art and was made possible in part by The Andy Warhol Foundation for the Visual Arts, the Herta and Paul Amir Art Foundation, and The Judith Rothschild Foundation. The catalogue is supported in part by the Pasadena Art Alliance.

EXHIBITION ITINERARY
Los Angeles County Museum of Art
November 10, 2005–February 20, 2006

Grey Art Gallery, New York University
April 25–July 15, 2006

PUBLISHED BY
Los Angeles County Museum of Art
5905 Wilshire Boulevard
Los Angeles, California 90036

DISTRIBUTED BY
D.A.P./Distributed Art Publishers, Inc.
155 Sixth Avenue
New York, New York 10013
(800) 338-2665
www.artbook.com



ISBN 0-87587-194-1

Director of Publications: Stephanie Emerson
Editor: Sara Cody
Designer: Sandy Bell
Rights and Reproductions: Piper Severance
Rights and Reproductions Supervisor: Cheryle T. Robertson
Photographer: Steve Oliver
Photography Supervisor: Peter Brenner
Printed and bound in Italy by Graphicom

JACKET FRONT: *Space* (detail), 1951, Los Angeles County Museum of Art
JACKET BACK: *Untitled*, 1950s, Luchita Mullican
FRONTISPIECE: Lee Mullican, c. 1980
TITLE PAGE: *Peyote Candle*, 1951, Luchita Mullican

# Contents

# Foreword

One of the most important aspects of LACMA's mission is to "interpret works of art representing the highest levels of achievement from all historical periods and cultures." The museum considers the exhibition of art made in southern California to be a very special part of that mission. LACMA is therefore proud to have organized *Lee Mullican: An Abundant Harvest of Sun* and to offer the public a comprehensive view of an extraordinary artist and influential teacher whose work has heretofore been unduly neglected, in large measure because he chose to work in Los Angeles at a time when New York was considered the epicenter of the American art world. In reassessing Mullican's paintings, drawings, and sculptures, not only are we better able to comprehend the history of art and culture in our own city and state, but we can also achieve a richer understanding of art made in the second half of the twentieth century all across the United States.

*Guardian of the Modern*, 1979, Los Angeles County Museum of Art

LACMA would like to thank The Andy Warhol Foundation for the Visual Arts, the Herta and Paul Amir Art Foundation, The Judith Rothschild Foundation, and the Pasadena Art Alliance for their generous sponsorship of *Lee Mullican*. The museum is likewise grateful to the many museums and private collectors (listed on p. 124) who kindly agreed to lend works to both the Los Angeles and New York venues of the exhibition. Finally, thanks are due to curator of Modern and Contemporary Art Carol S. Eliel, whose insight gave rise to the show's concept and whose scholarship and determination brought it to fruition.

Andrea L. Rich
*President and Wallis Annenberg Director*
Los Angeles County Museum of Art

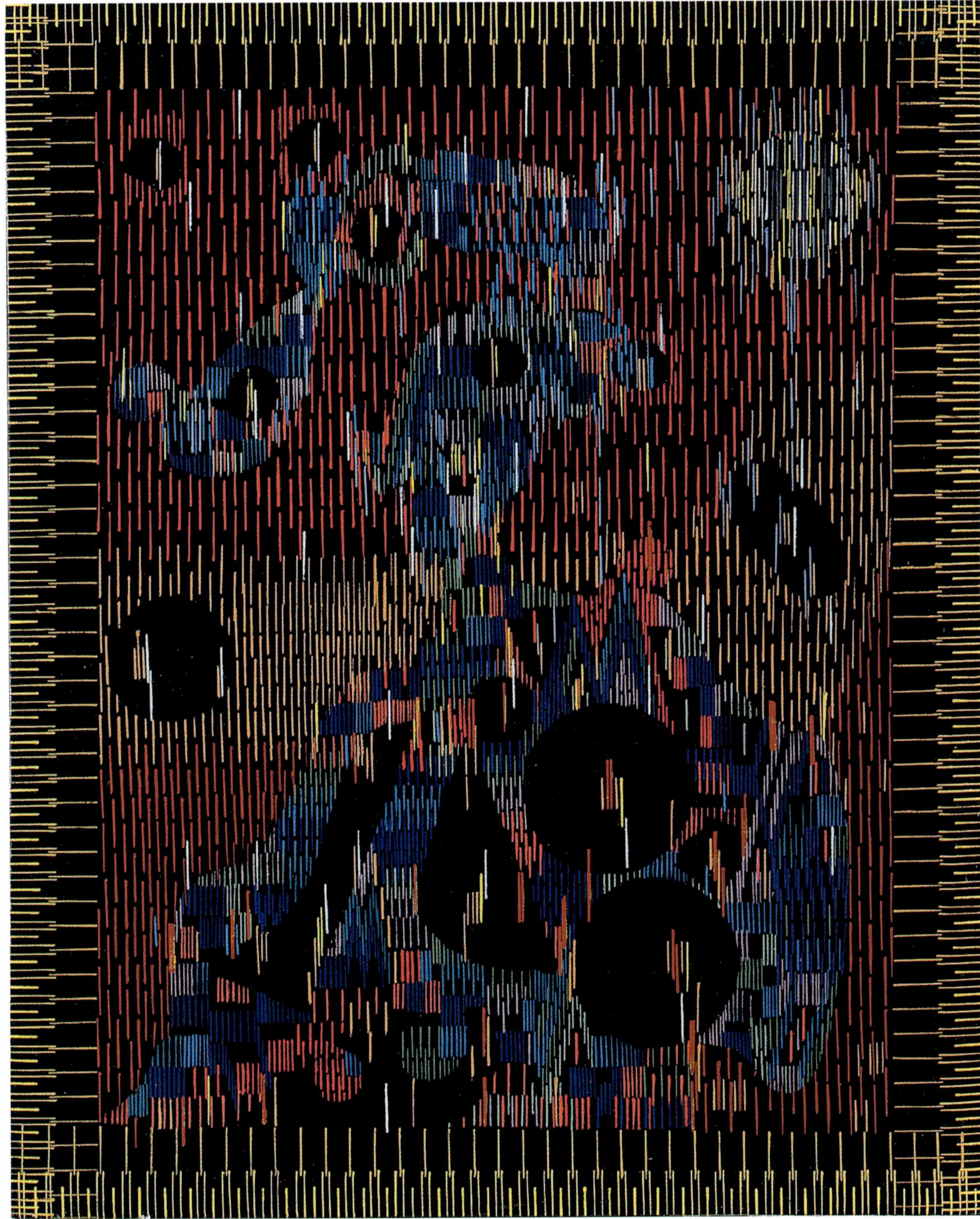

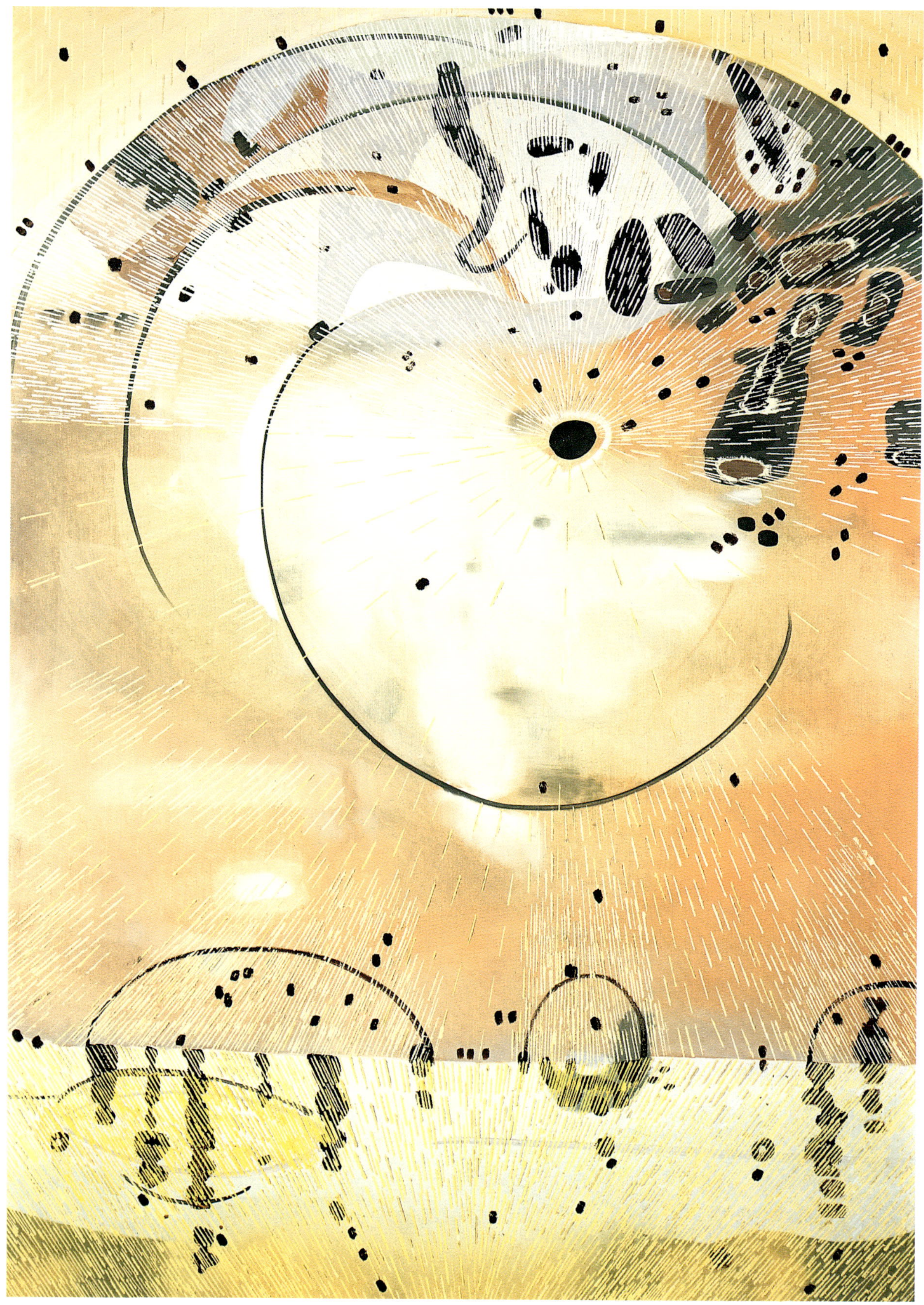

CAROL S. ELIEL

# His Feet Planted on Virgin Soil, His Head in the Clouds

In 1980, looking back over his artistic practice, Lee Mullican explained:

> I explored inner-space, outer-space. There were walks in landscapes that appeared from the depths of the mind. I found a new planet and there were galaxies to explore. There was an energy that moved from canvas to canvas and drawing to drawing. I am not sure this energy has ever been fully understood. Mystery of everything and a vision of all.[1]

The richness of Mullican's imagination, as evidenced by this statement, coupled with the breadth of his interests gave rise to a body of work created over some fifty years that simultaneously engages the eye, the mind, and the heart. His paintings, drawings, and sculptures—images of great beauty and shamanistic power—reveal not only a fine hand but also a broad range of influences and references, including Native American art and culture, modern art (particularly Surrealism), Zen Buddhism, Hinduism, and beyond. Throughout his work Mullican addressed the apparent conflict between abstraction and figuration, the absorption of Western and non-Western sources, and the relationship between form and content. In short, throughout his career he addressed issues central to the art of the second half of the twentieth century.

FIG. 1
*The Measurement*, 1951, Orange County Museum of Art

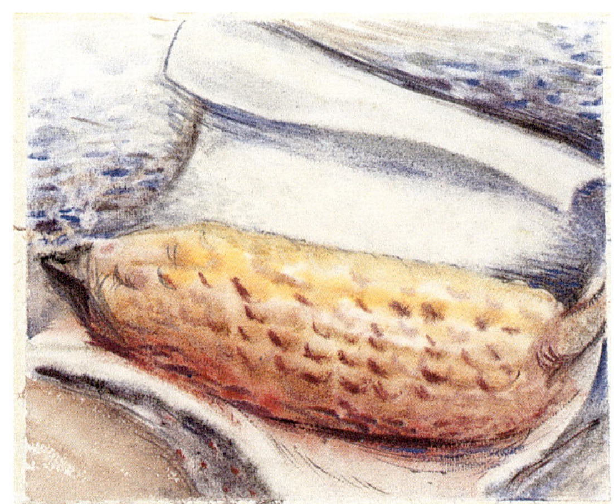

FIG. 2
*Still Life*, 1939, watercolor on paper, 10 x 8½ in., Fred Jones Jr. Museum of Art, University of Oklahoma

## Early years

The third of four children of a businessman and an amateur painter, Alva Lee Mullican was born on December 2, 1919 in Chickasha, Oklahoma, just south of Oklahoma City. Mullican literally grew up with Native American culture; as he later described it, Chickasha in the 1920s and '30s "was just a small town in Indian territory, with many Indian tribes centered in that area."[2] Already at an early age Mullican was interested in both theater and, inspired by his mother's oil painting kit, art.[3] He was never particularly absorbed in the academic aspects of his schooling but was instead drawn to pictures of all sorts: "Imagery was more important to me than anything."[4] After graduating from high school in Chickasha, Mullican enrolled at Abilene Christian College in 1937; in the school library Mullican became familiar with modern art through books on van Gogh and Picasso and articles on Cubism and Surrealism in magazines such as *Time* and *Life*. The college was quite conservative, however, and with his growing interest in modernism, Mullican came to the conclusion after two years at Abilene Christian that he "had to go somewhere else."[5]

After spending time during the summer of 1939 in Santa Fe, where nature and the landscape made a great impression on him, Mullican transferred that fall to the University of Oklahoma, enrolling in basic drawing and painting classes (fig. 2). Although he was able to work there for the first time from a live model, Mullican already was interested in nonobjective painting. He realized that his predilections were atypical for artists working in those years in the heartland of the United States. "I was not interested in what Thomas Hart Benton was doing or John Steuart Curry," he recalled, saying that those regionalists "didn't interest me in the least"; instead, he found that he was most interested in working with abstraction.[6] It was the freedom of abstraction that particularly appealed to Mullican, the fact that an abstract painting could "be upside down, it can be any way, and it's still okay."[7] At the same time he was fascinated with Surrealism, particularly the figurative Surrealism of Salvador Dali, which he called "far out" and "part of the modern age."[8] The seeds of Mullican's dual interest in both abstraction and figuration were thus planted already in his student years. During this same period he discovered modern music, foreign films, and the writings of Gertrude Stein; he became increasingly familiar with the work of Picasso; and he came to the realization that he "wanted to be different" from what he encountered in Oklahoma.[9] Mullican likewise became aware of the Southwest's influence as an environment on the art he was producing, particularly in terms of the vibrant colors of the land and the skies.[10]

Mullican also realized that he wanted to attend art school—not just a university with an art department—and so in 1941 transferred to the Kansas City Art Institute. As a teaching institution this too proved unsatisfying to the budding artist: "Lo and behold, when I got there the abstract world that I was interested in was not in Kansas City either."[11] He nonetheless profited from the excellent museum there—the nearby William Rockhill Nelson Art Gallery (as the Nelson-Atkins Museum was then called) with its outstanding collection of Chinese art—as well as a large Picasso exhibition that same year.[12]

### Army years

After graduating from the Kansas City Art Institute, Mullican returned to Chickasha, only to be inducted into the army almost immediately in June 1942. Following basic training in Missouri, he was sent to the army's topographic school in Fort Belvoir, Virginia. This proved to be a fortuitous posting; not only did he learn to make

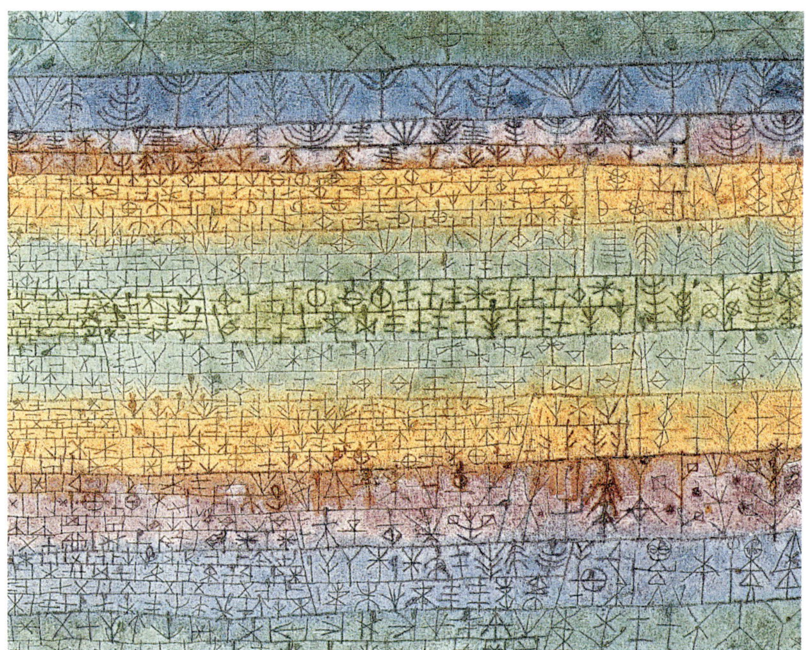

FIG. 3
Paul Klee, *Tree Nursery*, 1929, oil on canvas with incised gesso ground, 17¼ x 20⅝ in., The Phillips Collection, Washington, D.C.

maps there—which became enormously important for his later work—but he also was able to visit museums in Washington and Baltimore and take weekend leaves in New York City. "It was at the Phillips Gallery in Washington, D.C. at that time that I saw my first Paul Klees, a whole large exhibition of Paul Klee. . . . I never really got over that," he recalled. "That was one of the great revelations. . . . The sense of what he could do by making a mark, and then making another mark, and the use of color and abstraction . . . was a great influence" (fig. 3). Mullican was also impressed by the power that Klee was able to communicate even in very small works, saying that their scale "really attracted me."[13] Another lasting influence was that of Morris Graves, whose work Mullican first saw at this time at The Museum of Modern Art in New York. Graves, based in Seattle, was included in Dorothy Miller's *Americans 1942* exhibition at MoMA, and works such as *Purification*, included in the show and illustrated in its exhibition catalogue (fig. 4), seem to have had a material impact on Mullican's postwar mineral drawings (fig. 5).

In 1943 Mullican was assigned to Camp Maxey (near Paris, Texas) as part of a topographic battalion; his duty was to draw maps based on aerial photographs. Supplied with as much paper and ink and as many pens and pencils as he wanted, Mullican drew incessantly, not only while on duty but also for pleasure. "I was influ-

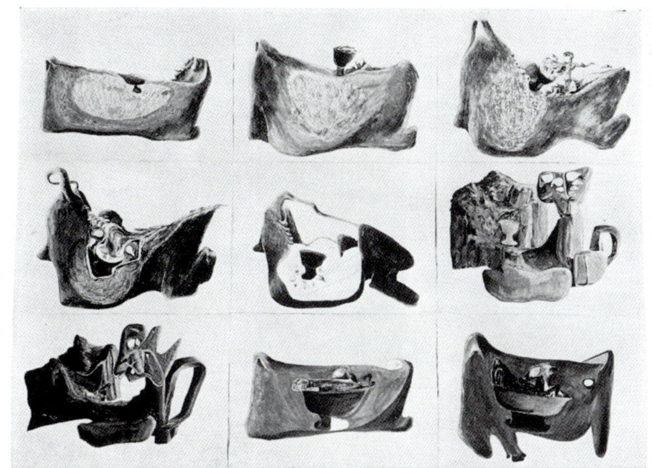

FIG. 4
Morris Graves, *Purification*, series of nine gouaches, 12½ x 16⅛ in. each, illustrated in The Museum of Modern Art's 1942 catalogue, *Americans 1942: 18 Artists from 9 States*.

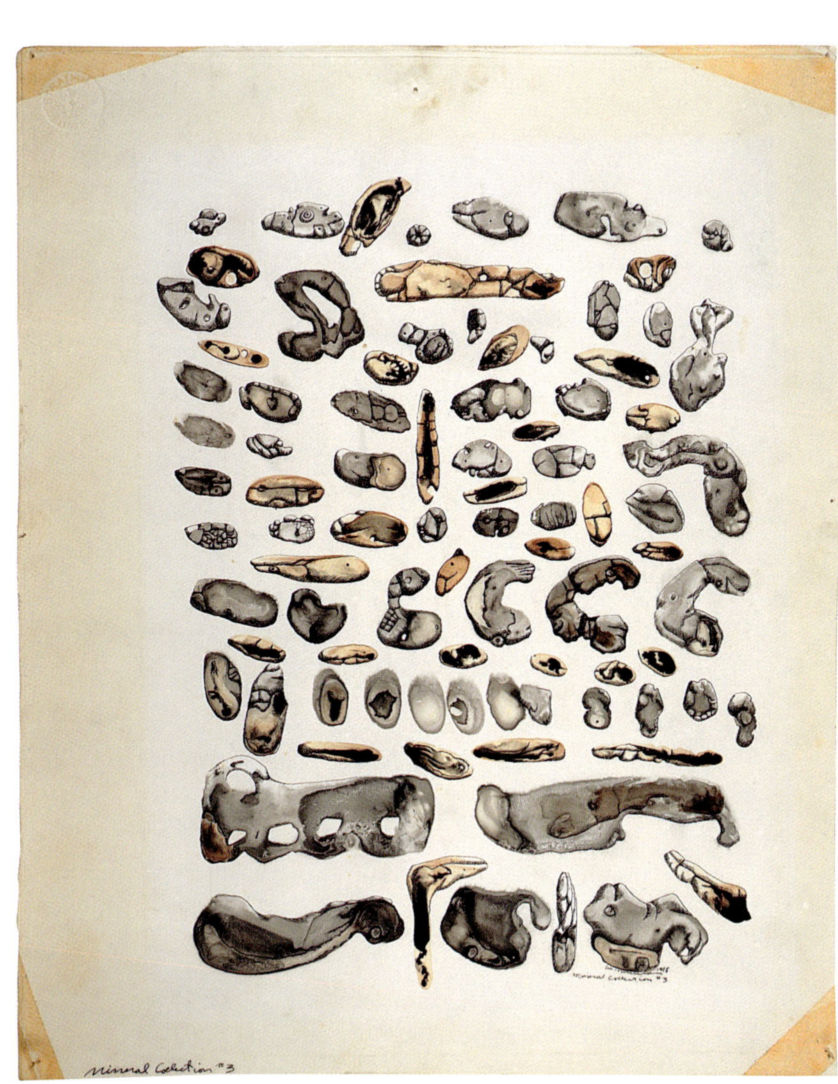


FIG. 5
*Mineral Collection #3*, 1948, Weatherspoon Art Museum, The University of North Carolina at Greensboro

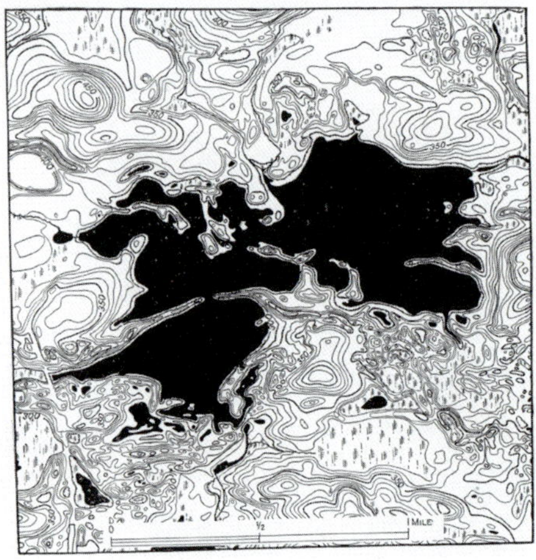

FIG. 6
Topographical map, U.S. Army, early 1940s

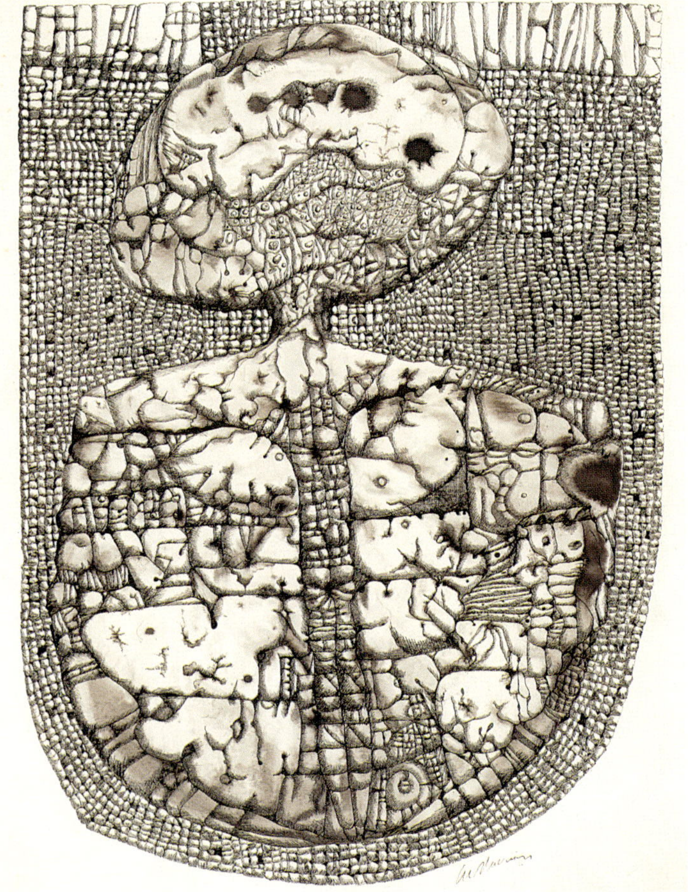

FIG. 7
*Personnage*, 1947, Los Angeles County Museum of Art

enced by techniques and materials which were a part of mapmaking. A lot of the drawing was done with crowquill pens, very fine line," he recalled. "For years after the war, I did a lot of drawing in this style and with this kind of technique."[14]

Mullican was subsequently transferred to Desert Center, California (not far from Palm Springs), where he started working with topographic mapping. While none of his topographic or contour drawings from this time have been identified, contour drawings made for the military during the same general period (fig. 6) suggest how influential such work was on Mullican's drawings of the immediate postwar years (figs. 7–9). Mullican remembers this period as one with "more time to draw, more time to think. . . . [I] made my first trips into Los Angeles, first trips into Hollywood, first into jazz clubs." He also appreciated the freedom to leave the base and spend time enjoying the natural environment of the desert.[15]

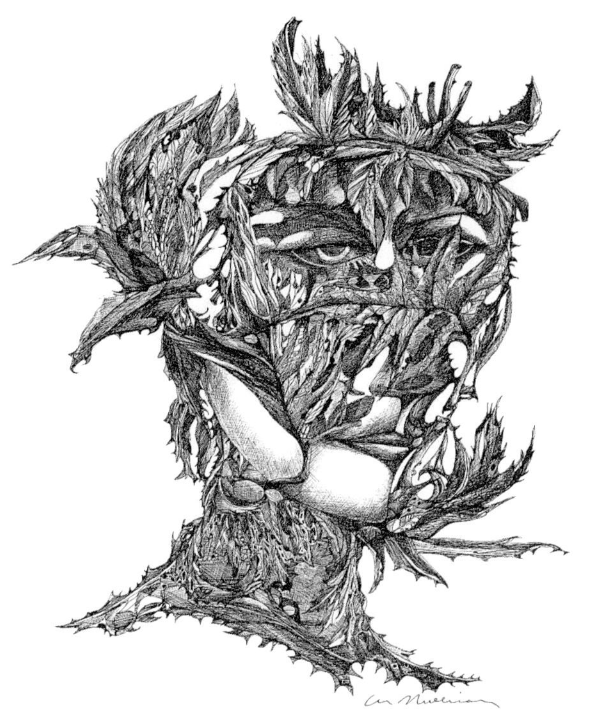

FIG. 8
*Untitled*, 1945, Los Angeles County Museum of Art

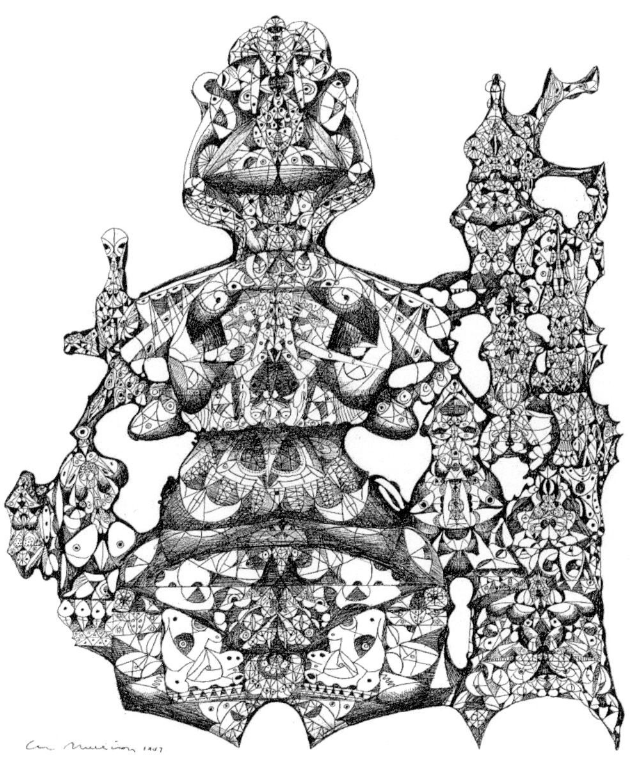

FIG. 9
*Untitled*, 1947, Los Angeles County Museum of Art

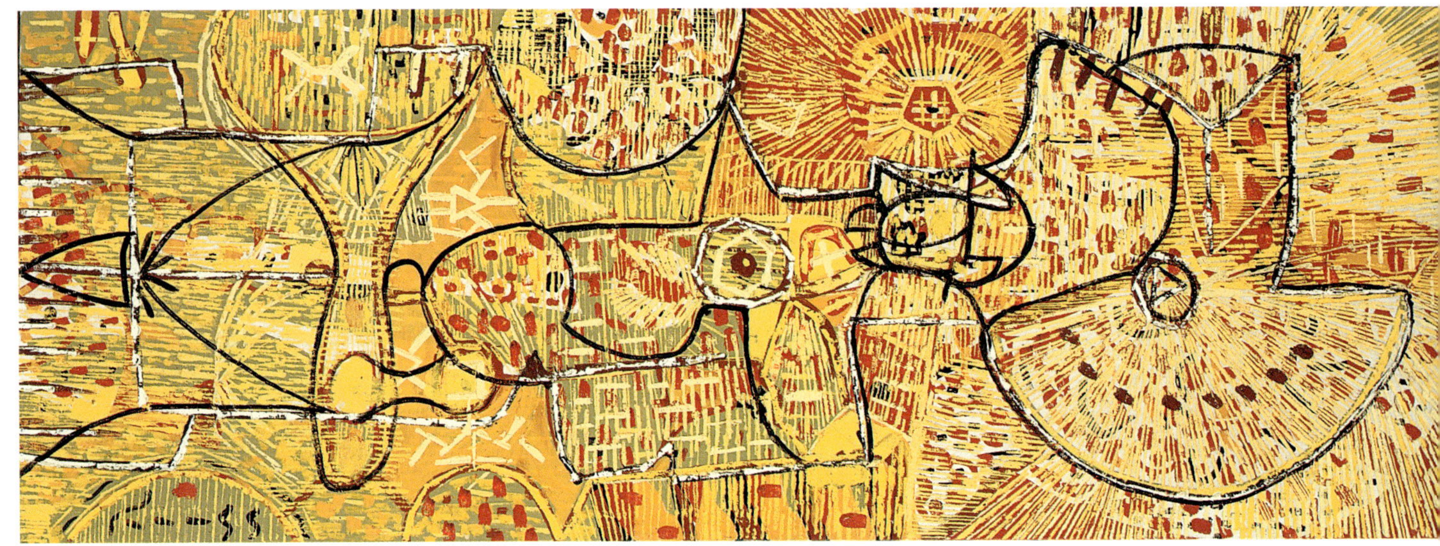

FIG. 10
*Untitled*, c. 1949, Lucid Art Foundation

Ironically, after training in the desert Mullican was sent to the lush environs of Hawaii, where he started drawing maps in earnest, again based on the kind of aerial photographs that would have such an influence on his later work.[16] In works such as *Untitled* of around 1949, *Section from the Burlap Plain* of 1951, and *Dynaton Triptych* of around 1952 (figs. 10–13), Mullican's interest in the "aerial view of pattern" becomes evident.[17] *Dynaton Triptych* in particular reflects the process the army topographers followed to make an image based on an aerial photograph: "We received the photographs, and we would make [them] into a mosaic," he later recalled.[18] Such paintings also reflect the continuing influence of Morris Graves, whose work suggesting abstracted aerial views of the landscape Mullican had already seen at MoMA in 1942 (fig. 14). The one known aerial drawing from Mullican's army service (fig. 15), imbued with the spirit of Mondrian and Constructivism, likewise suggests the affinity Mullican felt for modernist abstraction.

Being stationed in Hawaii was significant to the young artist in other ways as well. He appreciated the blend of Eastern and Western culture in Hawaii and actively explored Asian art, regularly visiting the Honolulu Academy of Fine Arts, where he spent a lot of time not only visiting the collection but also in the library looking at art periodicals. Altogether it was a highly influential time for his work.[19]

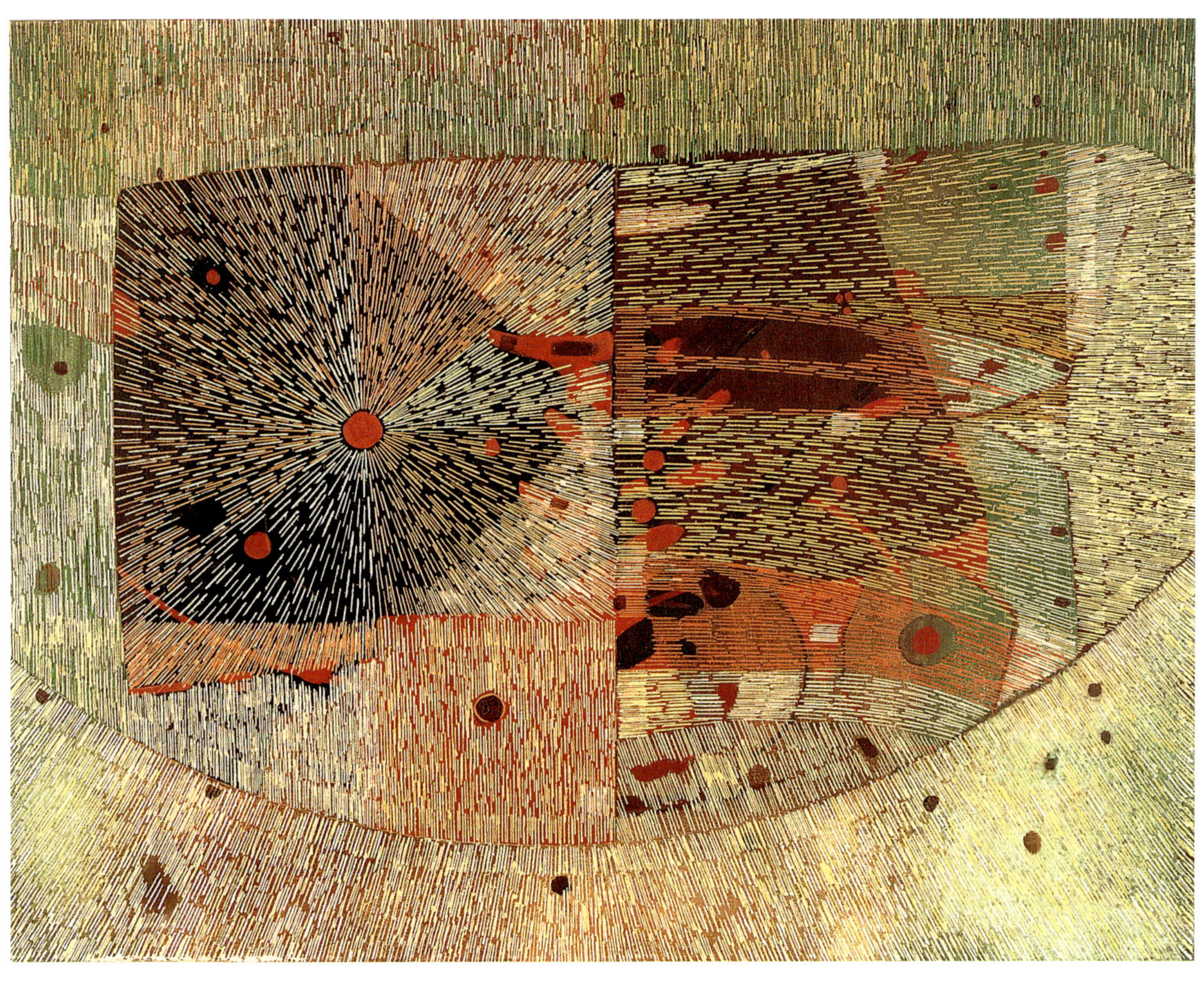

FIG. 11
*Section from the Burlap Plain*, 1951, Beverly and Mel Rosenthal

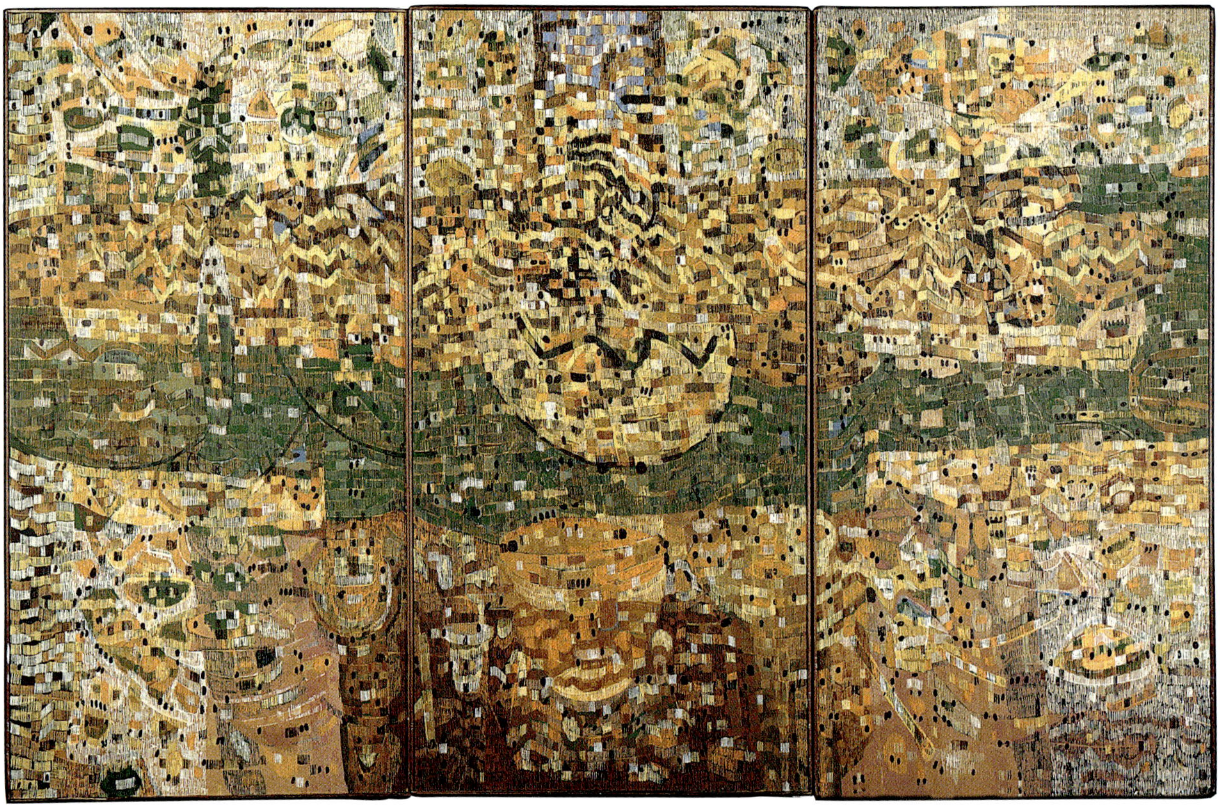

FIG. 12
*Dynaton Triptych*, c. 1952, Thomas Weisel and Emily Carroll

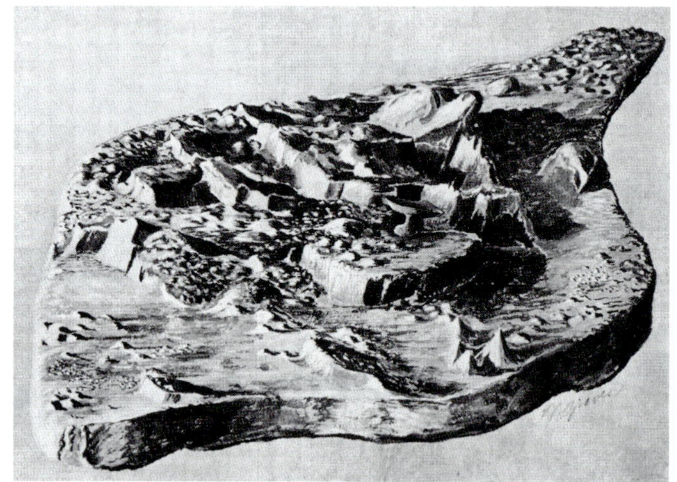

FIG. 14
Morris Graves, *Constant Journey*, gouache, $12\frac{5}{8}$ x $16\frac{1}{8}$ in., illustrated in The Museum of Modern Art's 1942 catalogue, *Americans 1942: 18 Artists from 9 States*.

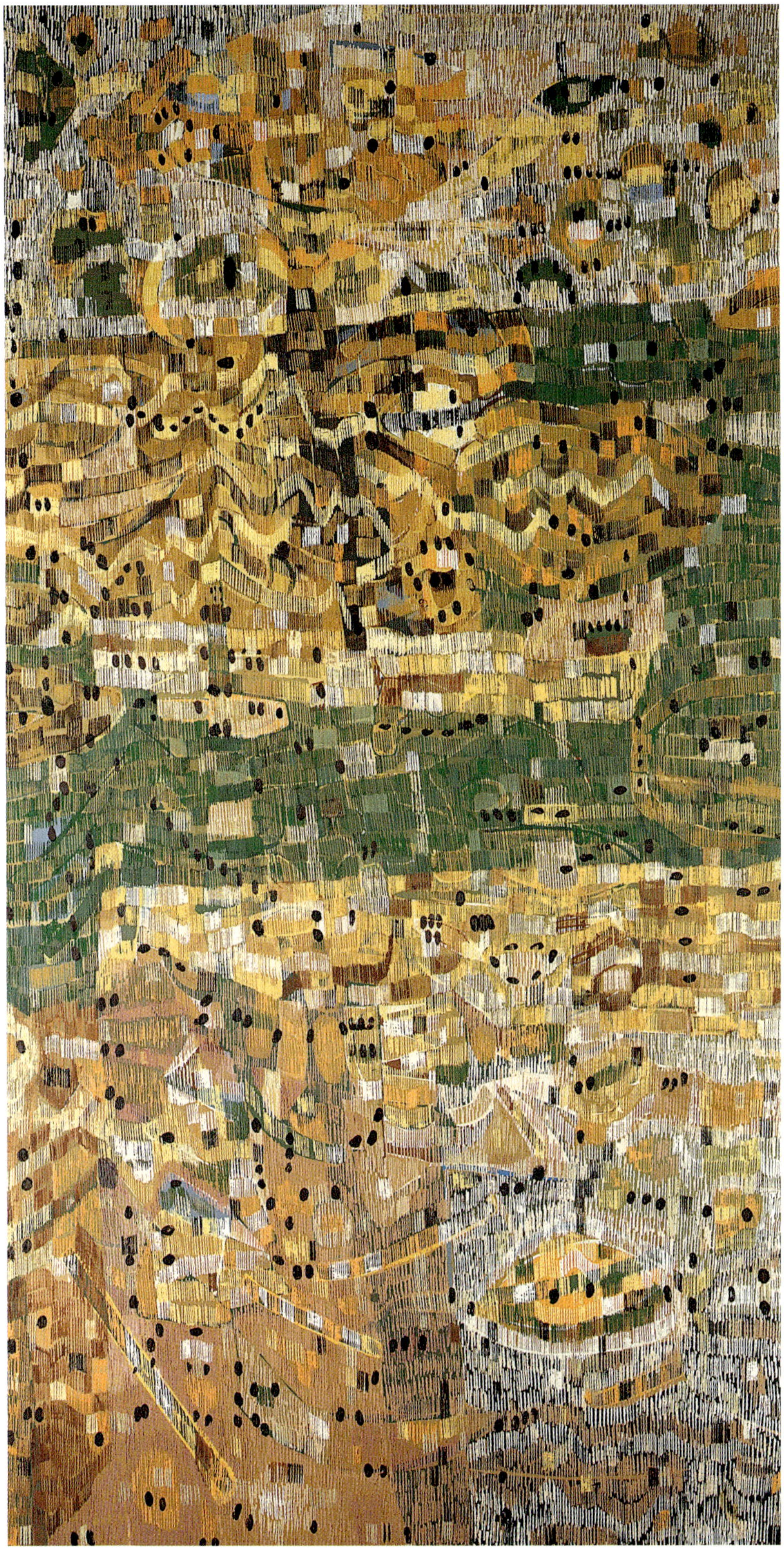

FIG. 13
*Dynaton Triptych* (detail)

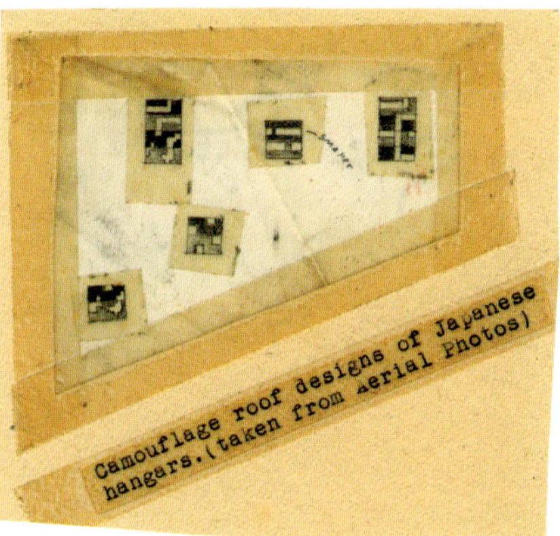


FIG. 15
Mullican's camouflage roof designs of Japanese hangars (based on aerial photos), pencil and typewriter on paper with cellophane tape, approx. 4 x 4 in., early 1940s, Collection Matt Mullican

## DYN, Paalen, and the influence of Native American art

Until this point Mullican's art had been informed largely by Cubism and Surrealism. This changed in Honolulu with what Mullican later called "the big event [in] my life." In the Honolulu Academy library, he first encountered an issue of *DYN* magazine, published by Wolfgang Paalen in Mexico City. "What I found in [*DYN*] was a part of what I wanted to do," he said. "I knew this."[20]

Austrian-born Wolfgang Paalen had been a protégé of André Breton's, and in 1935 became one of the youngest official members of the Surrealist circle in Paris. Four years later Paalen left Europe, traveling first to New York and then around western Canada and Alaska, where he collected Northwest Coast Indian art. In the fall of 1939 he moved to Mexico.[21] Unlike many of the European avant-garde artists who came to the United States (generally New York) in the late 1930s and early 1940s to escape Hitler's growing power in Europe, Paalen saw North America as a desirable destination rather than a place of involuntary exile. His profound interest in indigenous cultures (North and Central American) made both the United States and Mexico countries of choice for Paalen, and during his travels he amassed a truly significant collection of Native American objects.

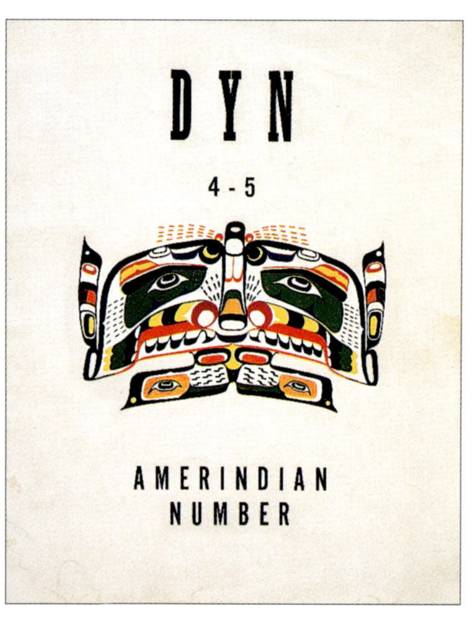


FIG. 16
*DYN*, no. 4-5, "Amerindian Number" (Dec. 1943), Getty Research Institute

Paalen published only six issues (including one double issue) of *DYN*; the first is dated April–May 1942 and the last was printed in November 1944. The periodical's title was meant to connote "a *potential* concept of reality ... a concept I call *dynatic* (from the Greek word *to dynaton*: the possible ... from which the name of this review *DYN* is derived)."[22] Mullican was attracted to the art he saw in *DYN* on first encounter; he correctly understood it to be "different than straight Surrealism. This was different than Cubism, which had always before been my big thing. Here was a magazine being published with articles and reproductions about things I was not aware of.... Through this magazine I became really interested in primitive art, folk art, pre-Columbian art, Northwest Coast art....There was a direct link between that and modern painting, for me."[23] For Mullican and many others the most influential issue of *DYN* was no. 4-5, the double issue printed in December 1943 and subtitled "Amerindian Number" (fig. 16). On seeing that issue, Mullican recalled, "Here was a primitive art that brought into focus a lot of the things that I had really begun to think about."[24]

This Amerindian issue of *DYN* includes sophisticated, richly illustrated, scholarly articles such as "Totem Art" (by Paalen) and "Tlatilco, Archaic Mexican Art and Culture" (by Miguel Covarrubias), among others. A brief, unsigned preamble to the issue, attributable to Paalen, states that "art can reunite us with our prehistoric past and thus only certain carved and painted images enable us to grasp the memories of unfathomable ages. So, too, in the direction of the future—as it is only through the imagination that thought can find its aim—it is art that often prefigures what might be."[25] The prophetic, forward-looking power of art would become central to the Dynaton group that Paalen formed along with Gordon Onslow Ford and Mullican in San Francisco around 1950, and it distinguishes their aesthetic from that of the better-known New York School.

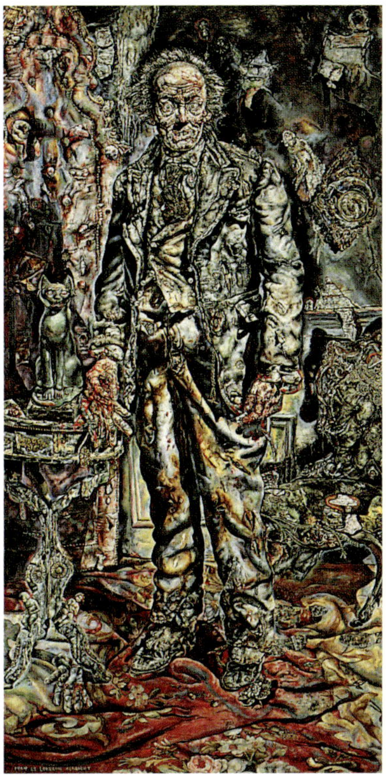

FIG. 17
Ivan Albright, *Picture of Dorian Gray*, 1943-44, oil on canvas, 85 x 42 in., The Art Institute of Chicago, gift of Ivan Albright

## Postwar years

Mullican was stationed on Guam when the atom bomb was dropped and the war in the Pacific ended. Before returning to the United States, he was sent to Tokyo for a month. He not only saw the destruction the war had caused there[26] but also traveled briefly to the countryside, visiting Shinto shrines and natural landmarks as he pursued his growing interest in Asian culture. Finally discharged early in 1946, Mullican returned temporarily to Chickasha. During this period he made his first trip to Chicago, where he was intrigued by Ivan Albright's paintings at The Art Institute (fig. 17). Mullican later recalled that he was "fascinated with the technique, and the intricate surface detail, and the patience with which [Albright] worked surfaces and patterns....I began to work out similar things in a much more abstract sense....I think that helped to develop my

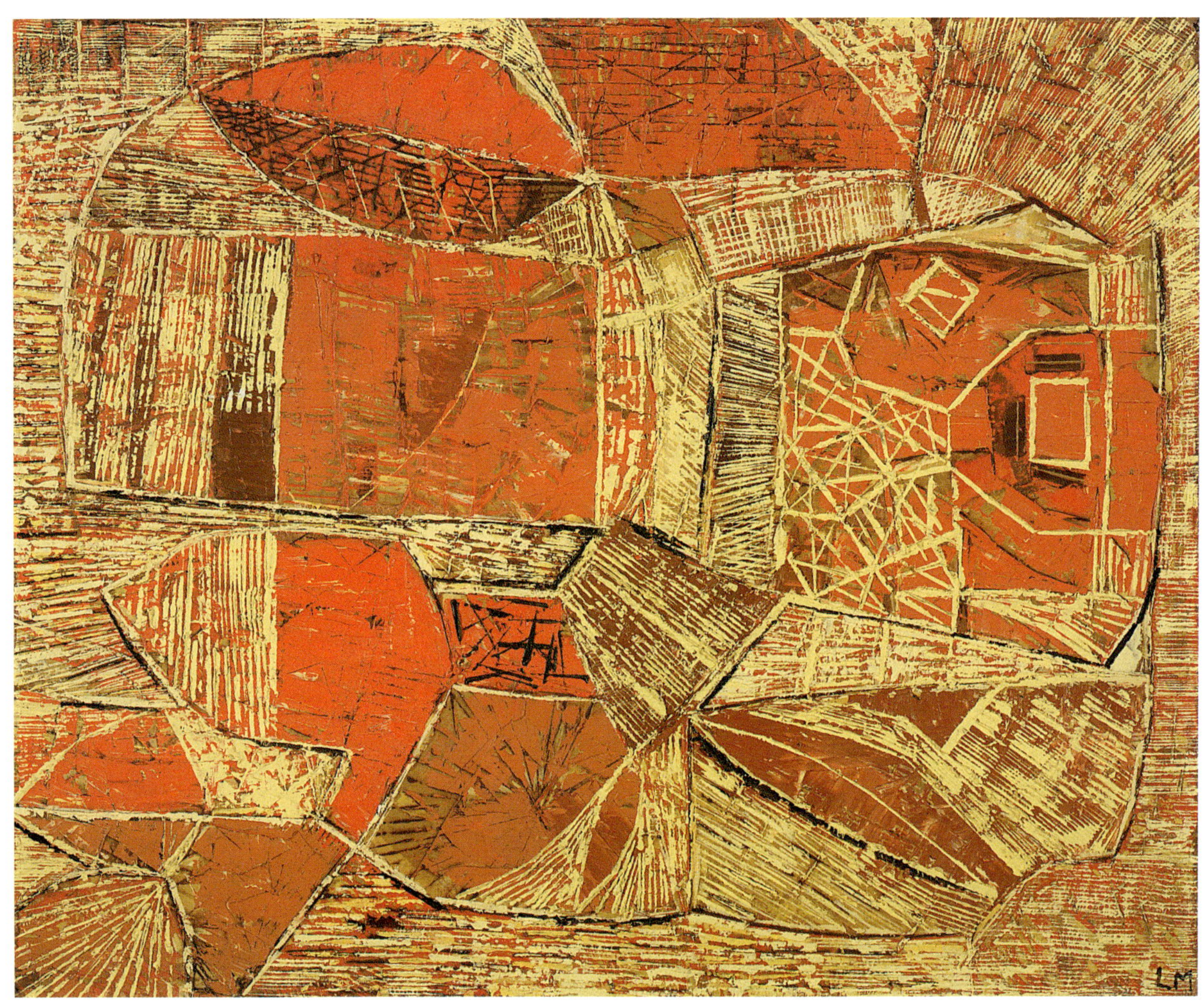


FIG. 18
*The Fossil Swims*, 1948, Estate of the artist, courtesy Marc Selwyn Fine Art

sense of an intricate and more tightly woven surface, which I really got involved with."[27] He also spent some time in Santa Fe and Taos, where he made his first purchases of New Mexican *santos* (folk art images of saints) as well as of Native American artifacts.[28]

Contemplating his future, Mullican felt he had two viable choices as a budding artist: to move to New York City or to go to California. When his army buddy Jack Stauffacher (whom Mullican had originally befriended because he saw Stauffacher reading *The Life of the Buddha* in the latrine) invited Mullican to live with him and his brother Frank near San Francisco, Mullican chose the West Coast. Referring to this decision years later, Mullican recalled that arriving in San Francisco "was a new beginning, [a] totally new beginning.... This was my Paris."[29]

Stauffacher ran the Greenwood Press, a small printing press that proved critical to Mullican's career in several ways. Having made many drawings during and immediately after his war service, Mullican started using oils again after he moved to California, making his first significant paintings. It was thanks to Stauffacher that Mullican began painting with a printer's ink knife, creating his unique method of applying fine, slightly three-dimensional, parallel uplifts of paint to create intricate images (figs. 18–21). "One day I told Jack that it would be nice if I had a palette knife ... to work on my paint with, and he said, 'Well, here.' He went into the print shop and brought back a little printer's ink knife, a knife that he used to put ink on the rollers with.... And that was the beginning of my striation technique."[30]

In these early paintings we see not only Mullican's creation of an idiosyncratic painting style but also his simultaneous attraction to abstraction and figuration. *The Fossil Swims* (fig. 18) reads not only as an abstracted aerial landscape but also as a fish, while *Luminous Loot* (fig. 19) and other early paintings such as *Happily the Chiefs Regard You* (fig. 22) suggest not only powerful primal forces but also the indigenous totems and other figures he had first seen illustrated in *DYN* as well as the kachinas he knew from Santa Fe. Later, Mullican confirmed that "throughout ... my work I have had a feeling that there's always been this battle, back and forth, between a sense

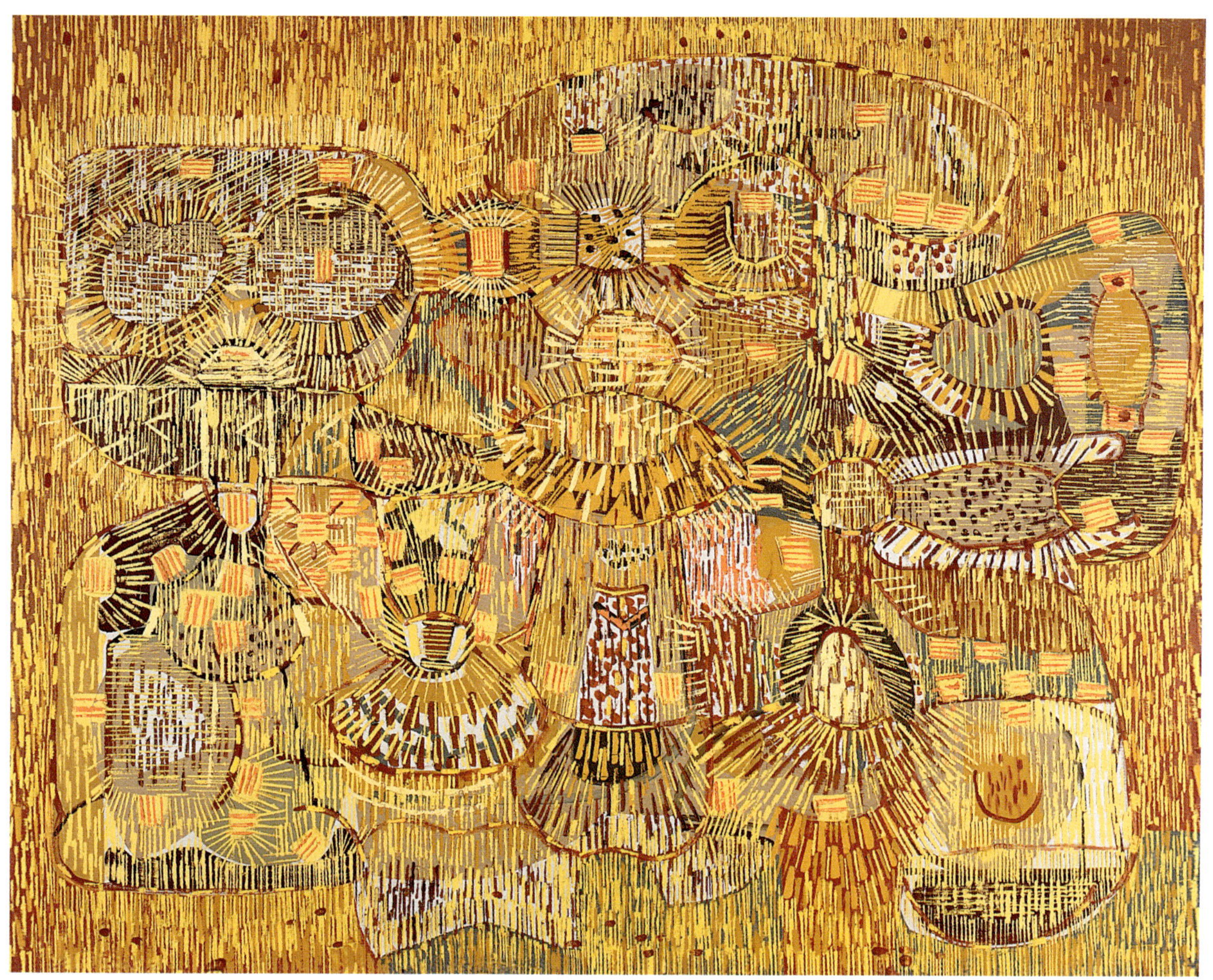

FIG. 19
*Luminous Loot*, 1948, Thomas Weisel and Emily Carroll

of pure abstraction and a need for some kind of image."[31] At the moment in the late 1940s when members of the New York School were resolutely adopting their signature abstract styles—with the lone exception of Willem de Kooning, who consistently acknowledged the validity of figuration as well as abstraction[32]—Mullican already understood intuitively the value of both vocabularies, that it was fundamentally inappropriate to distinguish between abstraction and figuration, that the two needed somehow to coexist.[33] Later in his career, when teaching first-year art students, Mullican would bring in slides he had shot of sand on the beach and close-up views of tide pools, images that are literally realistic but that function as abstractions (see fig. 74). He chose to show these to young art students "to get their minds around the idea . . . that there was no need to make a distinction" between the abstract and the figurative.[34]

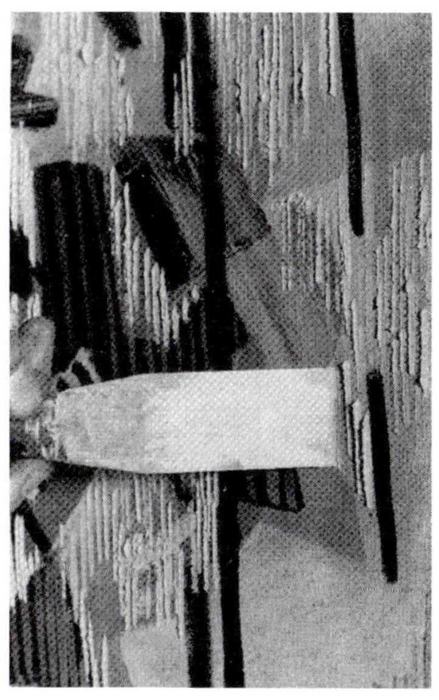

FIG. 20
Photo of Mullican using a printer's ink knife to apply paint to canvas, originally published in *Art News* (Oct. 1953)

FIG. 21
*Space* (detail), 1951, Los Angeles County Museum of Art

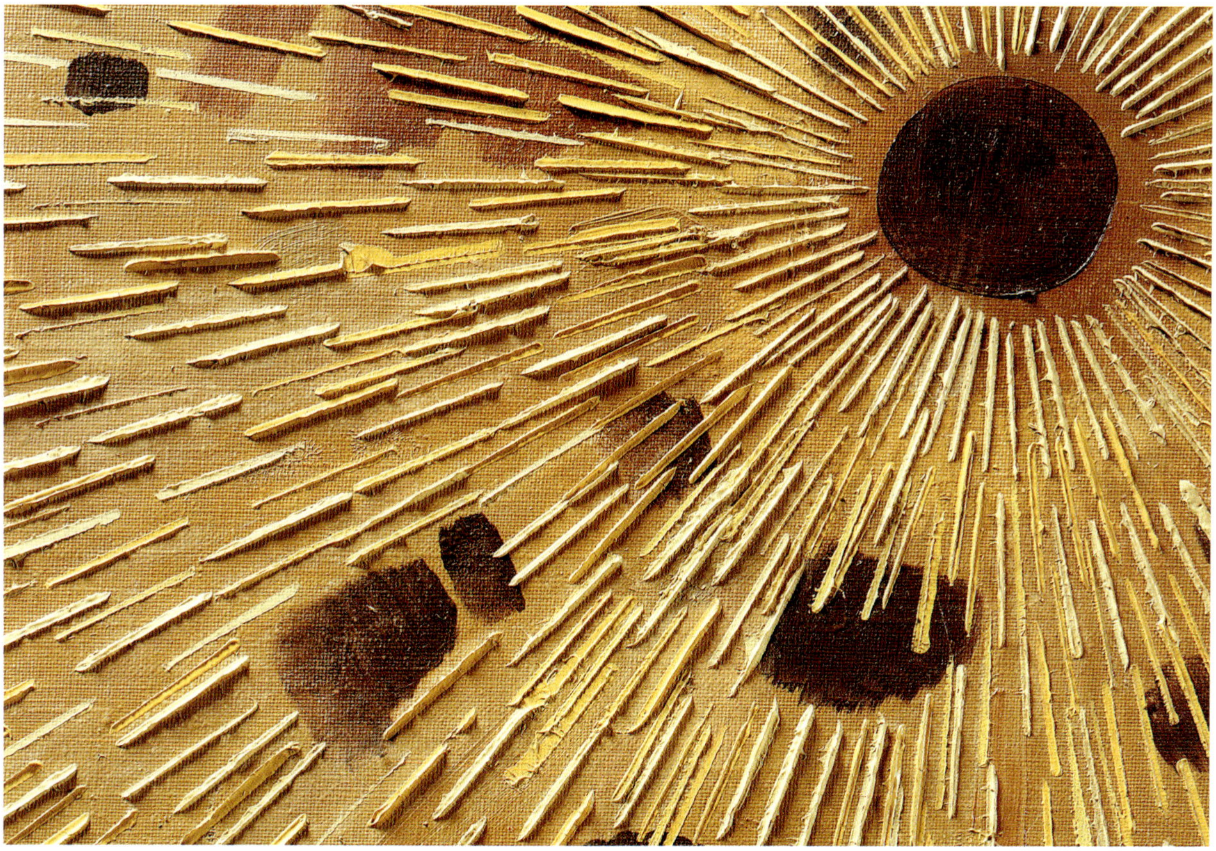

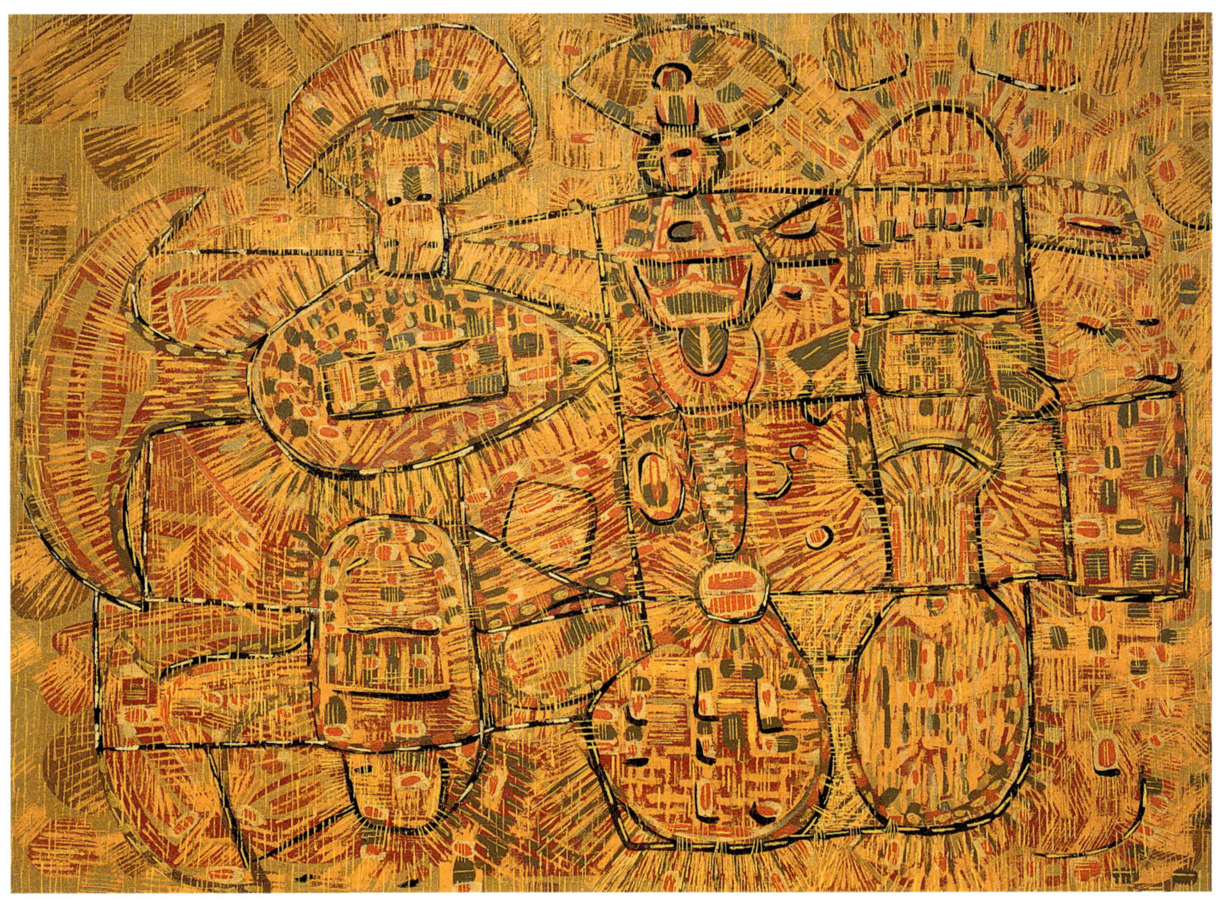

FIG. 22
*Happily the Chiefs Regard You,* 1949, Harold and Gertrud Parker

As the artist himself described his stance, "that's where my vision was. . . . One step is in the air, one step is on the earth."[35]

Greenwood Press proved significant for Mullican in a second way as well. Jack Stauffacher hung one of Mullican's paintings in his office at the press, where the British-born Surrealist Gordon Onslow Ford (by then living in San Francisco) saw it. Intrigued by the canvas (now lost), Onslow Ford immediately recognized that he had to meet Mullican;[36] a friendship began between the older European and the younger American that would last a lifetime. Both Onslow Ford and his wife, the writer Jacqueline Johnson, became mentors for Mullican, who spent many hours looking at works from Onslow Ford's significant collection of modern art, which included paintings by Picasso, Klee, Max Ernst, Paul Delvaux, Georges Braque, and others. Onslow Ford at this moment was completing *Towards a New*

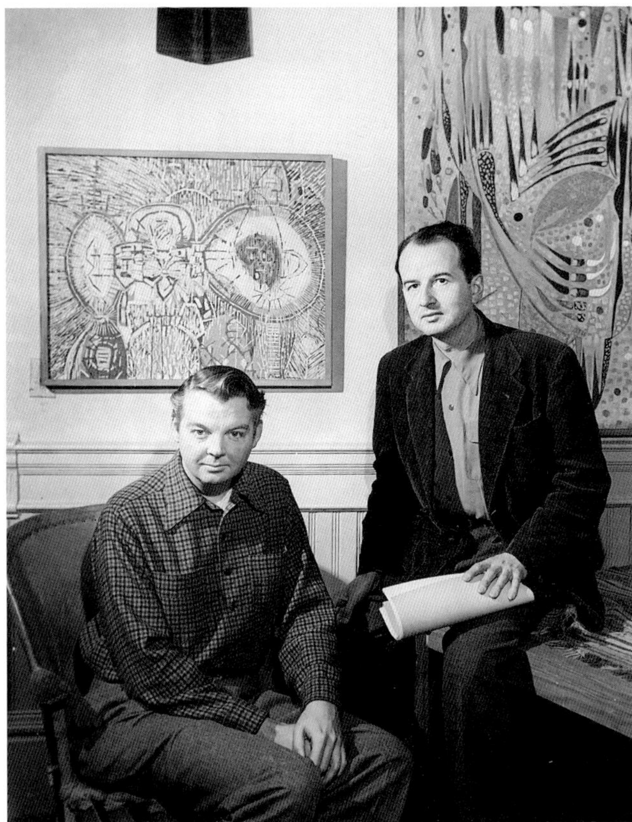

FIG. 23
Mullican and Paalen in front of their own canvases, Mill Valley, California, 1951

*Subject in Painting*, the book that accompanied his exhibition later in 1948 at The San Francisco Museum of Art. Mullican felt that Onslow Ford's text, which expresses a sense of communion with nature and emphasizes the importance of the spiritual and emotional in art, reflected his own still inchoate sense of art's important role. Onslow Ford also pays homage in the text to Surrealism and to specific artists whom Mullican revered, including Klee and Paalen. Mullican felt that he had found a soul brother in Onslow Ford and that he was coming of age as an artist.

Through Onslow Ford as well as through the Stauffacher brothers (Frank was a commercial artist, writer, and filmmaker), Mullican came into contact with the wider creative community in the Bay Area. Most importantly, it was through Onslow Ford that Mullican met Paalen (who had arrived in San Francisco from Mexico in 1948) at the time of his small solo exhibition that same year at The San Francisco Museum of Art (fig. 23). Mullican likened the experience of entering the one-room show—where he spent hours looking at Paalen's work—to "entering a chapel, entering a church,

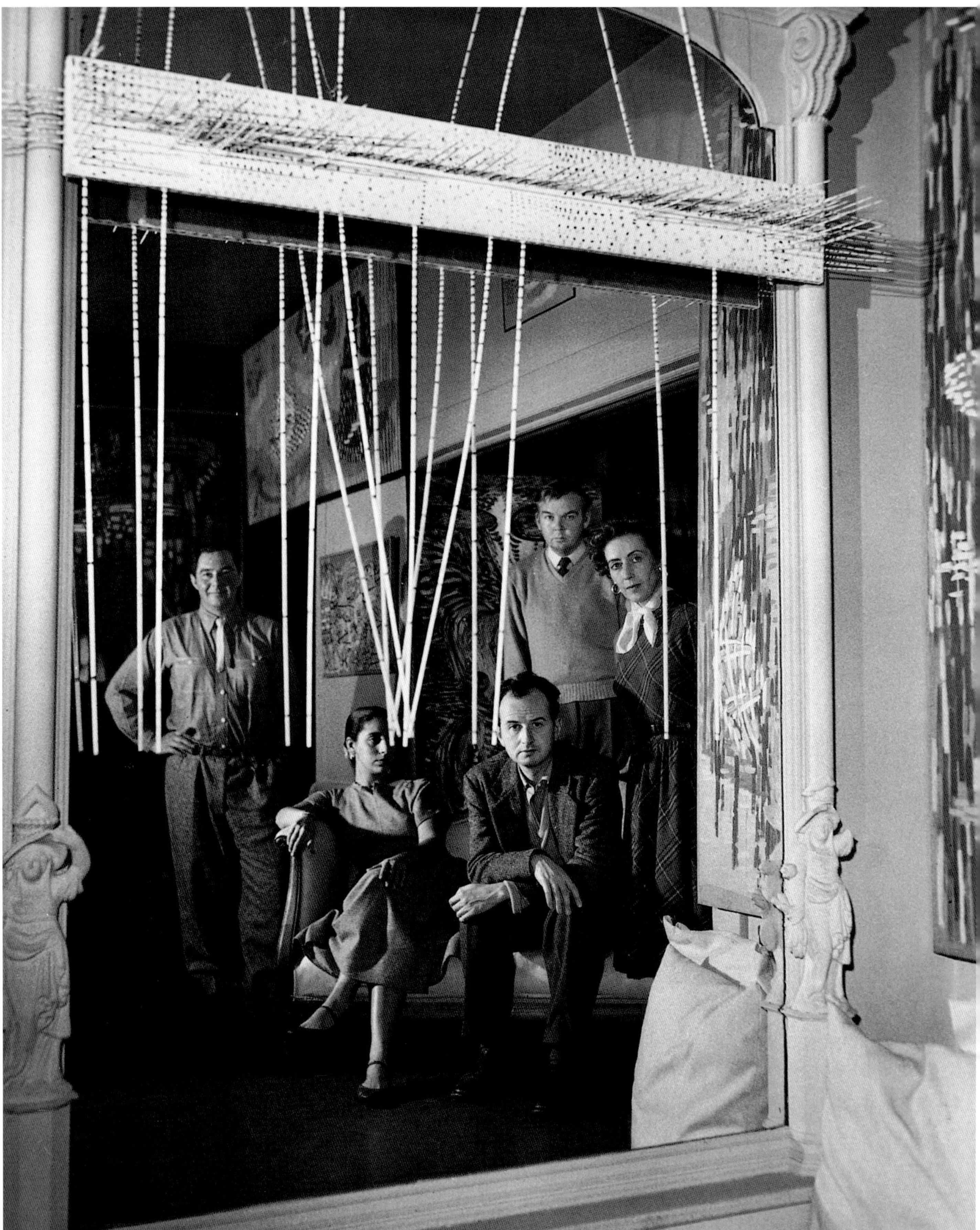

and being surrounded by these apostles of the spirit and mind."[37] Mullican met the publisher of *DYN* along with Paalen's wife Luchita Hurtado; shortly thereafter Paalen and Mullican traded paintings, Mullican moved into Paalen's grand Victorian house among the redwood trees of Mill Valley,[38] and Paalen agreed to write the text for the catalogue of Mullican's show of twenty-four paintings at The San Francisco Museum the following year. Not surprisingly, Paalen focused in this text on Mullican's relationship to and affinity for Native American and other indigenous imagery. As only an outsider can, Paalen understood intuitively that "this incomparable city [San Francisco] holds . . . a strategic position of inspiration between the currents of the great old cultures of the Pacific and the stirring forces of America."[39] He also noted that Mullican's year in San Francisco had been "a fecund year . . . an abundant harvest of sun."[40]

Mullican had long thought of himself as a dreamer[41] and repeatedly expressed interest in the spiritual and the metaphysical. Through art, he felt, one could transcend the mundane and create an alternative cosmos; one could achieve what he later called "the creation of a private world."[42] Mullican perceived his role of artist as akin to that of medium, through whom the work of art would appear. "The work of art [is] just a record of my being an artist. . . . I am standing on this particular metaphysical, almost unexplainable plane in my studio, and the canvas is there before me [and] . . . the painting appear[s]. And once it appears . . . you're not quite sure how it got there. . . . [You] just accept it."[43] This approach to painting was very much informed by his interest in Surrealist automatism and particularly by his growing relationship with both Onslow Ford and Paalen, whose work had long expressed similar interests (figs. 24–26). Despite the fact that the three artists worked in different styles, they felt an enormous affinity for each other's work and felt compelled to make some sort of collective public statement. As Mullican later recalled Paalen saying, "The time has come. We've got to do something."[44]

FIG. 24
Left to right: Gordon Onslow Ford, Luchita Hurtado, Wolfgang Paalen, Lee Mullican, and Jacqueline Johnson in Onslow Ford's home on Telegraph Hill, San Francisco, 1949 (the suspended sculpture is one of Mullican's *Tactile Estatics*); reproduced as the frontispiece of the 1951 *Dynaton* exhibition catalogue

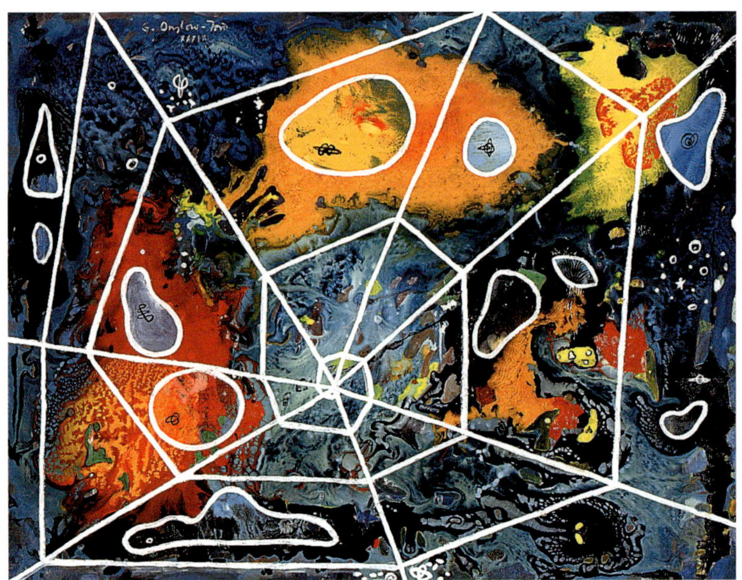

FIG. 25
Gordon Onslow Ford, *Space Web*, 1939, Ripolin enamel on canvas, 28¾ x 36½ in., Franz von Braun

## Dynaton

The "something" they did was the *Dynaton* exhibition at The San Francisco Museum of Art in 1951 (figs. 27–29). After stating that painting at its core addresses issues of mark-making and image-making (i.e. of abstraction and figuration),[45] Paalen explained in the exhibition catalogue that

> the *Dynatón* [*sic*] is a limitless continuum, in which all forms of reality are potentially implicit.... I call our concept of painting *metaplastic*, because although our means consist in direct plastic expression, our *aims* are not solutions of formal problems, but a new meaning.... Painting is the adventure into an inner space which can not be measured by yardsticks nor light-years. A space where thought travels faster than light, where the nearest is also the farthest, where the smallest sea-shell curves [are] as meaningful as the galactic spiral and the eye of the mind at once beholds worlds gone and to come.[46]

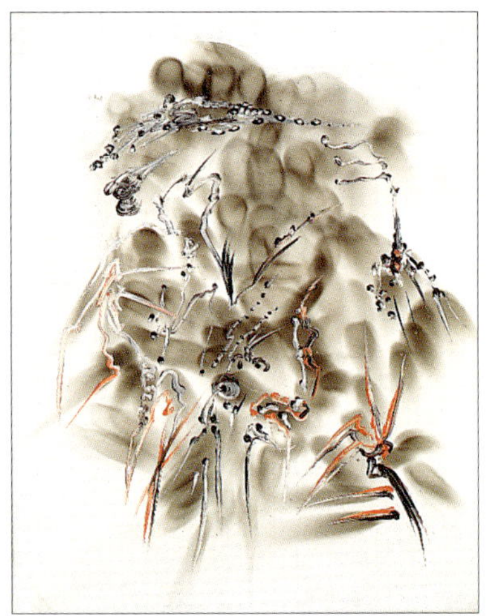

FIG. 26
Wolfgang Paalen, *Untitled (Fumage)*, 1938, fumage and oil on canvas, 16⅜ x 13 in., Collection of Harold and Gertrud Parker, Tiburon, California

The notion of a galactic spiral is particularly relevant for several of the works Mullican showed in the *Dynaton* exhibition, including *Quartette of Spider Sounds*, *Oblique of Agawam*, and *The Splintering Lions* (figs. 30, 32, and 71), all of which suggest celestial bodies hurtling through space, spinning out from a more or less

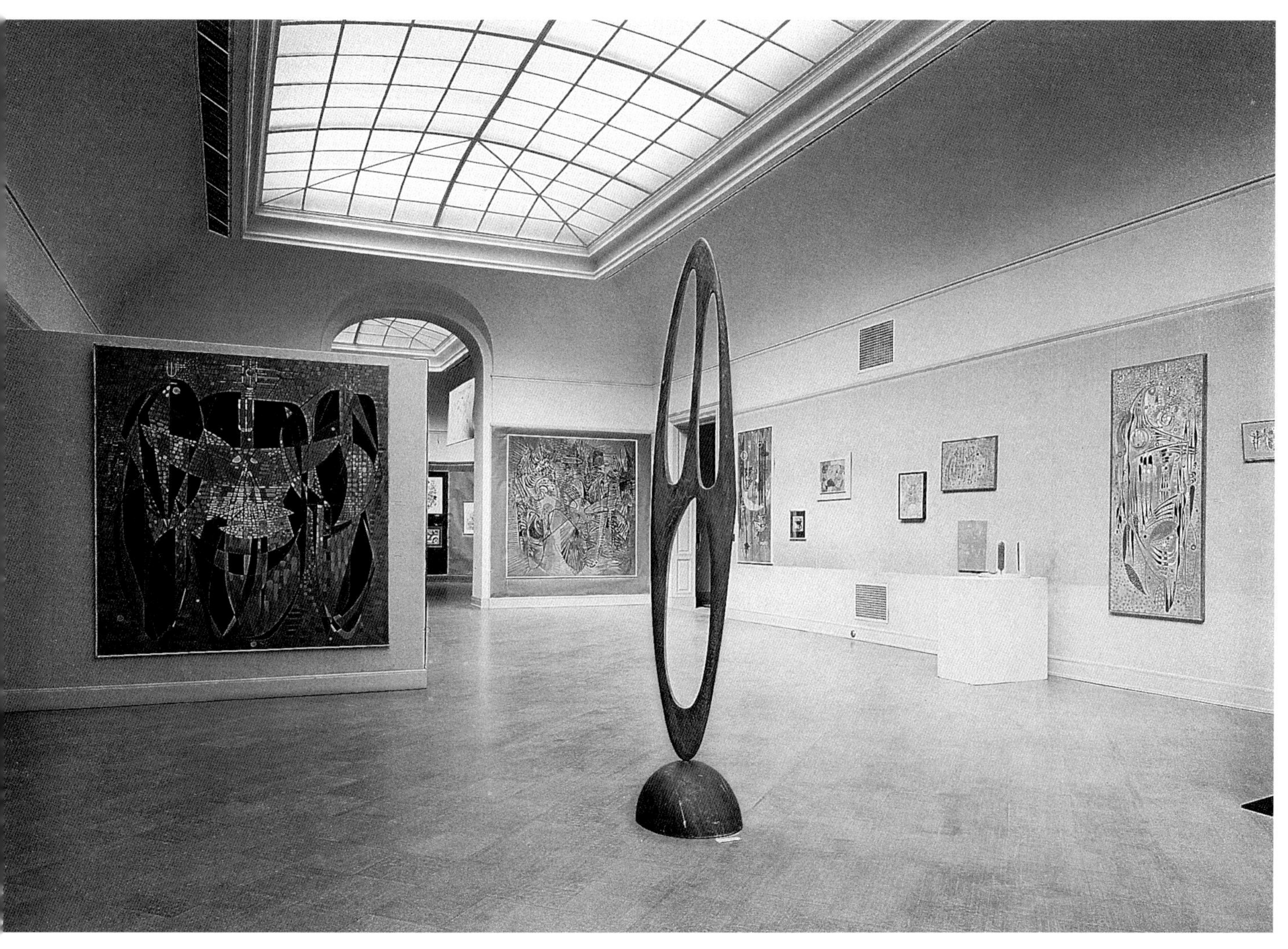

FIG. 27
View of the *Dynaton* exhibition, The San Francisco Museum of Art, 1951, with Paalen's *Messengers from the Three Poles* (1949) on the left, *The Cosmogons* (1944) in the center background, and *Project for a Monument* (1945) in the foreground

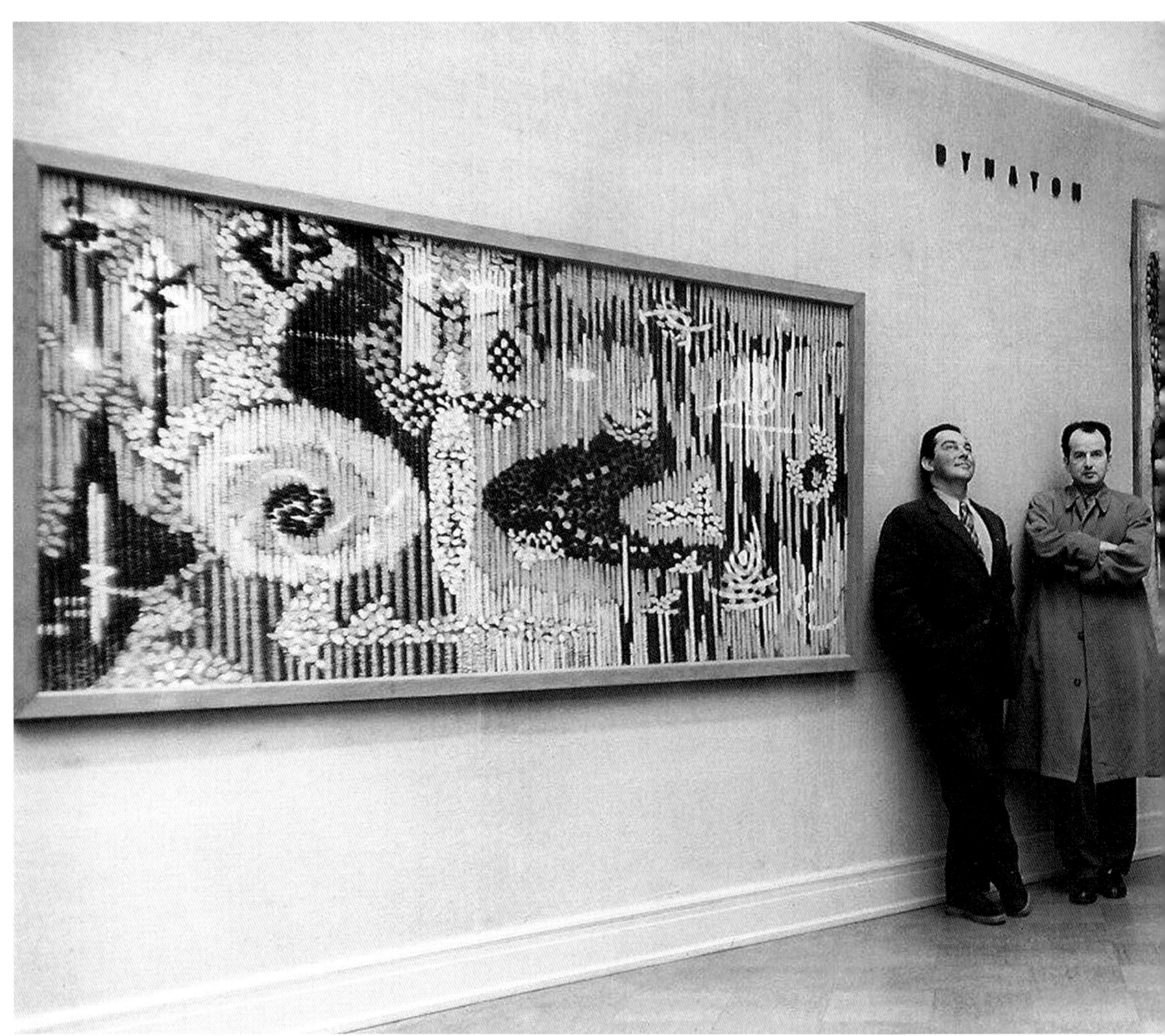


FIG. 28
Onslow Ford, Paalen, and Mullican in the *Dynaton* exhibition, with Onslow Ford's *The Great Haunts* (1950) on the left

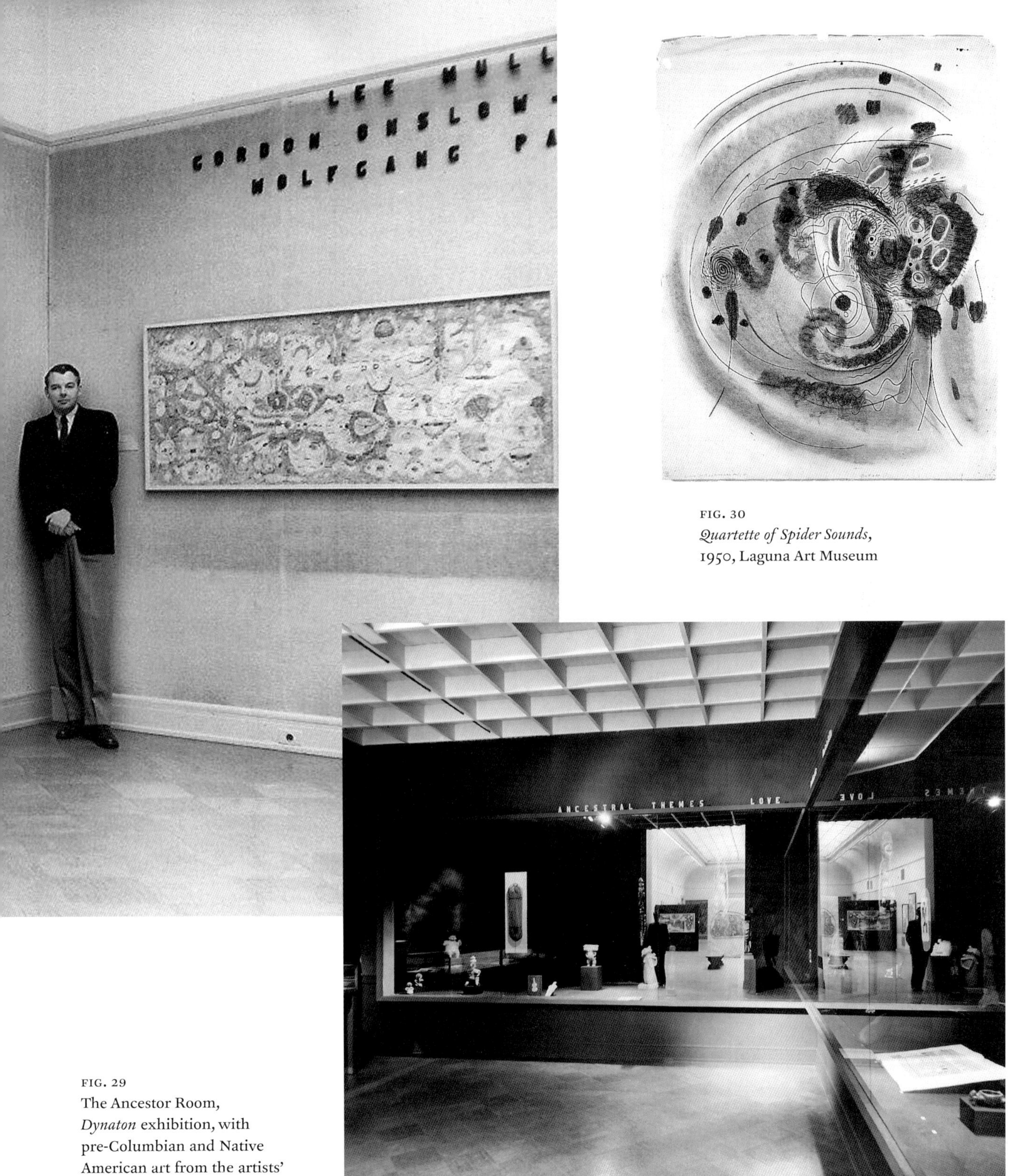


FIG. 29
The Ancestor Room, *Dynaton* exhibition, with pre-Columbian and Native American art from the artists' collections

FIG. 30
*Quartette of Spider Sounds*, 1950, Laguna Art Museum

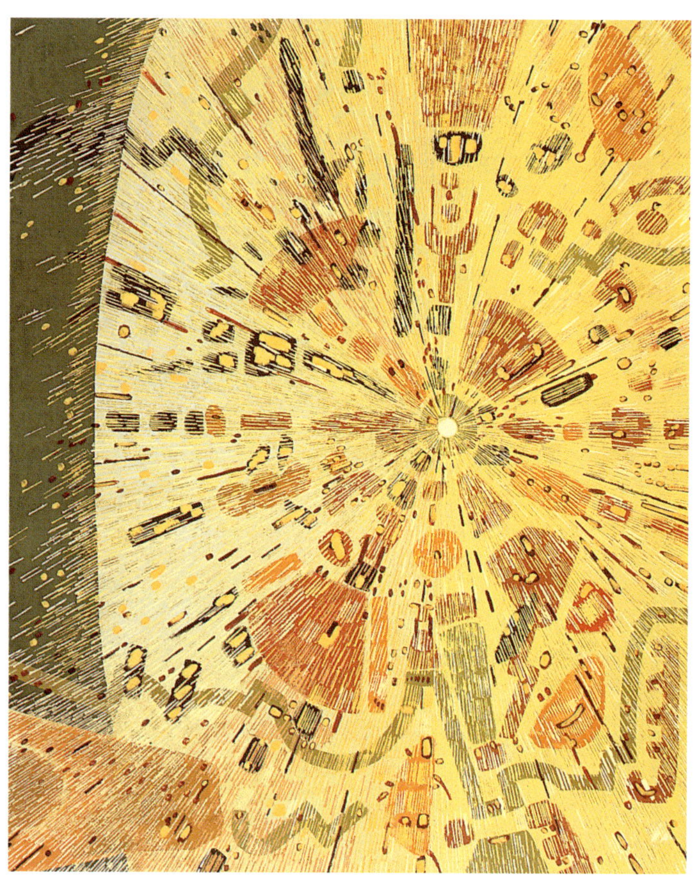

FIG. 31
*Agawam (First Quarter)*, 1950 (left section of *Agawam Triptych*), Collection of the Trenton Family Trust

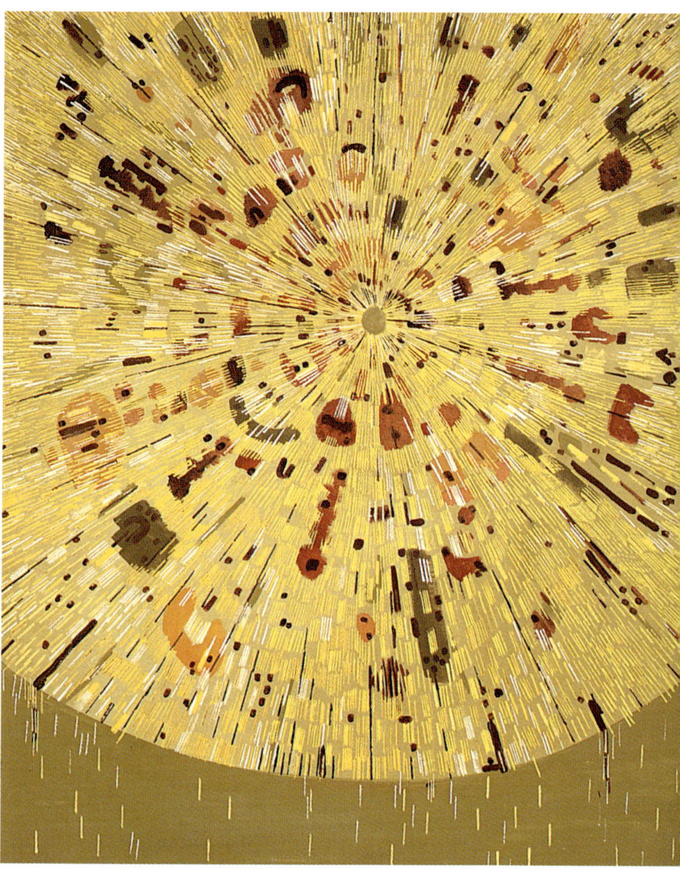

FIG. 32
*Oblique of Agawam*, 1950 (center section of *Agawam Triptych*), Miani Johnson, Willard Gallery

FIG. 33
*Third Quarter*, 1950 (right section of *Agawam Triptych*), Harlan and Natasha Levine

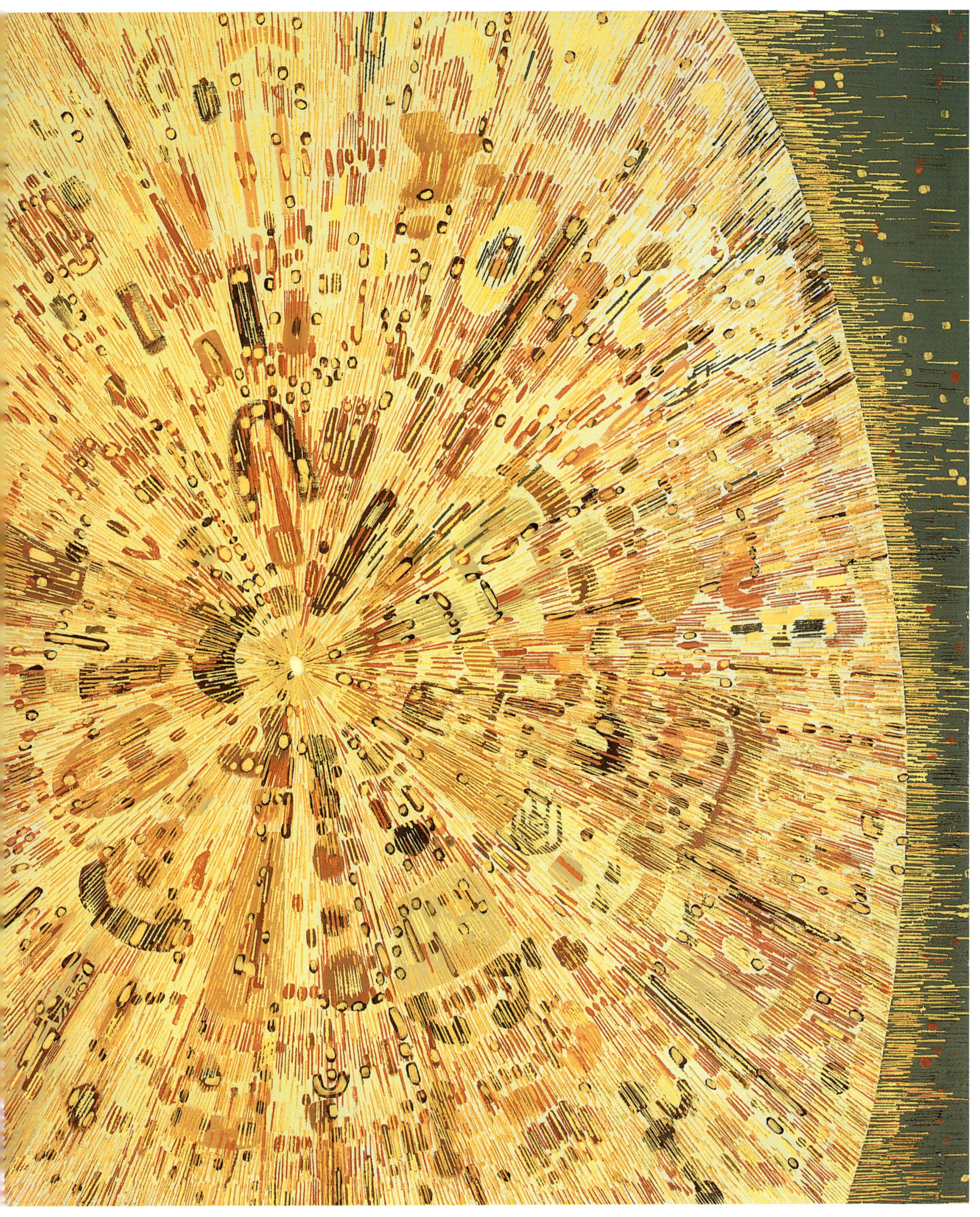

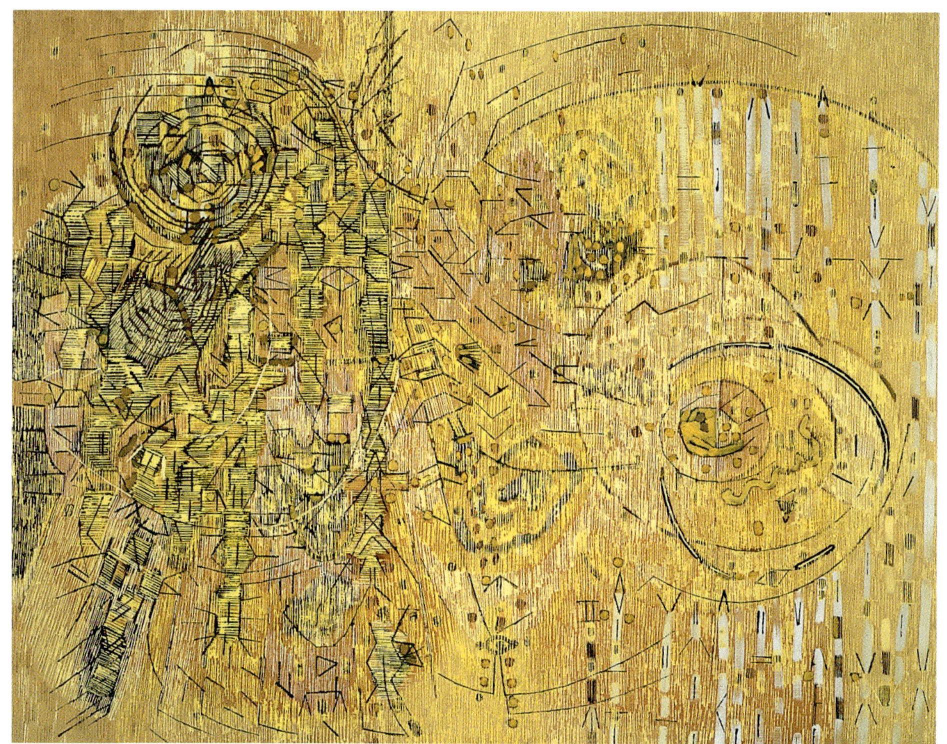

FIG. 34
*Turning Worlds*, 1950, Allan M. Jalon and Mary Tricarico Jalon

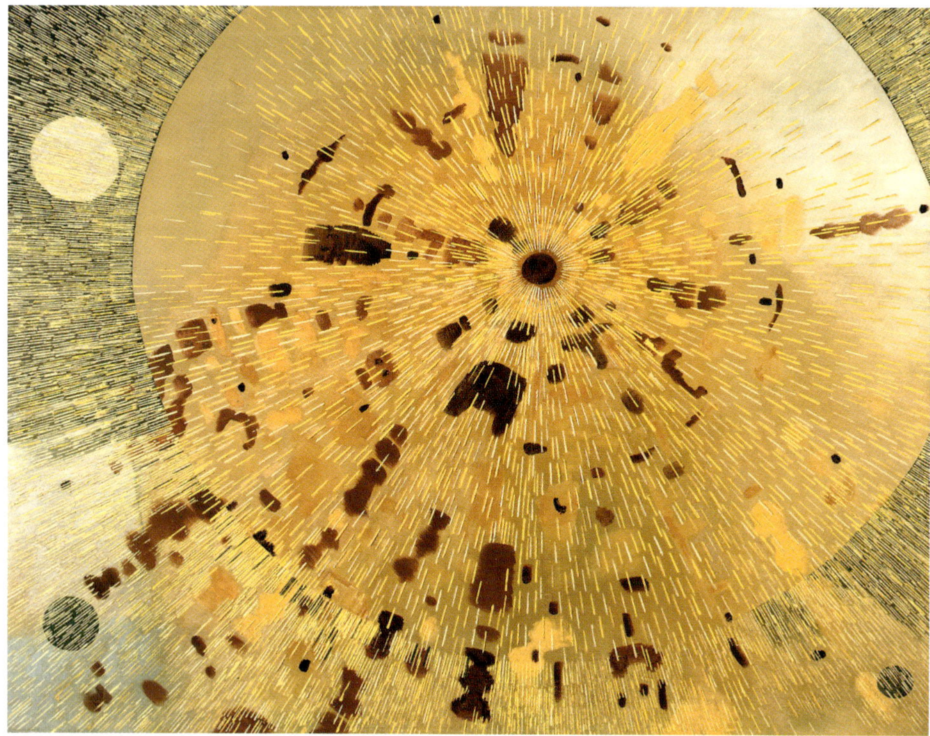

FIG. 35
*Space*, 1951, Los Angeles County Museum of Art

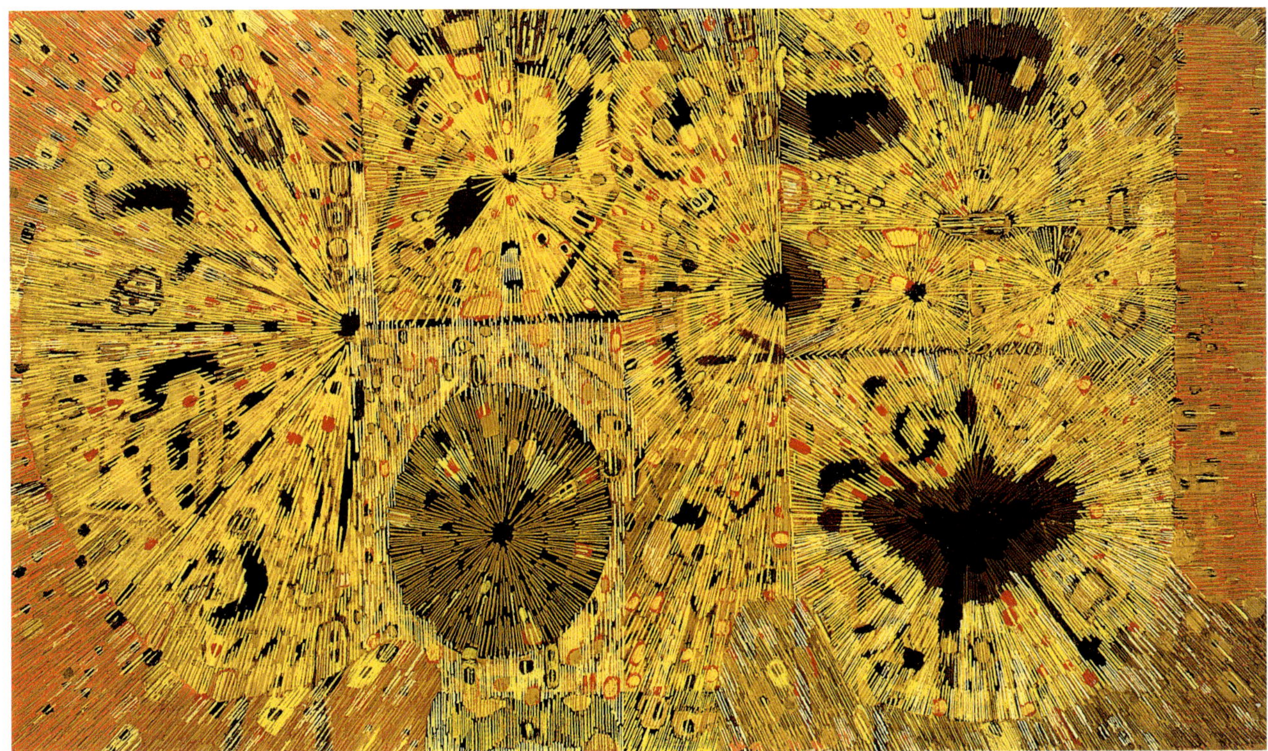

FIG. 36
*Ninnekah Calendar*, 1951,
William Resnick, M.D. and
Douglas Cordell, M.D.

clearly defined central point.[47] *Oblique of Agawam* is in fact the central panel of Mullican's 1950 Agawam triptych, including *Agawam (First Quarter)* on the left and *Third Quarter* on the right (figs. 31 and 33). The terms "first quarter" and "third quarter" evoke heavenly bodies as they wax and wane over time, while "agawam," a Native American word meaning "crooked river" (and also the name of a town in Oklahoma), harks back to Mullican's interest in topography and aerial photography.

Mullican similarly conjures cosmic images of planets and galaxies in other paintings of this period, some with explicit and others with rather mysterious titles. Titles such as *Turning Worlds* and *Space* (figs. 34 and 35) are clear in their references; the titles of *Ninnekah Calendar* and *The Measurement* (figs. 36 and 1) suggest the parsing of time and space, while *The Ninnekah* (fig. 37)—along with *Ninnekah Calendar*—refers to a small town in Oklahoma just south of Chickasha. Though lacking a descriptive title of any sort, *Untitled* (fig. 38) clearly evokes the same planetary imagery as the Agawam triptych. *Peyote Candle* (p. 2) likewise "has to do with cosmic space, with the creation of new planets."[48] The title of *Peyote Candle* also evokes hallucinogenic drugs and the Native American shamans who used

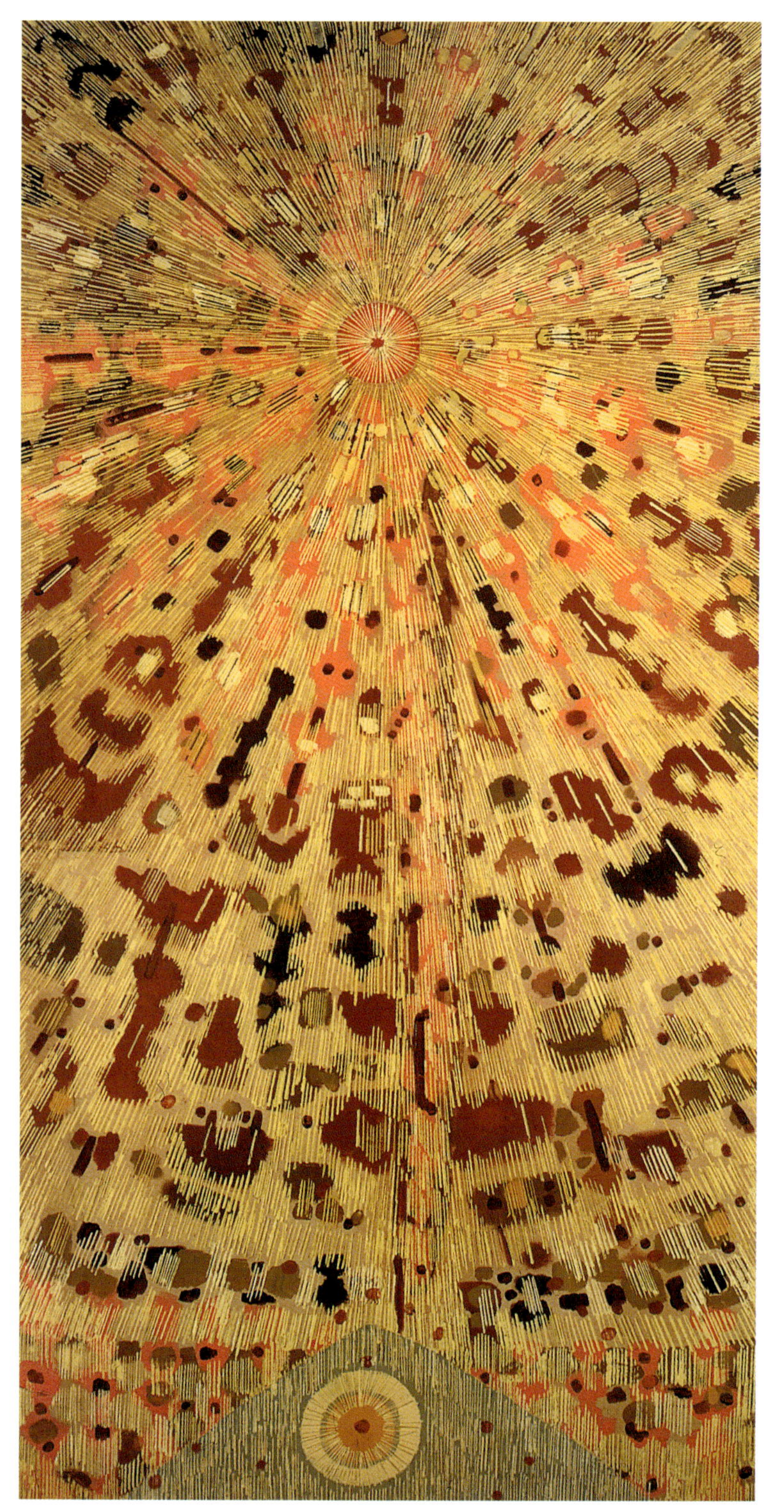

FIG. 37
*The Ninnekah*, 1951, Nora Eccles Harrison Museum of Art

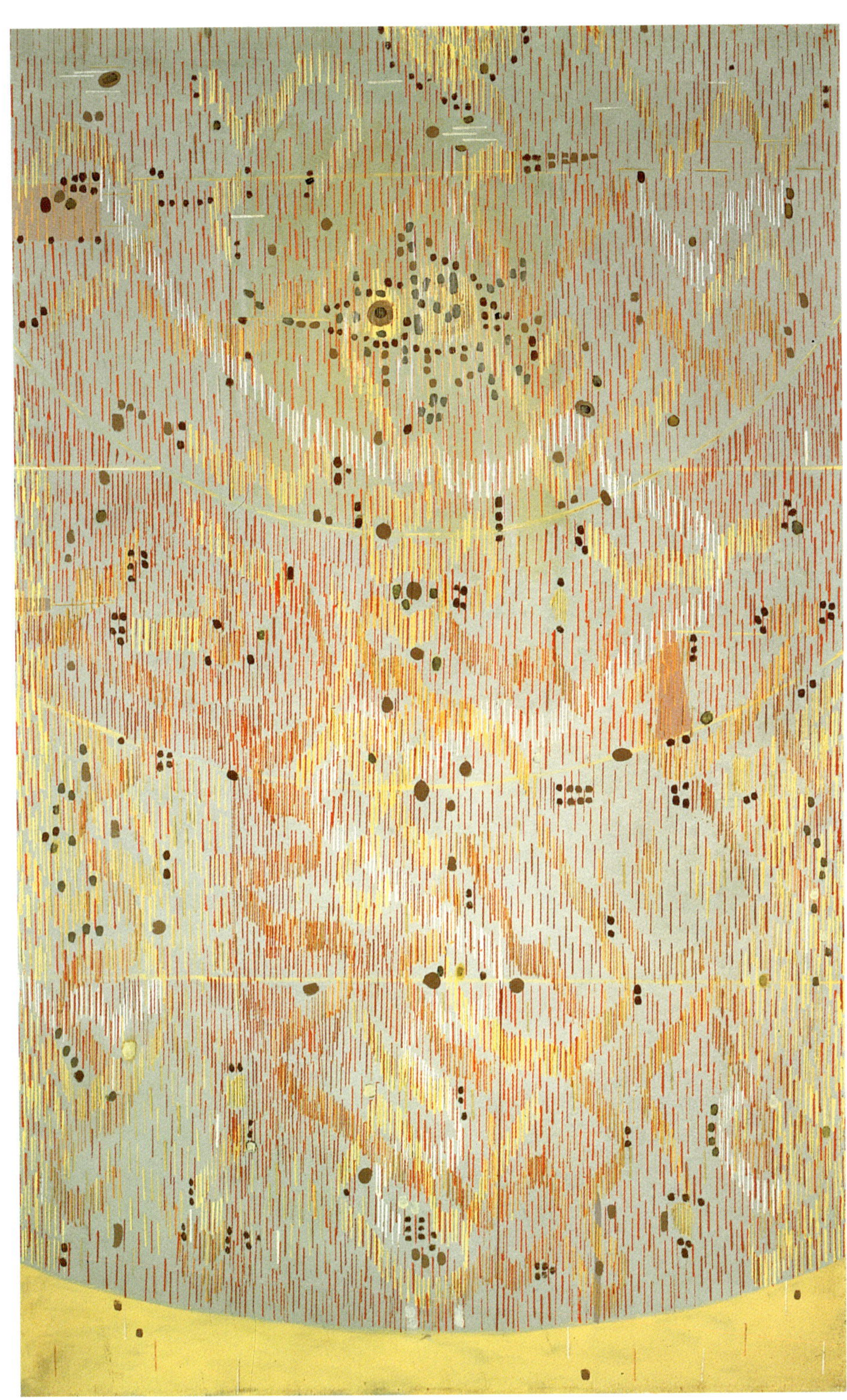

FIG. 38
*Untitled*, 1951, Orna and Keenan Wolens

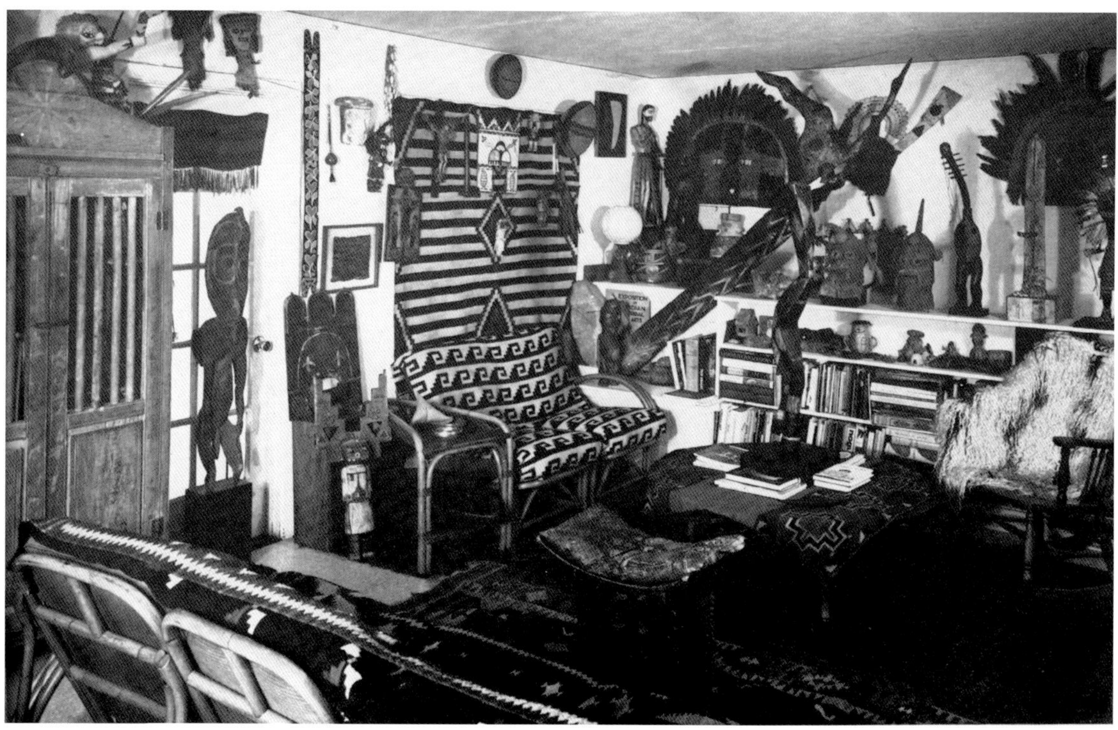

FIG. 39
The Mullicans' living room, Santa Monica, c. 1975

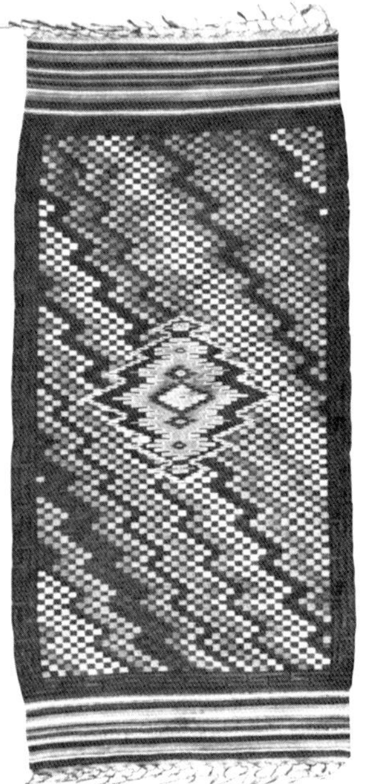

FIG. 40
Serape-style blanket (*saltillo*), Mexico, c. 1900, from the Mullicans' collection

such means to achieve transcendent states. All of these paintings express Mullican's stated desire to seek "the opening of a new world, opening of the mind into a kind of cosmic thought, ideas that went beyond what one saw, beyond form."[49]

The Ancestor Room of the *Dynaton* exhibition was also extremely important for Mullican (fig. 29). Displayed in this small gallery were pre-Columbian and Native American objects from the collections of the three Dynaton artists (mostly from Paalen's very fine collection), including Olmec, Aztec, Maya, Haida, Kwakiutl, Plains Indian, and numerous other pieces. The importance of indigenous art for Mullican cannot be overstated; many times he stressed his fascination with pre-Columbian and Northwest Coast art, and he himself collected not only kachinas but also Zuni wood carvings, Sioux pictographs, Plains Indians peyote (feather) fans, Navajo rugs, Rio Grande blankets, Brazilian masks, and other objects that significantly informed his own work (fig. 39). Mullican's love of the intricate stitching and elaborate patterning of Native American rugs and textiles (fig. 40) certainly informed his lifelong use of his printer's knife technique (fig. 41), while Sioux pictographs doubtless

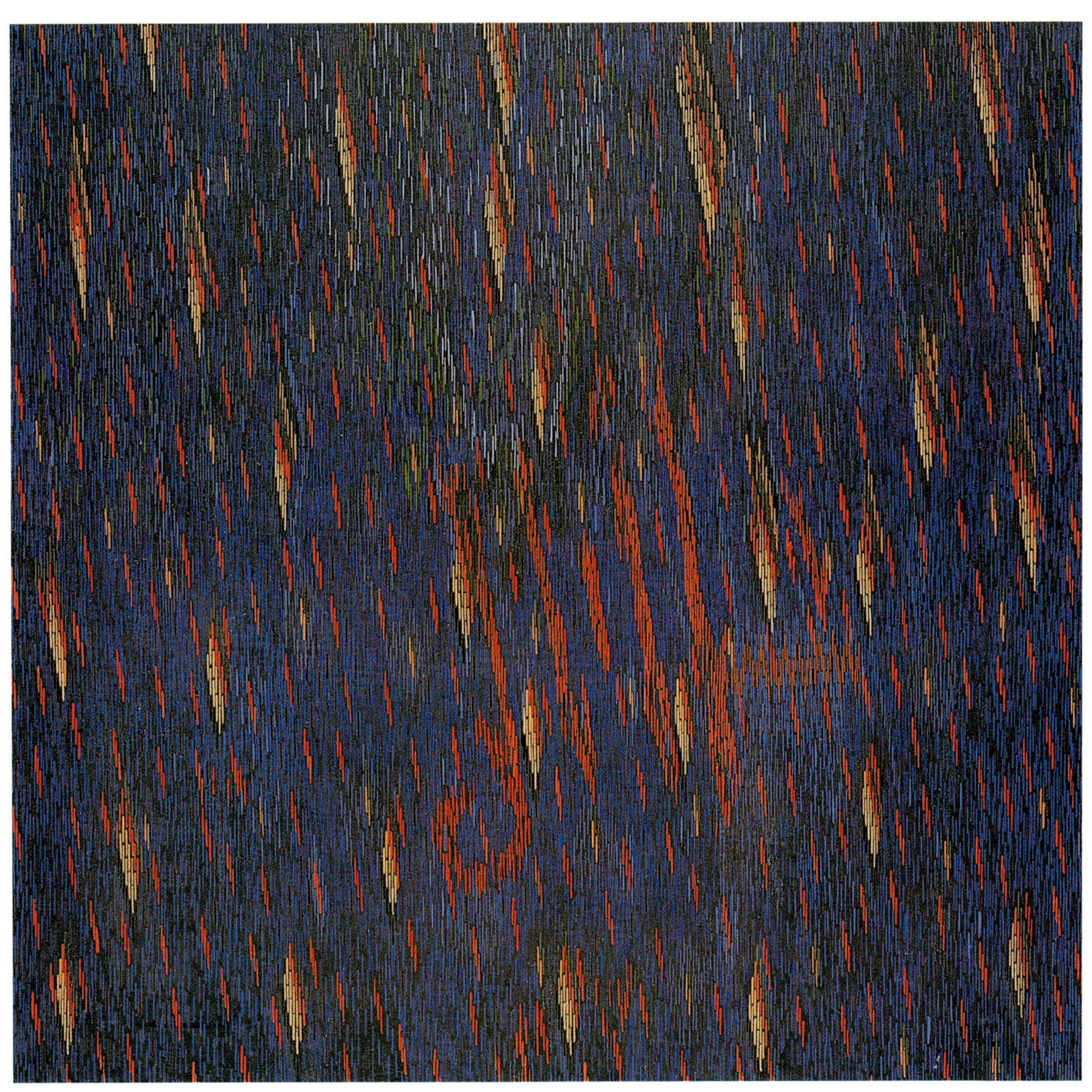

FIG. 41
*Untitled*, 1972, Luchita Mullican

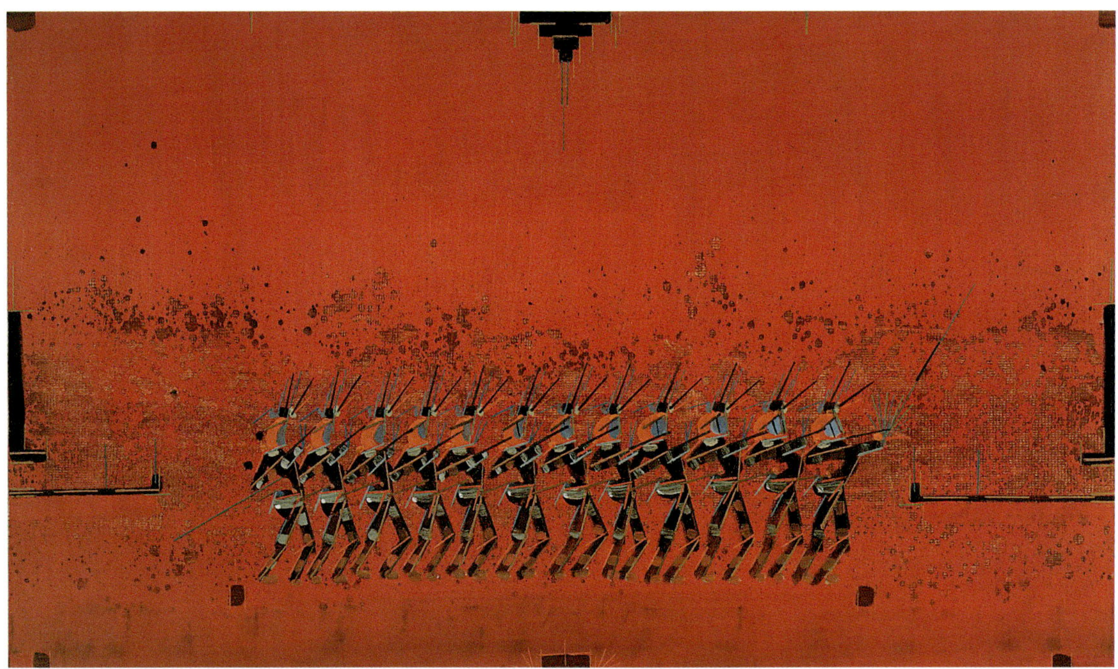

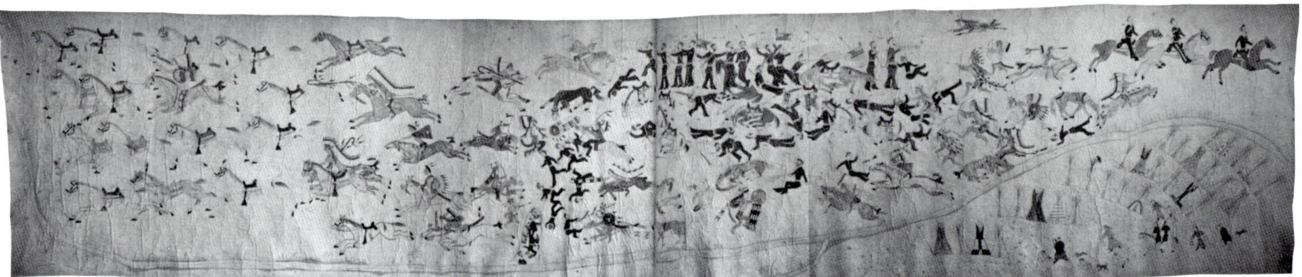

FIG. 42
*Untitled*, 1970, Santa Barbara Museum of Art

FIG. 43
Battle of Little Bighorn pictograph, Sioux (South Dakota), after 1876, from the Mullicans' collection (as illustrated in *The Artist as Collector* catalogue, 1975)

influenced a series of friezelike paintings Mullican made in the early 1970s (figs. 42 and 43). It has likewise been suggested that the figure on the right side of *Magic Night* (fig. 44) is based on a doll from the Chimu civilization in Peru (c. 1100–1500).[50] Mullican also borrowed titles—such as *Happily the Chiefs Regard You* (fig. 22) and *He-Rain* (fig. 45)—from Navajo poetry. Yet the importance of indigenous cultures for Mullican was not a question simply of copying motifs or styles; rather it was a total absorption of what Paalen called "the powerful rhythms"[51] of Native Americans and particularly (for Mullican) of the American Southwest. As Mullican clarified, "I never consciously copied Indian motifs or designs. It was a matter

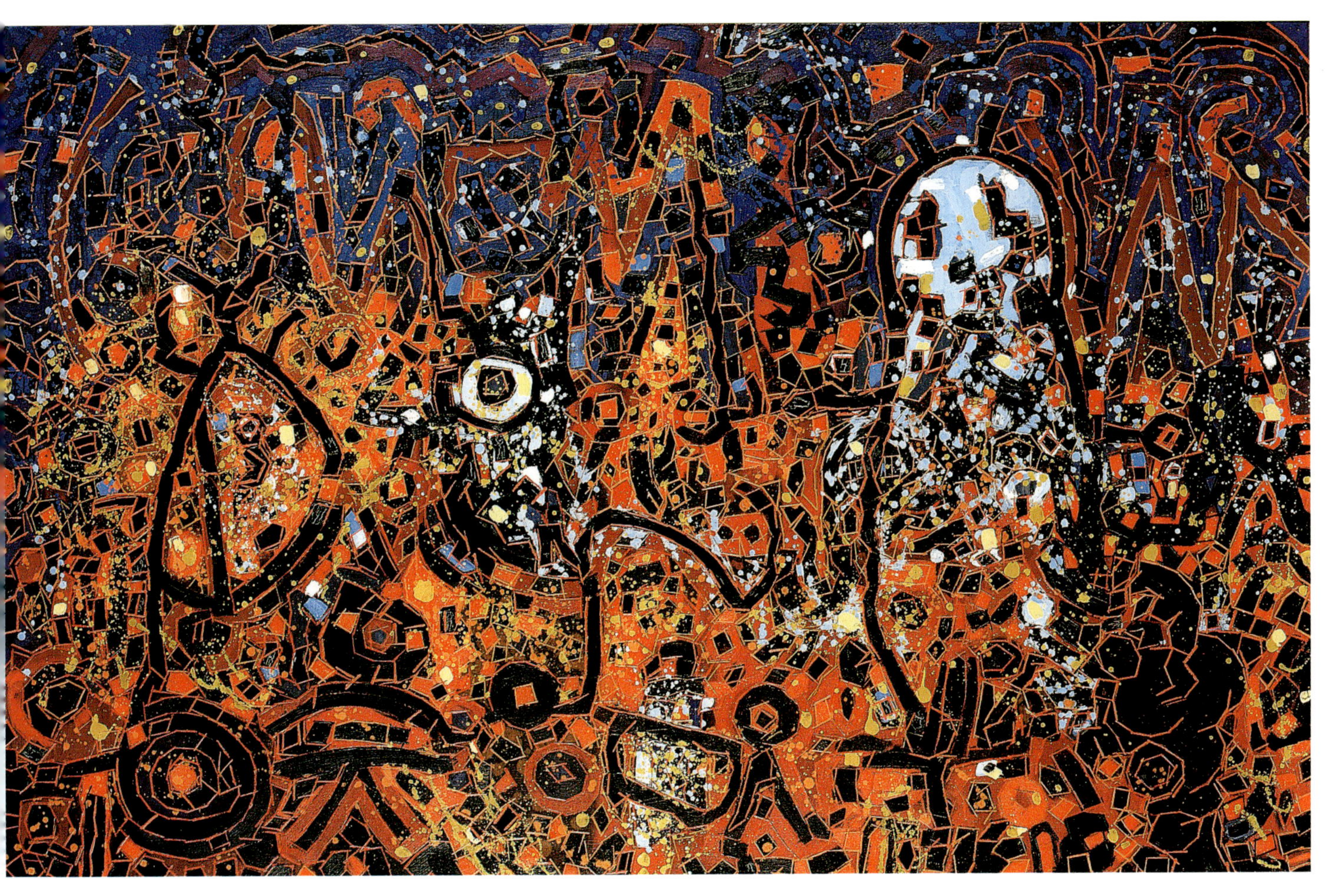

FIG. 44
*Magic Night*, 1966, Smith College Museum of Art

of extracting from nature what I saw and felt about the Southwest, just as the Indians must have. I create a new landscape of my own, instead of painting obvious reality."[52]

Mullican's sculptures of the early 1950s (figs. 46–50) were also very much informed by Native American artifacts as well as by Surrealist objects. These stick sculptures, collectively given the name *Tactile Ecstatics* by Wolfgang Paalen,[53] allowed Mullican the freedom to move away from the two-dimensional surface of the canvas into the three-dimensional volume of the real world. Mullican clearly acknowledged the Native American roots of these sculptures, which were "constructed out of dowels and spiked sticks.... Later I added string, feathers, etc., trying to create some kind of shamanistic objects—influenced by feathers, fans, Indian wands and staffs."[54] Yet even this three-dimensional "reality" was extremely fragile; according to Mullican, the sculptures were conceived as "temporary, put together with string and glue, perhaps to be destroyed ... even as I had seen a Navajo sand painting brushed away as the sun went down."[55]

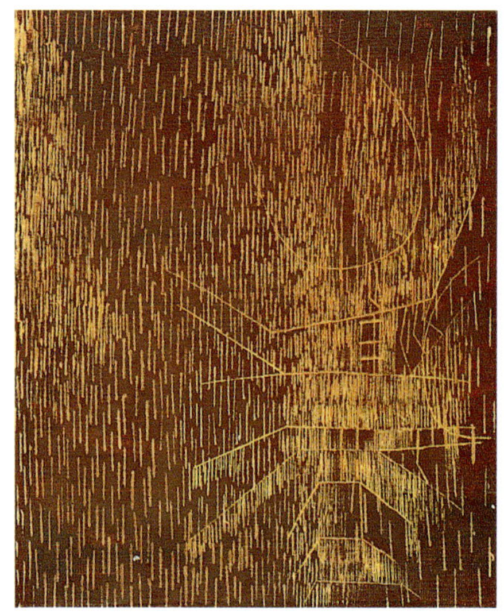

FIG. 45
*He-Rain*, 1949, Estate of the artist, courtesy Marc Selwyn Fine Art

## Dynaton vs. the New York School

So much of what Native American image-making was about—a meditative reflection on nature and man's place in the universe—was what Mullican strove to achieve in his own work: "We [the Dynaton painters] were involved with ... a kind of meditation, and for me this had a great deal to do with the study of nature, and the study of pattern.... We were dealing with art as a way of meditation."[56] While Mullican's East Coast contemporaries who formed the New York School were also interested in Native American art,[57] the meditative ethos of Mullican and his Dynaton colleagues distinguishes their work from the more heroic, even grandiose nature of Abstract Expressionism. The West Coast artists "assumed a transcendental and abstracted point of view outside the self-expressive ethos of the emergent New York School. In retrospect, Dynaton offered a holistic vision, meditative rather than self-assertive. The artists often used the word 'awareness' to describe a state of oneness with nature and with their plastic materials and means."[58] Along with other

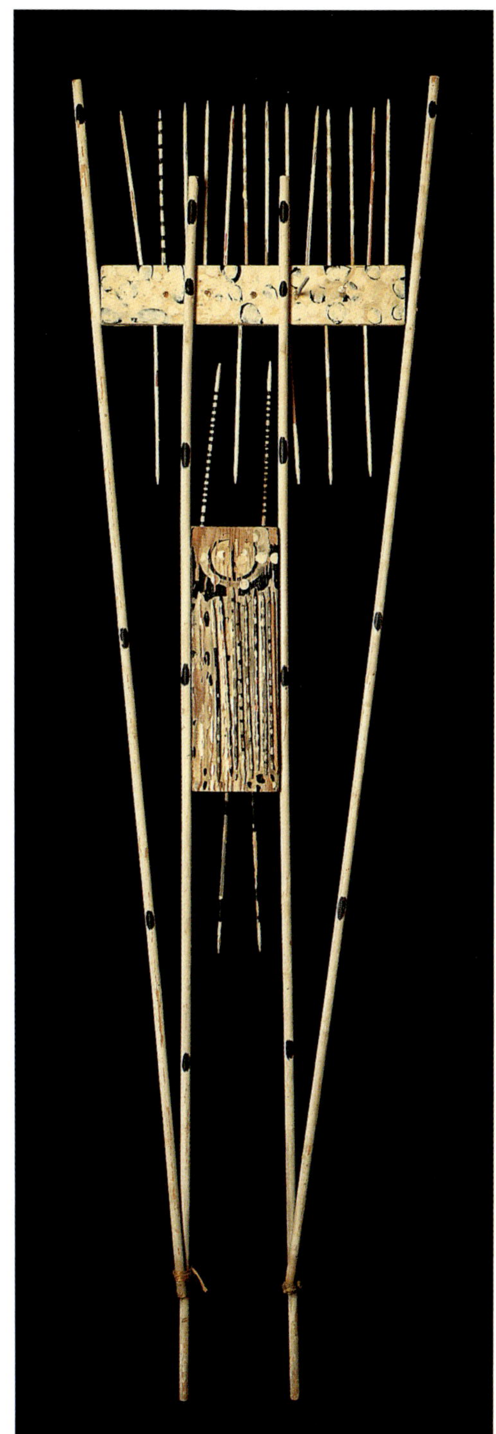

FIG. 46
*Untitled*, c. 1950–55,
Los Angeles County Museum of Art, promised gift of Mr. and Mrs. Gifford Phillips

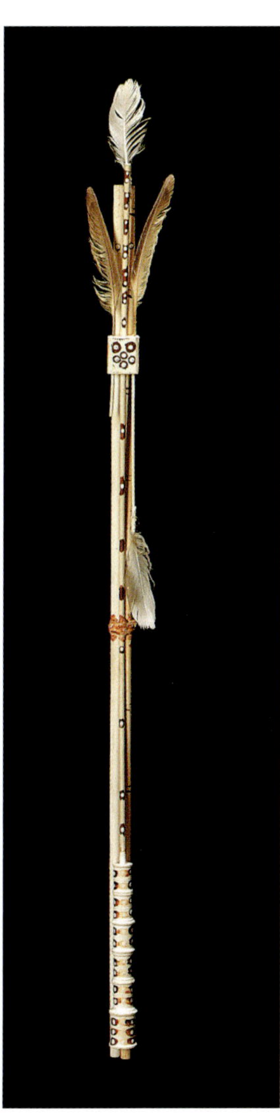

FIG. 47
*Untitled*, c. 1950–55,
Los Angeles County Museum of Art, promised gift of Mr. and Mrs. Gifford Phillips

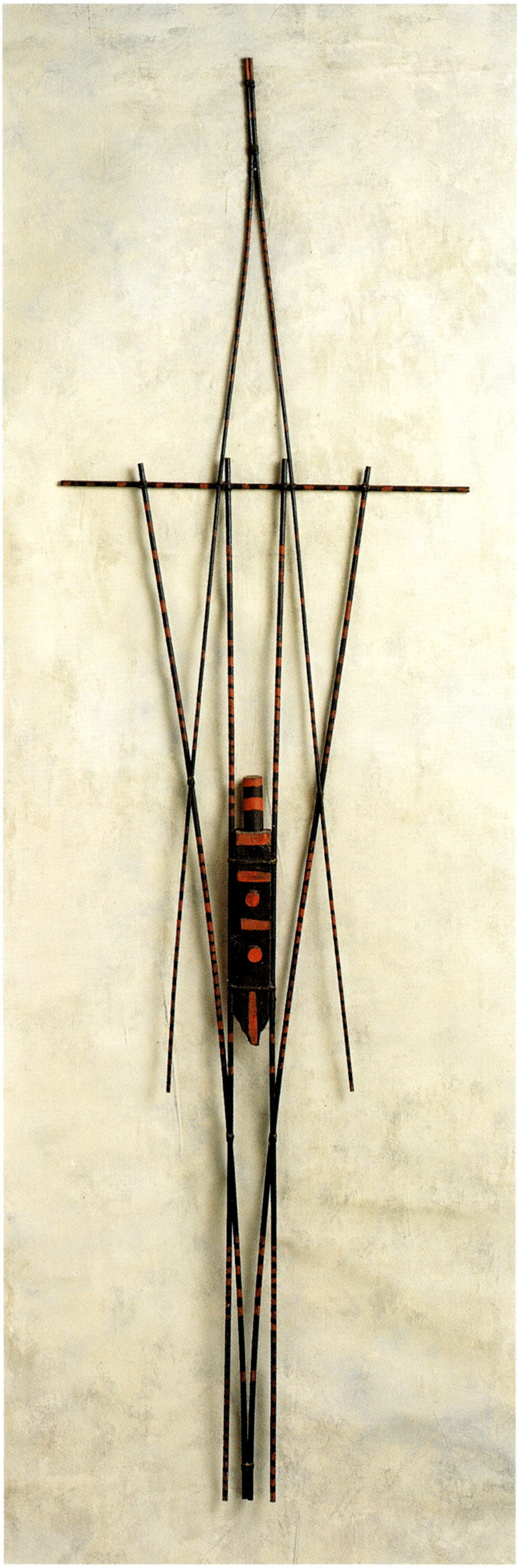

FIG. 48
*Untitled*, c. 1950–55,
Luchita Mullican

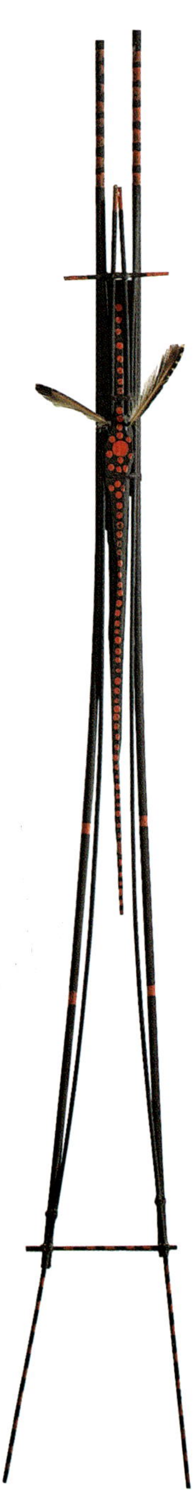

FIG. 49
*Untitled*, c. 1950–55,
Donna J. Cramer

West Coast artists such as Mark Tobey and Morris Graves, the Dynaton artists "created a holistic meditative art resonant with the special touch and calligraphic signature of the artist's hand but without the tragic overtones and violent gestural disruptions of the pictorial plane"[59] that was seen in New York-based Abstract Expressionism.

Mullican understood another important difference between the San Francisco-based Dynaton group and the New York-based Abstract Expressionists to revolve around the importance of content in painting. As he explained it, "What we [Dynaton artists] felt, what we were doing ... was this content of the possible.... It did not just include the formal use of the brush, like [Franz] Kline or [Clyfford] Still and so forth. They really didn't want any content. They didn't want it to be known. They were insulted if you even suggested there was such a thing. We were totally involved with our content."[60] The intimate, necessary connection of Mullican's paintings to nature and the world around him stood in contrast to the Abstract Expressionists, who "didn't want to say that [their painting] came from nature or that it came from the city or that it came from the sea or that it came from the mountain or from a cloud.... They wanted to disassociate from everything," Mullican said. To the Abstract Expressionists, painting was "an action that just came out of the paint tube."[61]

Already before the *Dynaton* exhibition in San Francisco, Mullican had his first solo exhibition in New York, at the Willard Gallery, where he had six shows between 1950 and 1967.[62] Willard in the 1950s and '60s also represented David Smith, Mark Tobey, and Morris Graves among many others. Although being a part of this stable of artists gave Mullican automatic entrée into New York

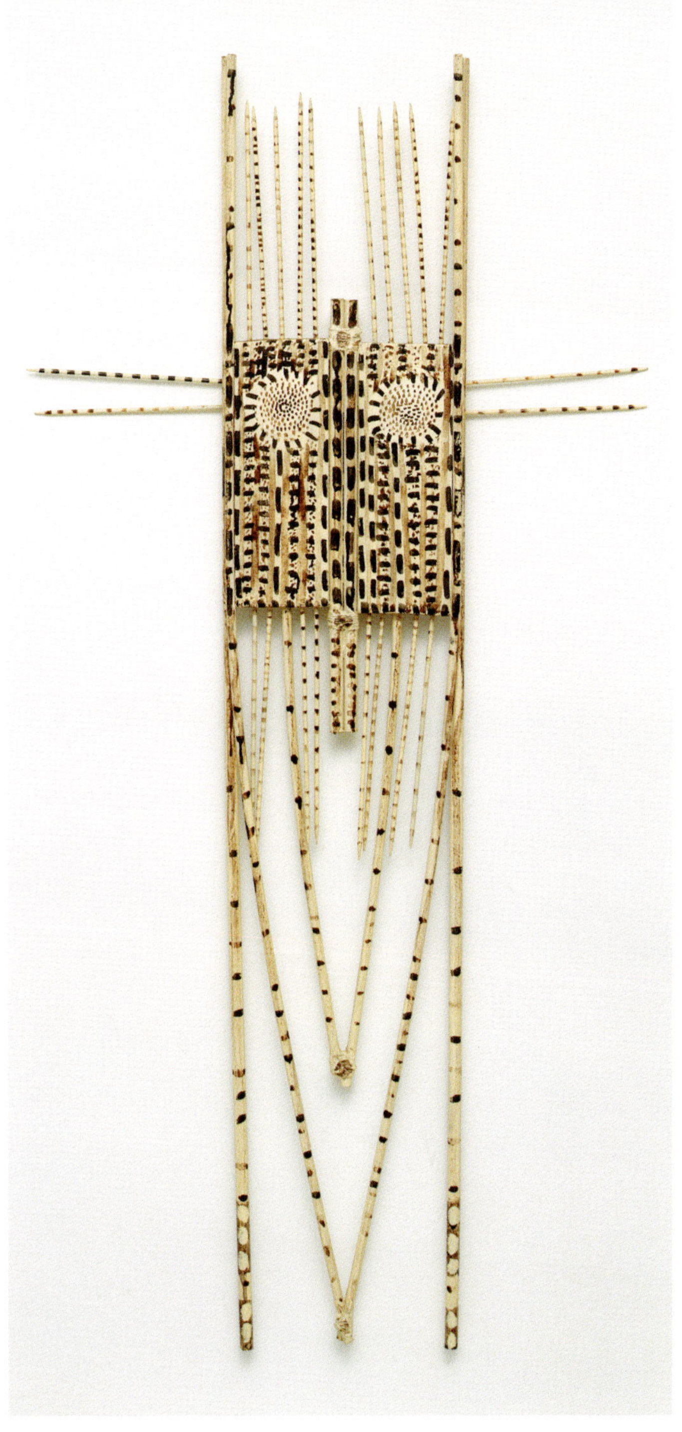

FIG. 50
*Presence*, 1955, The Museum of Modern Art

art circles, he nonetheless felt "awkward, kind of out of place.... Partly because of my youth, partly [because] of my insecurity, partly [because] I was still feeling my way, not really quite sure what I wanted to do."[63] His sense of isolation also stemmed from the fact that he was a California artist:

> [It] was rather difficult to deal with ... because if you weren't a part of the New York group it was very difficult. ... We all knew it.... [It] was as much as saying, "Well, we are a spiritual group, and we are just outweighed" by what was happening in Abstract Expressionism.... We were all kind of pushed down in relation to what was happening around us.... [It] was all the New York School ... that's all the curators, collectors, that's all they were interested in. So it was very difficult. Although several museums bought my paintings, The Museum of Modern Art bought one of my wooden constructions [fig. 50], and I would be included in exhibitions.... But as far as really being visible it was very limited. [64]

## Southern California and Zen Buddhism

Mullican nonetheless made an active decision to stay and build his career in California. After the close of their group show in 1951, the three Dynaton artists followed separate paths. Onslow Ford remained in the Bay Area, settling in the secluded and extraordinarily beautiful woods of Inverness. Paalen and Luchita Hurtado divorced. Paalen returned to Mexico; Mullican and Hurtado, who had fallen in love with each other, moved to Southern California (Hurtado directly to Santa Monica in 1951 and Mullican via Oklahoma the following year) and eventually married. They moved south, as Mullican later explained, because they "wanted to have a new beginning."[65]

Early on, Mullican had ambivalent feelings about Southern California. In August 1952 he wrote to Marian Willard Johnson (owner of the Willard Gallery) that he liked it so far: "The sun, the beaches, the summer never really hot, are all of the advantage." But,

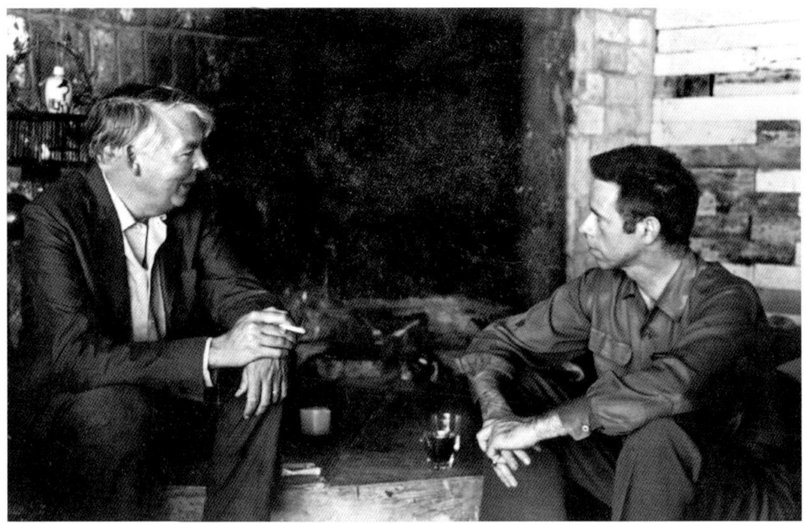

FIG. 51
Mullican with Alan Watts in the Bay Area in the early 1950s

he continued, "there is little else unless you take part in the Movie Industry—there is a certain respect for vulgarity and to be sure the human element is really not very clean, there are [too] many naked torsos in Cadillacs and the rest as I expected blotched out in sordid real estate developments. It is not quite so bad in this Santa Monica area, at least the air is clean and the fog cool."[66] Despite these misgivings, Mullican found a niche for himself in the Los Angeles art world; dealer Paul Kantor asked Mullican to join his stable (along with Richard Diebenkorn, Emerson Woelffer, Ynez Johnson, and others), and he associated with artists, writers, designers, and others including Charles and Ray Eames, Chistopher Isherwood and Don Bachardy, Jean Renoir, and James Agee. During the same years, however, Mullican railed against what he saw as the insularity and provincialism of Los Angeles: "What is seen [in New York] counts for more, what I show [in New York] is 'for keeps' and God knows I want to try and make it.... Here [Los Angeles] ...who the hell cares? (I'm very bitter about this whole Southern California so it is bound to creep in....)"[67]

Mullican nonetheless continued to make important work, informed not only by Native American sources but also increasingly by Zen Buddhism. Already in San Francisco, through Onslow Ford, Mullican had met Alan Watts, a foremost interpreter of Eastern philosophies (Zen Buddhism in particular) for the West (fig. 51). Watts

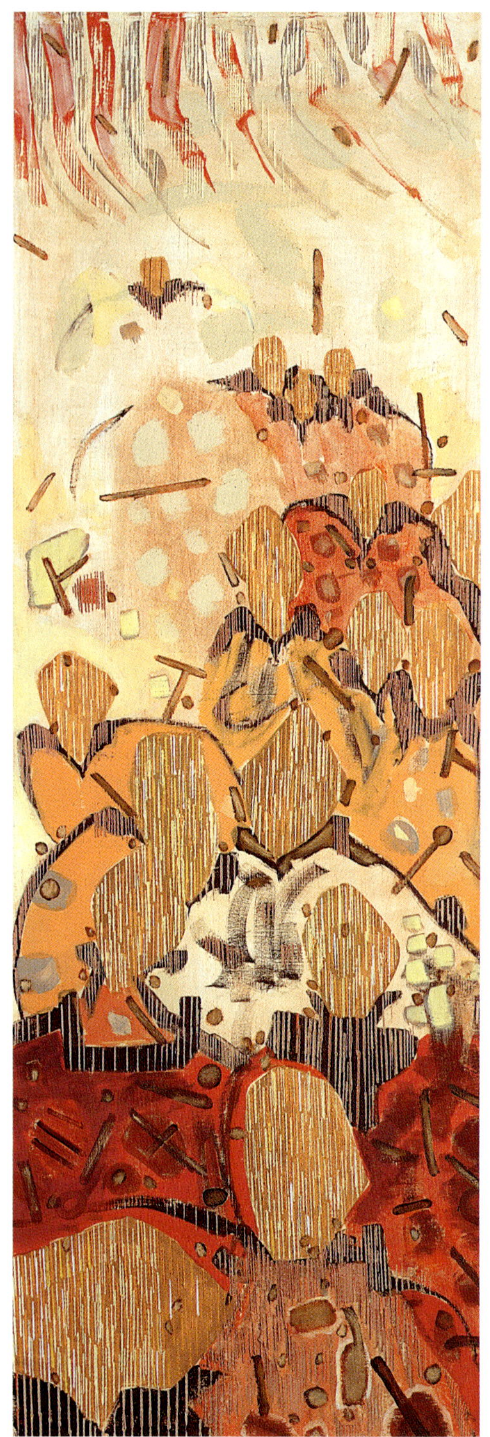

FIG. 52
*Zen Walk*, 1955, Betye Monell Burton

introduced Mullican to the 1953 English translation of *Zen in the Art of Archery* by Eugen Herrigel; Mullican realized that what the book described was exactly how he operated as a painter. In Herrigel's words, as a student becomes a master, "under the influence of Zen his proficiency becomes spiritual, and he himself, grown ever freer through spiritual struggle, is transformed."[68] Mullican's response to the book was immediate: "From that moment on, I became interested in Zen," he recalled, noting its impact on his art-making process.[69] A direct result of this influence can be seen in *Zen Walk* (fig. 52); in addition to the title's specific reference to Zen, the format and composition of the painting refer to Japanese hanging scrolls and Zen rock gardens. A series of almost completely white paintings from 1958 (figs. 53–55) suggests Mullican's continuing interest in the asceticism of the Zen sensibility, particularly as it was transmitted to the American audience in the 1950s.[70]

Zen seemingly influenced Mullican differently at different moments in his career. The title of *Mondo Interior* (fig. 56), made some dozen years after the white paintings, may refer to the Zen technique of *mondo*, a rapid question-and-answer method by which a Zen master attempts to help his student break out of the fetters of traditional patterns of thinking.[71] The medium and technique of *Mondo Interior*, which Mullican used in only an extremely small number of drawings, may well reflect the artist's attempt to free himself from the constraints of his usual means of image making. Although Mullican never formally practiced Zen, as he wrote to Marian Willard Johnson's husband Dan Johnson, "I don't practice it ... but I think I've *got it*."[72]

Mullican sought to expand his creative world in Southern California in other ways as well. He had been interested in theater since childhood, and in the early 1950s audited a playwriting class at UCLA and wrote several one-act plays. In 1955 Rachel Rosenthal (later acclaimed as a performance artist, though the term did not exist at the time) arrived in Los Angeles, first teaching at the Pasadena Playhouse and then starting the Instant Theatre, her own workshop for avant-garde improvisational theater/performance. Visual artists Wally Berman, John Altoon, and George Herms were

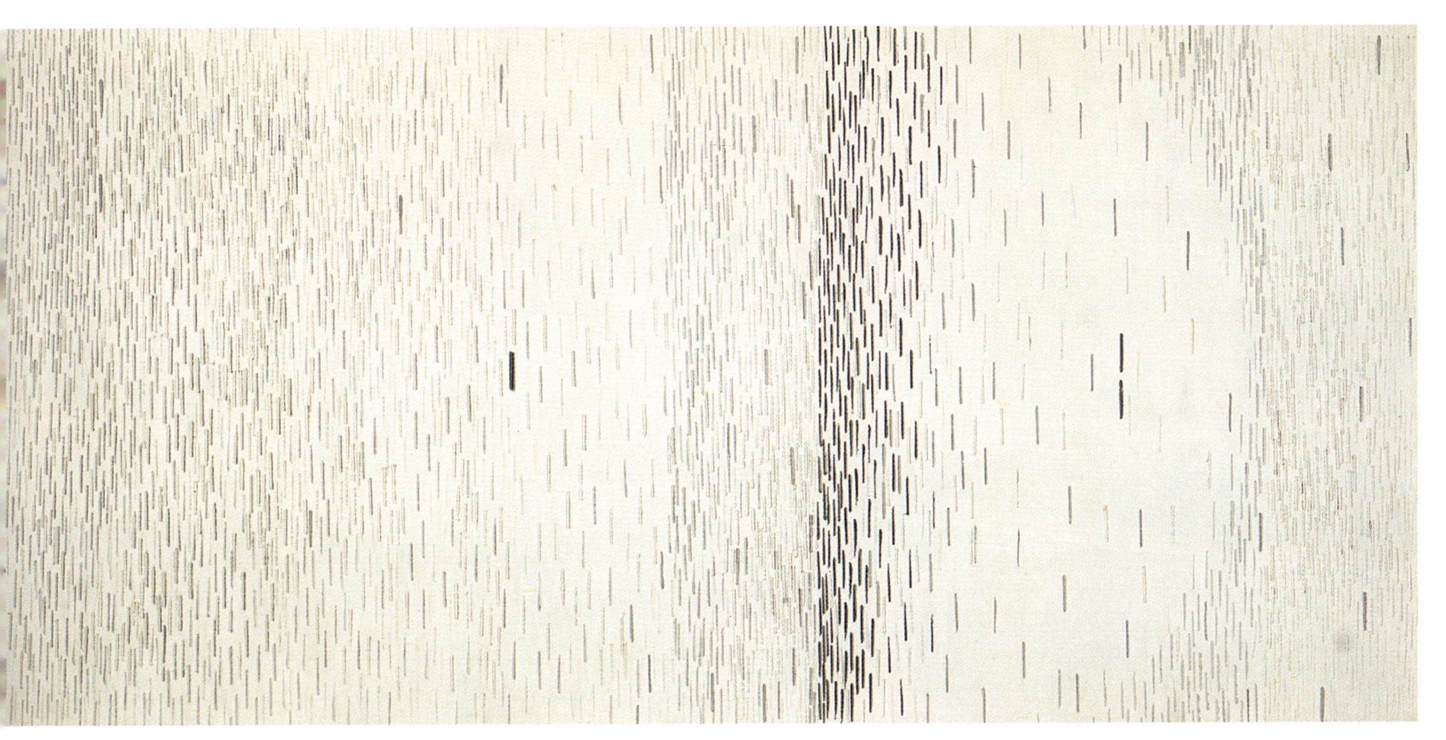

FIG. 53
*Untitled*, 1958, William Resnick, M.D. and Douglas Cordell, M.D.

FIG. 54
*Untitled*, 1958, Estate of the artist, courtesy Marc Selwyn Fine Art

FIG. 55
*Untitled*, 1958, Lucid Art Foundation

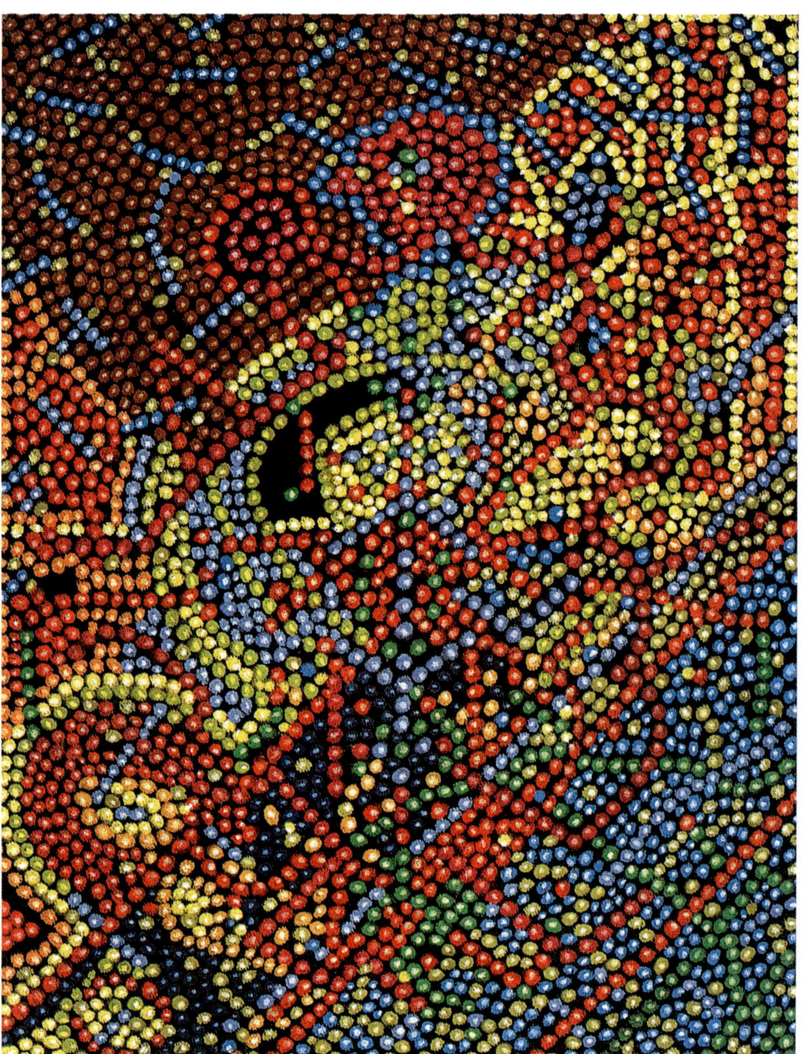

FIG. 56
*Mondo Interior*, c. 1970, Estate of the artist, courtesy Marc Selwyn Fine Art

among the regulars at Rosenthal's performances.[73] Mullican participated in Rosenthal's Instant Theatre for over a year (fig. 57), performing in a weekly improvised show with found objects as props and sets made of "junk assemblages."[74] He had stopped painting during this period, with his visual art production limited to objects he would use as part of his performances.[75] Ultimately, however, Mullican came to the conclusion that he could not do justice to both painting and performance. "I had to choose," he said. "Really I was a painter more than anything else. I could continue to write if I wanted to, but I was really a painter."[76] Following this realization, he resigned from Instant Theatre.

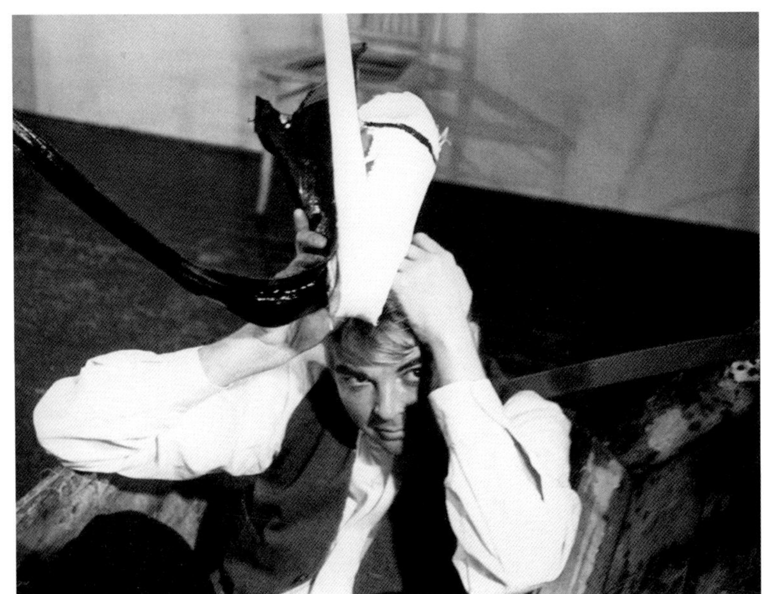

FIG. 57
Lee Mullican in Rachel Rosenthal's Instant Theatre, c. 1956–57

## Later work

The late 1950s and 1960s were years of flux for Mullican. In 1959 he began teaching at UCLA Extension, a continuing education program at the university. Soon thereafter he was awarded a Guggenheim Fellowship and spent the better part of a year in Rome with his family (Luchita, their first son Matt, and her son Daniel). Before coming back to the United States, they went on a camping tour of Europe, visiting numerous important prehistoric sites, including Altamira, Lascaux, and in Brittany. Rather than returning directly from these travels to a teaching job awaiting him at the University of Southern California, Mullican spent the first part of 1961 in upstate New York.[77] The family returned to Southern California in the summer so Mullican could teach at USC. Already by the fall of 1961, however, he had moved from USC to a permanent position in the art department at UCLA. By 1968 Mullican and his family were abroad again, this time on a year-long exchange program between UCLA and the University of Chile in Santiago. All of this change is reflected in Mullican's work of the late 1950s into the 1960s, when he experimented with a variety of styles. Paintings such as *California Landscape* and *The Chalk Garden* (figs. 58 and 59) are lyrical in tone and gentle in tonality; in other works from this same period Mullican relied much more heavily on his crisp printer's knife technique and a brighter palette (figs. 60–63), while in yet others he used a much looser, almost Expressionist vocabulary (figs. 64–66; see also fig. 44).

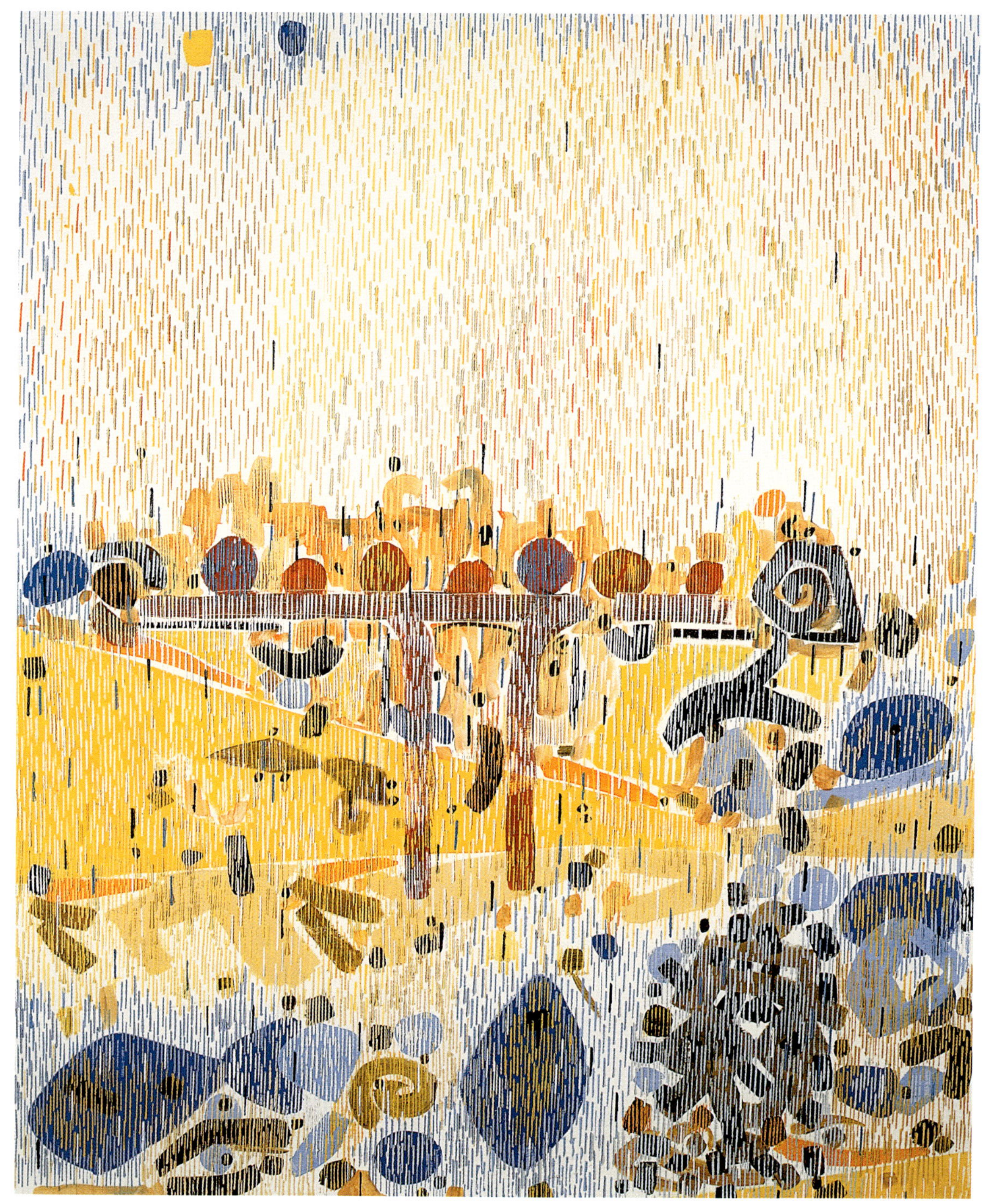

FIG. 58
*California Landscape*, 1958,
Estate of the artist, courtesy
Marc Selwyn Fine Art

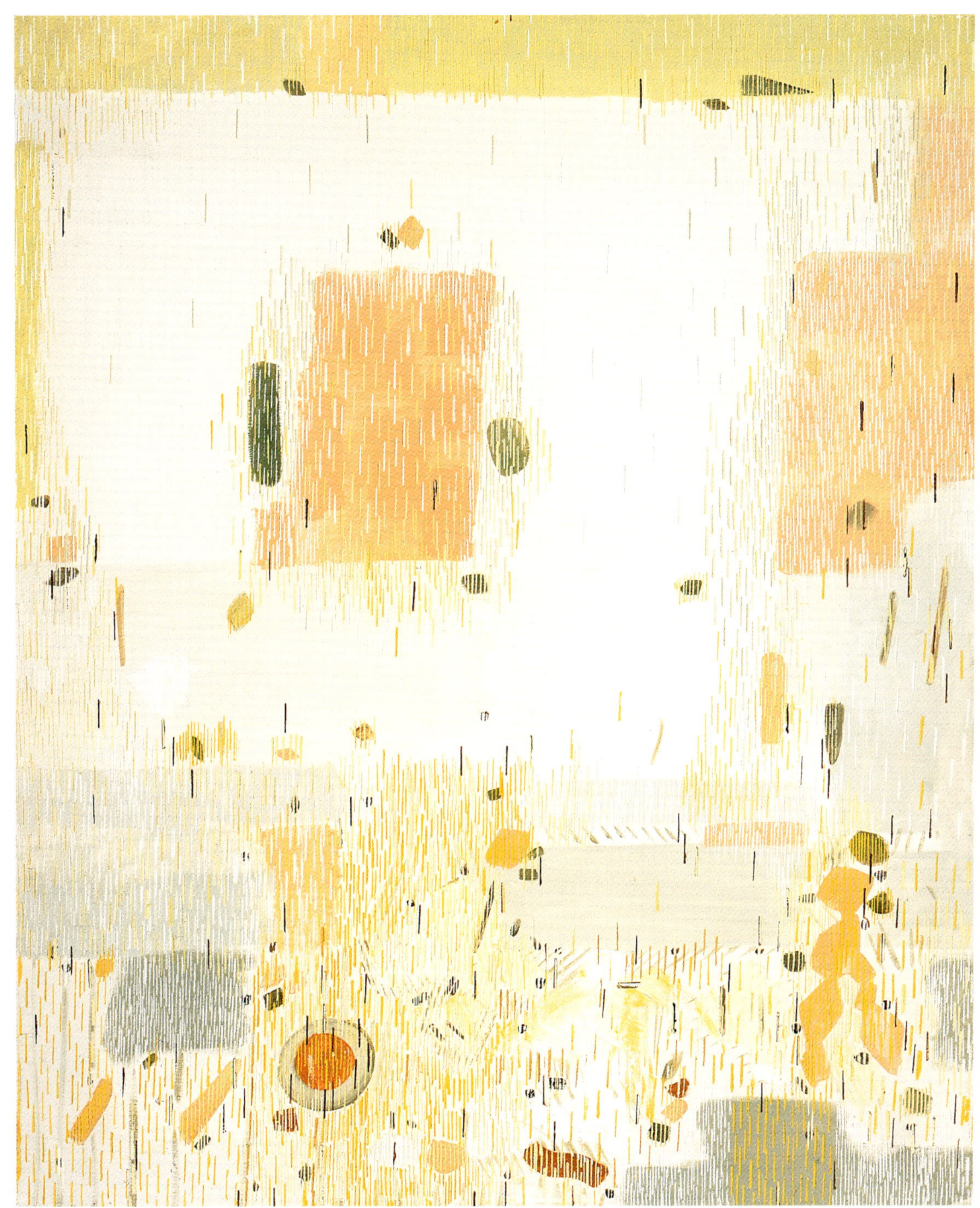

FIG. 59
*The Chalk Garden*, 1958,
Aimee Knowlton and
Jason Asch

FIG. 60
*Summer Fall*, 1961, Estate of the artist, courtesy Marc Selwyn Fine Art

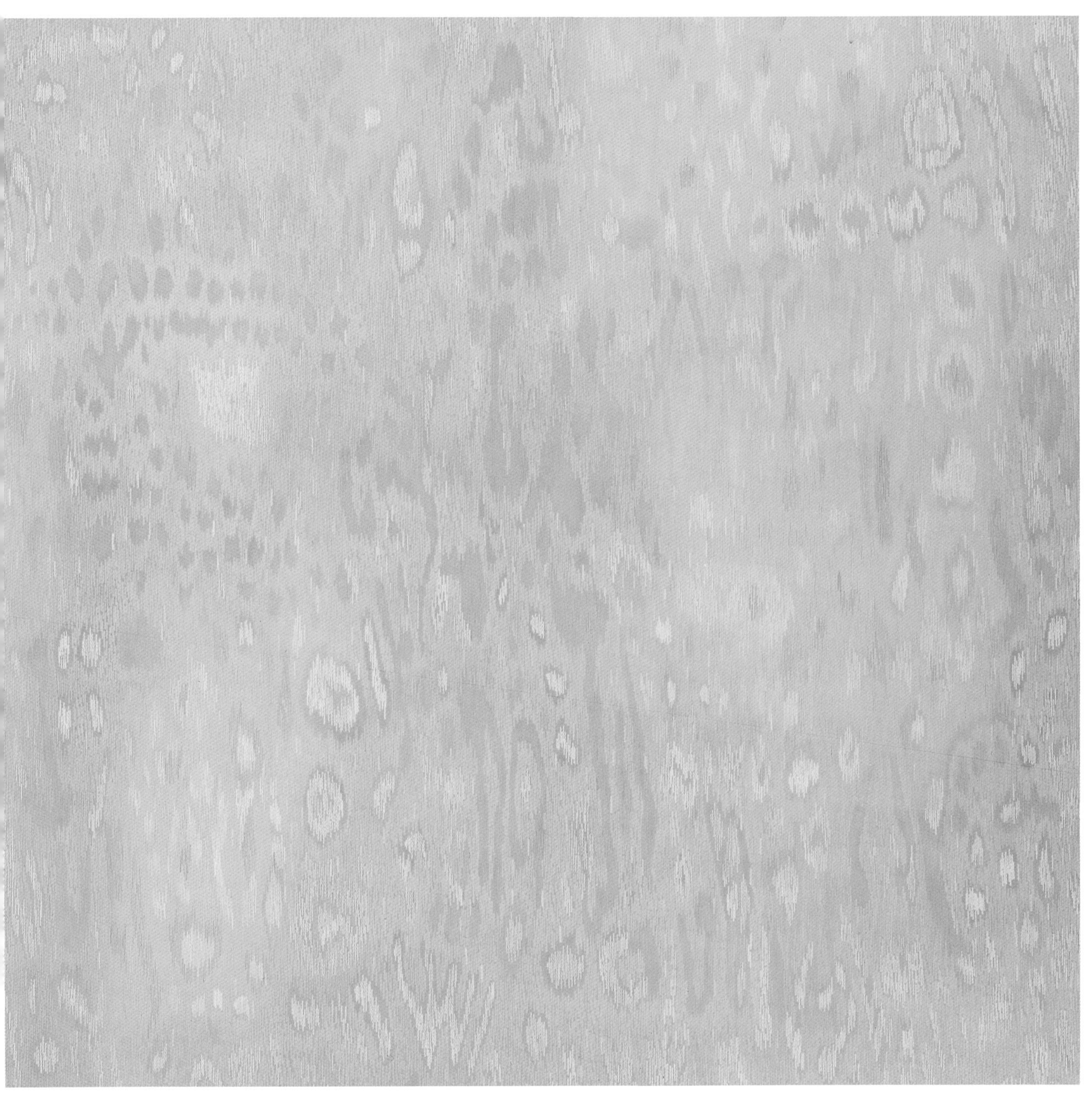

FIG. 61
*Paradise Gardens: A Walk,*
c. 1962, Dana and Stephen Sigoloff

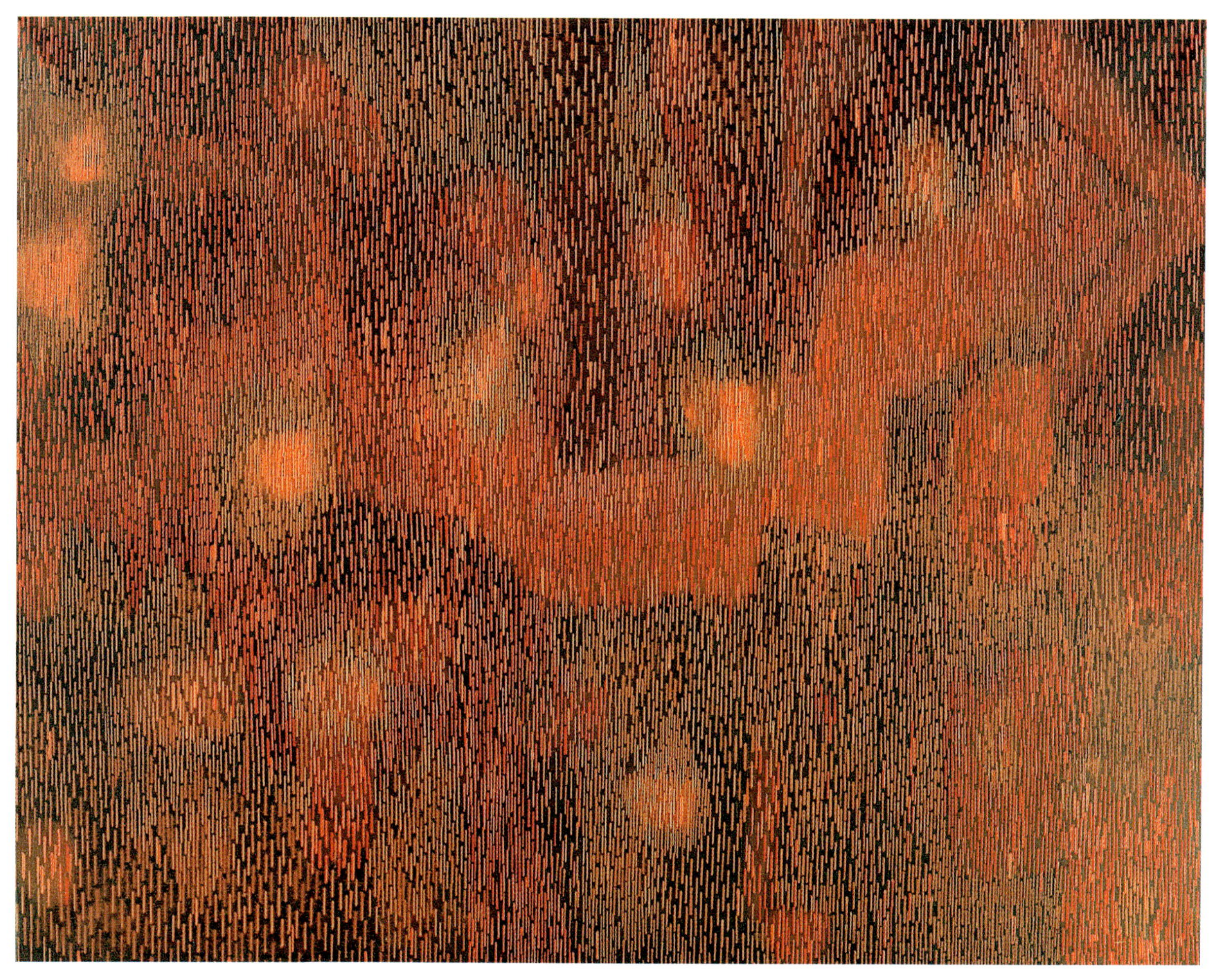

FIG. 62
*Evening Raga*, 1962,
Luchita Mullican

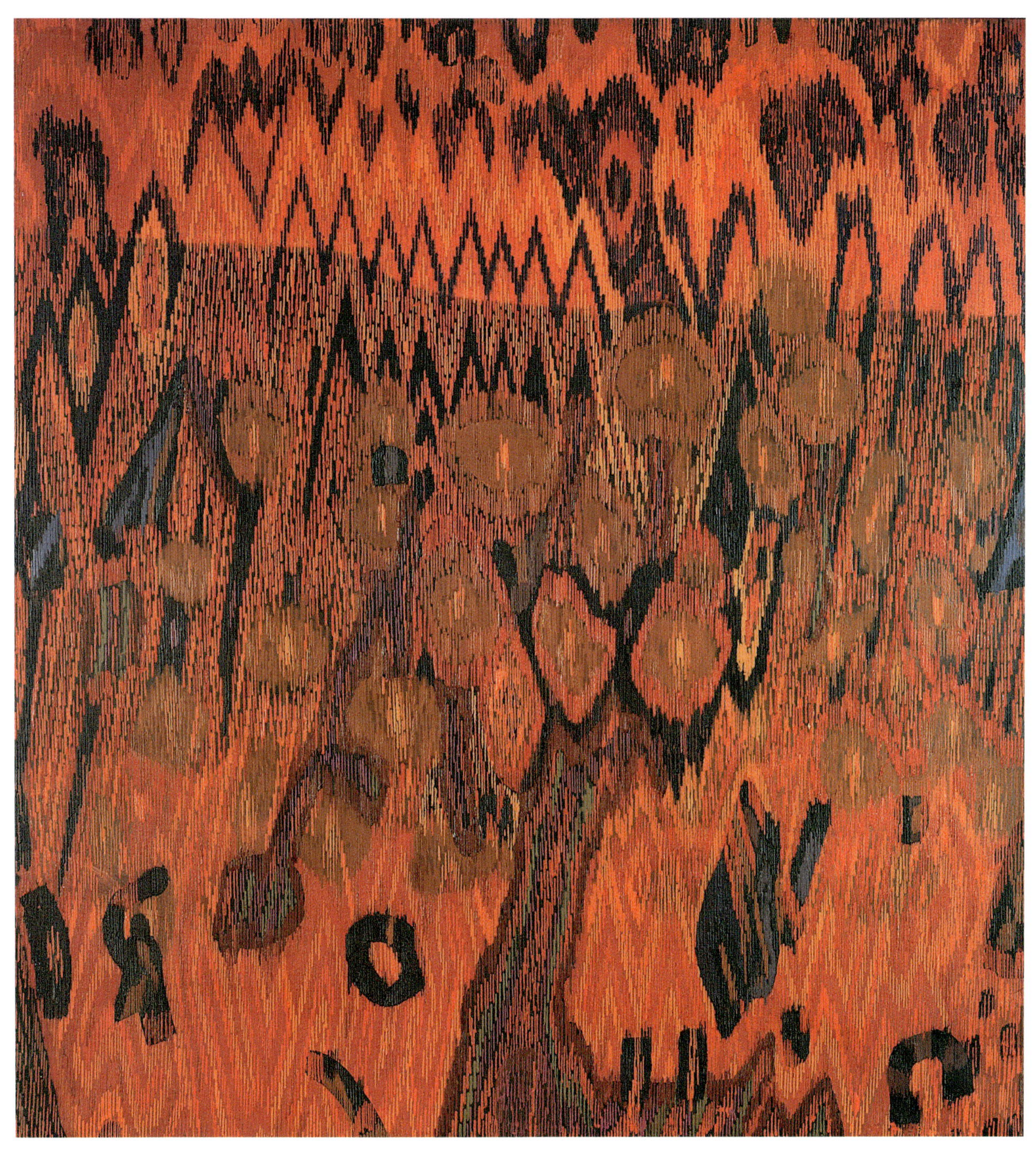

FIG. 63
*Untitled* (from the *Raga* series), c. 1962, Donna J. Cramer

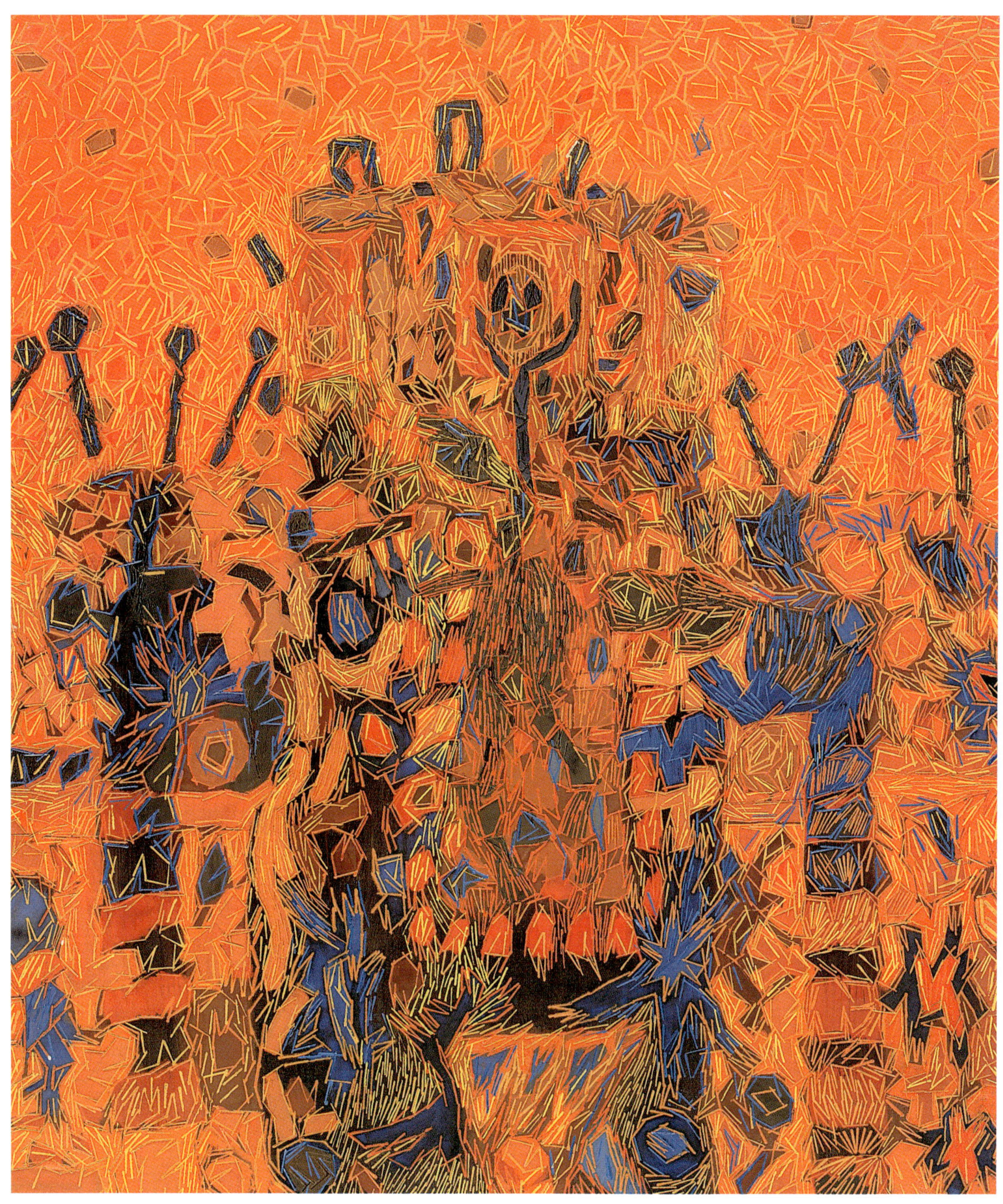

FIG. 64
*Fable*, 1963–64, Estate of the artist, courtesy Marc Selwyn Fine Art

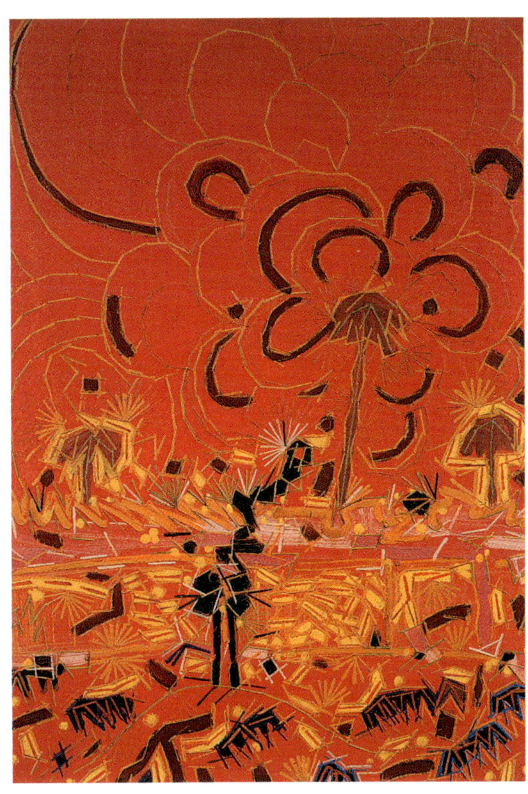

FIG. 65
*Landscape #5*, 1966,
Cecilia Dan

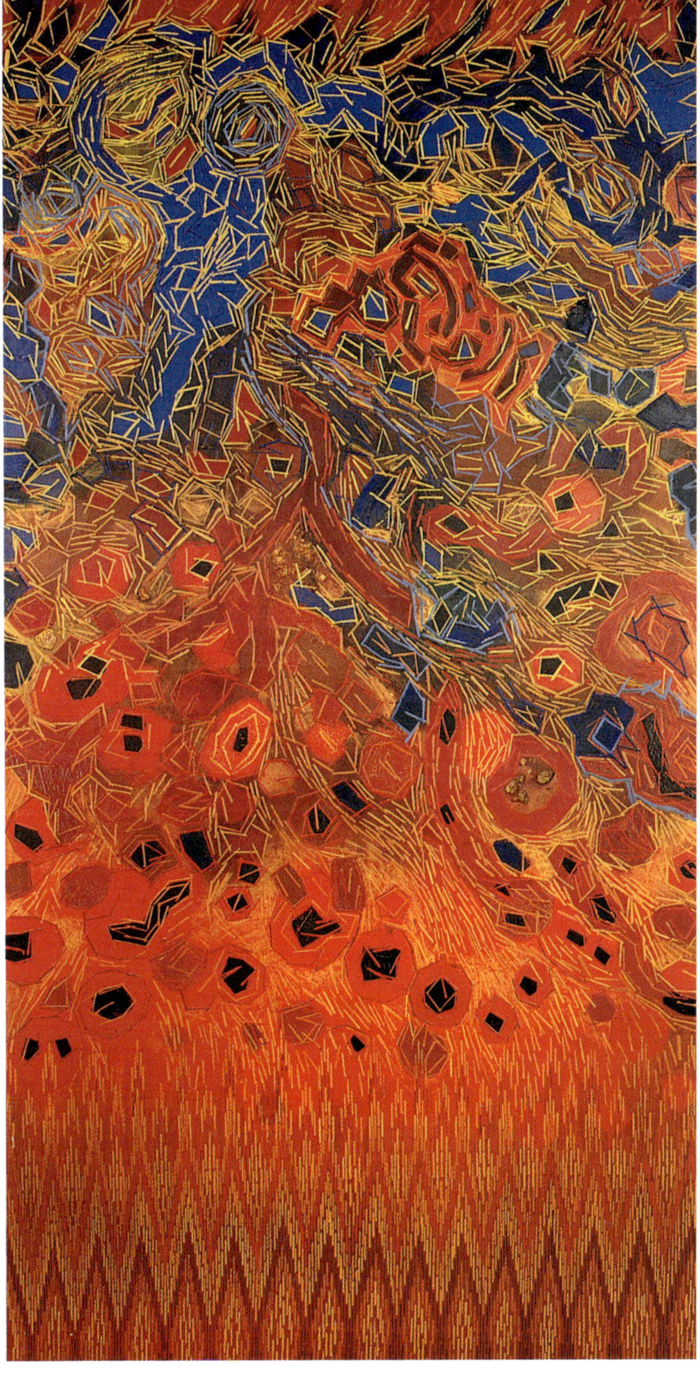

FIG. 66
*Pacific Rhythms*, 1964,
Nina Anthoine

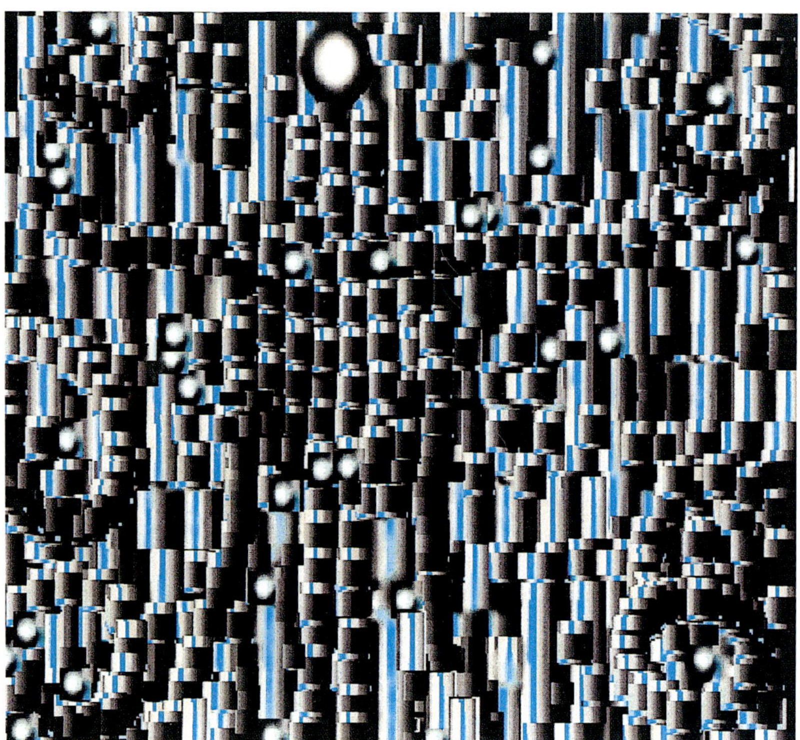

FIG. 67
*Untitled*, 1988, ink jet print on paper, 24 x 30 3/16 in., collection of Luchita Mullican, on loan to the Grunwald Center for the Graphic Arts, Hammer Museum, Los Angeles

By the late 1970s Mullican had embarked on his series of *Guardian* paintings, returning once again to his knife-stroke technique and using a limited and dark palette. *Guardian of the Modern* (p. 7), with its abstracted suggestion of a figural presence (the eponymous guardian), is typical of this series. Mullican painted these can-vases from the top down, flat on a table. He did not make any preliminary sketches or studies but rather allowed the image to materialize as he worked, akin to the Surrealists' automatist methods.[78]

The notion of allowing oneself the freedom to experiment, of not forcing oneself to adhere to a signature style, was as significant for Mullican the teacher as it was for Mullican the artist. Over the course of four decades he became an important mentor to a host of students including Tony Berlant, Vija Celmins, Michael McMillen, and Lari Pittman. His open, self-effacing, and supportive manner of teaching allowed his students to find their own strengths and their own paths, rather than forcing them to work in a particular style or to follow "in the master's footsteps."[79] Mullican also felt he could learn from his students just as they could learn from him. Tony Berlant remembers Mullican spending hours studying the Native

American blankets in Berlant's world-class collection, recalling that "he didn't say much but he looked very carefully."[80] Similarly, Mullican was willing to experiment with the computer as an art-making tool in the late 1980s, something that many students and young artists—but far fewer painters born in 1919—were open to at that time. Although he never exhibited them publicly, Mullican made an extensive series of unique computer-generated images (fig. 67) using equipment made available in the UCLA art department for just such experimentation.[81]

## South Asian influences

Mullican's openness, his willingness to consider new options and possibilities, is also evident in his growing interest after 1980 in India and its art and culture. The titles of certain Mullican paintings or series of works from two decades earlier already suggest his interest in Indian themes, specifically ragas (figs. 62 and 63).[82] In 1980 he and Luchita made the first of several trips to India, where they stayed with the Sarabhai family (friends of Luchita's of many years' standing), who were textile manufacturers and founders of the Calico Museum of Textiles in Ahmedabad. Given Mullican's interest in Native American textiles, it is not surprising that he would also have been intrigued by Indian textiles with their intricate dying and weaving techniques (fig. 68). The Sarabhais' longtime interest in and familiarity with Western modernism (they had worked at various moments with Frank Lloyd Wright, Alexander Calder, and Charles and Ray Eames, among many others) facilitated Mullican's increasing understanding of Indian art and culture, as did the fact that Grace McCann Morley—who had been director of The San Francisco Museum of Art during the Dynaton years—by then was head of the National Museum in New Delhi. With a growing interest in Indian culture after his first trip there, Mullican returned numerous times in connection with an official governmental exchange program between India and the United States through which he was to organize an exhibition of contemporary Indian painting for the U.S. *Neo-Tantra: Contemporary Indian Painting Inspired by Tradition*, mounted in 1985, was the result.[83]

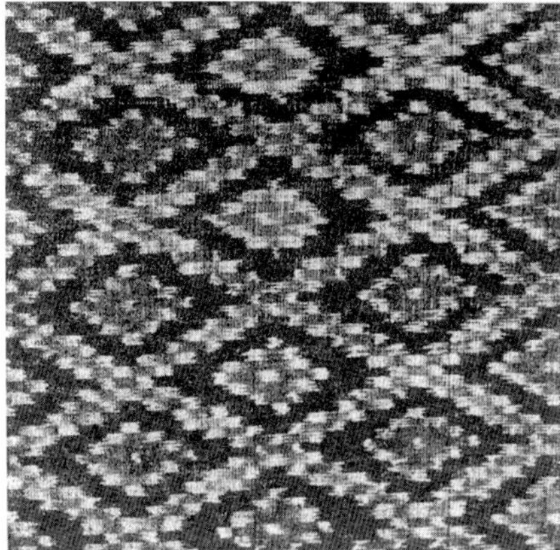

FIG. 68
Detail of cotton ikat *rumal* (cloth cover) from Pochampalli, Andhra Pradesh, India, c. 1950, Calico Museum of Textiles, Ahmedabad, Gujarat, India

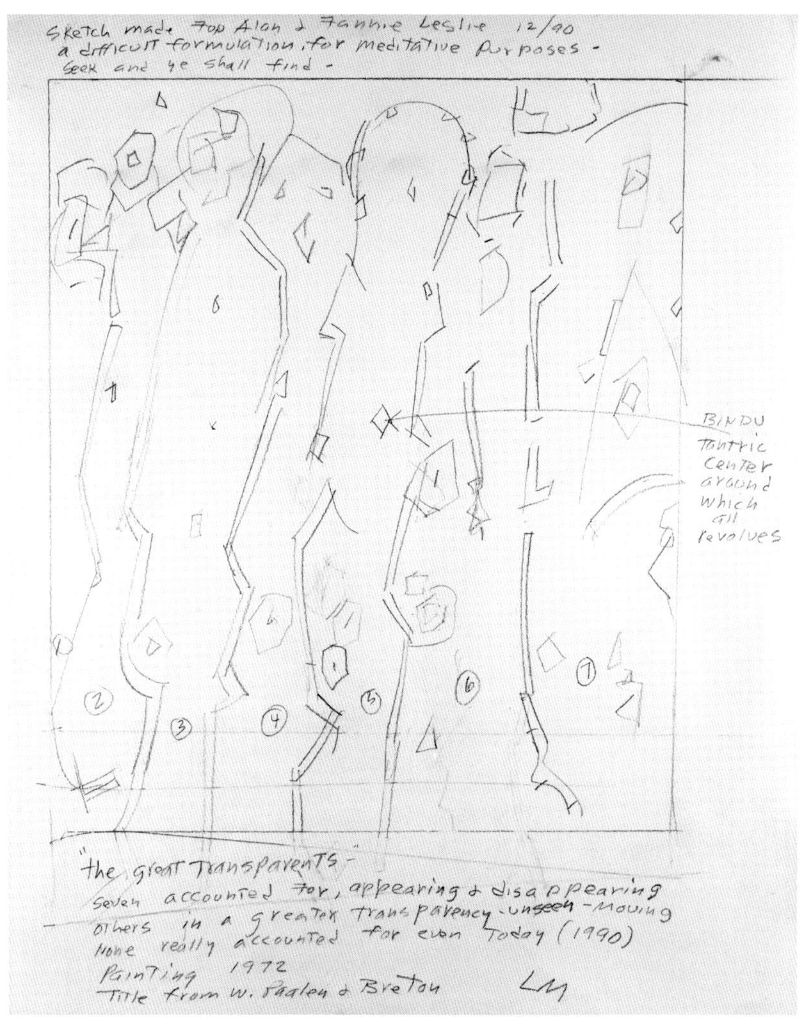


FIG. 69
*The Great Transparents,*
1990, graphite on paper,
14 x 11 in., The Museum
of Contemporary Art, Los
Angeles, gift of Fannie and
Alan Leslie

Traditional tantra is both a philosophy and an actual type of meditation practiced by certain Hindu as well as Buddhist sects. As described in the *Neo-Tantra* exhibition catalogue:

> The most important concept found in the tantras is the necessity of unifying (ceasing to separate) apparent opposites in order to attain enlightenment. These opposites are usually represented as male energy (*Shiva*) and female energy (*Shakti*) or as the individual (*purusha*) and nature (*prakriti*). Thus the equality, or complementarity, of male and female is a foremost aspect of tantric practice, as the union of both is required in order to achieve the highest understanding. According to the tantras, male and female (or the individual and nature) are not really separate, but are only seen that way from the viewpoint of worldly phenomena. When one has achieved a state of perfect enlightenment the two will be seen as completely integrated.[84]

Mullican doubtless understood this integration of opposites as akin to his goals of integrating abstraction and figuration as well as integrating the cosmic and the individual. Indeed, "another important tantric concept is that of the equality of macrocosm and microcosm. According to this principle everything in the external universe is represented in some form internally,"[85] which almost literally parallels Mullican's notions of "outer-space" and "inner-space."[86]

The *Neo-Tantra* project led in turn to an exhibition entitled *Visions of Inner Space* that Mullican coorganized in 1987 as another cultural exchange between India and the U.S.[87] Devoted to Western artists who shared Mullican's sensibilities, the show included works by Onslow Ford as well as by Graves, Tobey, and others interested in the spiritual and the mystical. Mullican spoke of the time he spent in India over these years as "one of the richest spiritual experiences . . . [based on Indians'] respect for life, their respect for religion, their respect for nature."[88]

It is interesting to consider Mullican's explication, in the form of a drawing dated December 1990 (fig. 69), of his 1972 painting

*The Great Transparents II* (fig. 70). According to the notes Mullican made on his 1990 drawing, the title of his 1972 canvas derived from Surrealism and Paalen; however, in 1990 he identified the central yellow diamond of the 1972 composition not as something evolving out of Surrealism and the Dynaton but as a *bindu,* which Mullican defined as the "tantric center around which all revolves." Based on the Sanskrit word for dot, *bindu* metaphysically

> represents the unity of the static (male, *Shiva*) and the kinetic (female, *Shakti*) cosmic principles, which expand to create the infinite universe of matter and spirit. A meeting-ground of subject and object, this is exactly the kind of spiritual oneness that the tantra artist strives for. A region where art and artist, creator and viewer merge into a single identity, becoming one with the cosmos as a whole.[89]

In 1993 Mullican very specifically stated that after his travels to India he referred to as a *bindu* what he earlier "would have called ... a focal point or something in the center of the canvas [around] which ... everything can revolve, evolve."[90] It is not that Mullican's fundamental concerns changed over time but that his cultural vocabulary expanded.

At its core Mullican's art is about what it meant to be a human in the second half of the twentieth century, a period bracketed by the deployment of the atom bomb in 1945 and Mullican's own death in 1998. His artistic concerns were simultaneously as expansive as the entire cosmos and as minute as the thousands of printer's knife strokes out of which he built his imagery; his artistic interests ranged equally widely, from Native American to South Asian art, from Surrealism to Zen Buddhism. Mullican sought both within himself and throughout the cosmos for the familiar as well as the awesome; he then strove to express the specific as well as the universal through his art, which encompassed both abstraction and figuration. As Mullican himself described it, "You might call my paintings landscapes of the mind. Anything can happen; there can be caves in space, or mountains in the sky, or stars on the ground. It's rather like playing God, myself."[91]

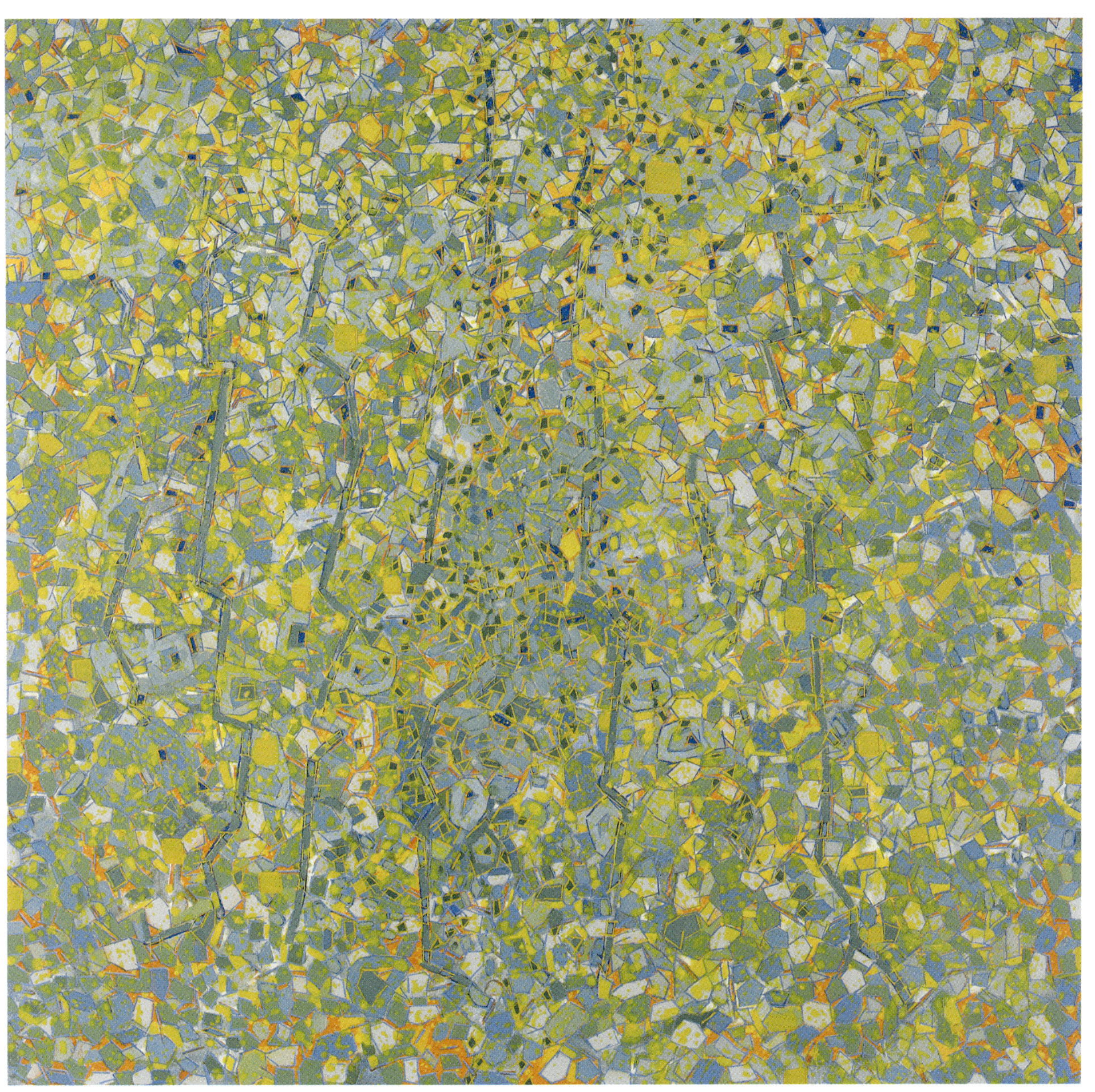

FIG. 70
*The Great Transparents II*, 1972, oil on canvas, 75 x 75 in., The Museum of Contemporary Art, Los Angeles, gift of Fannie and Alan Leslie

## NOTES

The title of this essay derives from a brief, unpublished testimonial to Mullican penned in 1985 by his friend and fellow artist Isamu Noguchi:

> For Lee Mullican,
> I have always known Lee as a shaman. Transformed. He knows but says little. More American it seems than others. Indian. With his feet planted on the virgin soil, not in our polyglot cities. His head is in the clouds, far above any skyscrapers. Lee remembers the reality that was here before. He gives us metaphors to hear again small sounds. And leads us into reverie.

I am grateful to Luchita Mullican for giving me access to this typescript.

1 Lee Mullican, unpublished typescript, July 1980.

2 Mullican, interviewed by Joann Phillips, in *Los Angeles Art Community: Group Portrait: Lee Mullican* (Los Angeles: UCLA Oral History Program, 1977), 3.

3 Lee Mullican, interviewed by Paul Karlstrom (May 22, 1992 and January 26, February 11, and March 4, 1993), transcript, Oral History Program, Archives of American Art/Smithsonian Institution. This quote from May 22, 1992.

4 Mullican, Karlstrom interview, May 22, 1992.

5 Mullican, Karlstrom interview, May 22, 1992.

6 Mullican, Karlstrom interview, May 22, 1992.

7 Mullican, Karlstrom interview, May 22, 1992. Mullican recounted a story about an abstract painting in a University of Oklahoma exhibition that was (erroneously) reproduced upside down in publicity materials for the show; in response, the artist hung the painting to match the publicity image. As Mullican recalled, "That [was] an attitude that really hit home."

8 Mullican, Karlstrom interview, May 22, 1992.

9 Mullican, Karlstrom interview, May 22, 1992.

10 Mullican, Phillips interview, 12–13.

11 Mullican, Karlstrom interview, May 22, 1992.

12 Mullican, Karlstrom interview, May 22, 1992. See also Phillips interview, viii.

13 Mullican, Karlstrom interview, May 22, 1992.

14 Mullican, Phillips interview, 29–30.

15 Mullican, Karlstrom interview, May 22, 1992.

16 Mullican, Karlstrom interview, May 22, 1992.

17 Mullican, Karlstrom interview, May 22, 1992.

18 Mullican, Karlstrom interview, May 22, 1992.

19 Mullican, Phillips interview, 34–35.

20 Mullican, Karlstrom interview, May 22, 1992.

21 For detailed accounts of Paalen's life and career, see Andreas Neufert, *Wolfgang Paalen 1905–1959: Denker und Visionär im Medium der Malerei/The Painter as Thinker and Visionary,* trans. Thomas J. Minnes (Dresden: Galerie Döbele, 2001) and Amy Winter, *Wolfgang Paalen: Artist and Theorist of the Avant-Garde* (Westport, CT and London: Praeger, 2003).

22 Wolfgang Paalen, "During the Eclipse," *DYN* 6 (Nov. 1944): 20; quoted in Winter, *Wolfgang Paalen*, 124.

23 Mullican, Karlstrom interview, May 22, 1992.

24 Mullican, Phillips interview, 36.

25 *DYN* 4-5 (December 1943), n.p.

26 The specter of the atom bomb specifically influenced Mullican's postwar drawings, as seen in *Personnage* (fig. 7), which clearly refer-

ences a mushroom cloud.

27 Mullican, Phillips interview, 49–50.

28 See *The Artist as Collector: Selections from Four California Collections of the Arts of Africa, Oceania, the Amerindians and the Santeros of New Mexico*, exh. cat., ed. James B. Byrne (Newport Beach, CA: Newport Harbor Art Museum, 1975), 22. Collecting these sorts of objects became a lifelong interest of Mullican's; see also the brochure "Mullican Collection" (Los Angeles: The Egg and The Eye, Inc., 1969).

29 Mullican, Karlstrom interview, May 22, 1992.

30 Mullican, Karlstrom interview, May 22, 1992.

31 Mullican, Phillips interview, 107.

32 It has been suggested that Jackson Pollock also might have returned to figurative imagery had he not died in a car accident in 1956. Already in June 1951 he tentatively returned to figuration in his work, writing to collector and fellow artist Alfonso Ossorio, "I've had a period of drawing on canvas in black—with some of my early images coming thru—think the non-objectivists will find them disturbing . . ." (See *Jackson Pollock*, exh. cat., Kirk Varnedoe with Pepe Karmel [New York: The Museum of Modern Art, 1998], 63.)

33 For Mullican, the intimate connection between abstraction and figuration was inherent in landscape. When asked whether he attempted to depict emotions or emotional states in his art, Mullican replied, "Yes, from landscape. . . . Landscape has always been a great influence on what I wanted to paint. . . . This kind of emotional impact is my . . . trying to grasp the essence of [nature]. . . . So whether it was crossing the Pacific, walking off into the desert, or whatever, I felt a sense of pattern and light and sky and cloud formations—all of that. I looked for it in an abstract way." Mullican, Phillips interview, 36–37.

34 Matt Mullican in conversation with the author, November 4, 2003.

35 Mullican quoted in *Realizing the Possible: The Art of Lee Mullican*, exh. brochure, David L. Witt (Taos: The Harwood Foundation Museum of the University of New Mexico, 1990), n.p.

36 Mullican, Karlstrom interview, January 26, 1993. Onslow Ford hyphenated his name early in his career, then dropped the hyphen later. For consistency, we have spelled his name without the hyphen. Hyphenation has been retained in the citation of published works where it originally occurred.

37 Mullican, Phillips interview, 66.

38 Mullican later reminisced about seeing and living with Paalen's collection of art and artifacts in this house, and about the experience of "opening case after case, crate after crate, of all these extraordinary things. . . . The collection was installed. The walls were covered in every corner; it was quite an atmosphere to live in." Mullican, Phillips interview, 77.

39 Wolfgang Paalen, in *Lee Mullican*, exh. cat. (San Francisco: The San Francisco Museum of Art, 1949), n.p.

40 Paalen, *Lee Mullican*, n.p.

41 Mullican, Karlstrom interview, May 22, 1992.

42 Mullican, Phillips interview, 71. See also the quotation at the beginning of this essay.

43 Mullican, Karlstrom interview, February 11, 1993.

44 Paalen as quoted by Mullican, Karlstrom interview, February 11, 1993.

45 Wolfgang Paalen, "Metaplastic," in

*Dynaton*, exh. cat. (San Francisco: The San Francisco Museum of Art, 1951), 1.

46 Paalen, "Metaplastic," 22, 26–27.

47 Mullican also indicated that the word "lions" in *The Splintering Lions* was meant "to represent a certain force and tension in the painting." Nan White, "Winning Painter is Optimist," *San Francisco News* (April 15, 1950), 10. I am grateful to Miani Johnson for allowing me access to the Willard Gallery archives, New York, where this clipping is located.

48 Mullican quoted in *Turning the Tide: Early Los Angeles Modernists 1920–1956*, exh. cat., Paul Karlstrom and Susan Ehrlich (Santa Barbara, CA: Santa Barbara Museum of Art, 1990), 145.

49 Mullican, Phillips interview, 84.

50 Information according to Smith College Museum of Art.

51 Paalen, *Lee Mullican*, n.p.

52 Mullican quoted in White, "Winning Painter," 10.

53 Mullican, Karlstrom interview, February 11, 1993.

54 Mullican quoted in Amy Winter, "DYNATON—The Painter/Philosophers," in *DYNATON, Before & Beyond*, exh. cat., ed. Nora Halpern (Malibu, CA: Frederick R. Weisman Museum of Art, Pepperdine University, 1992), 36.

55 Mullican, "Thoughts on the Dynaton, 1976," in *California: 5 Footnotes to Modern Art History*, exh. cat., ed. Stephanie Barron (Los Angeles: Los Angeles County Museum of Art, 1977), 40.

56 Mullican, Phillips interview, 85.

57 See W. Jackson Rushing, *Native American Art and the New York Avant-Garde* (Austin: University of Texas Press, 1995).

58 Susan C. Larsen, "Lee Mullican," in *Moderns in Mind: Gerome Kamrowski, Lee Mullican, Gordon Onslow-Ford*, exh. cat. (New York: Artists Space, 1966), 14.

59 Larsen, 17.

60 Mullican, Karlstrom interview, February 11, 1993.

61 Mullican interviewed by Amy Winter, January 7 and 8, 1990, Santa Monica, CA. I am grateful to Amy Winter for allowing me access to the tape recording of this interview.

62 The catalogue for the 1950 Willard Gallery show reprinted Paalen's text from the catalogue accompanying Mullican's show the previous year at The San Francisco Museum of Art.

63 Mullican, Karlstrom interview, January 26, 1993.

64 Mullican, Karlstrom interview, January 26, 1993.

65 Mullican, Karlstrom interview, January 26, 1993.

66 Letter from Lee Mullican to Marian Willard Johnson, August 29, 1952 (Willard Gallery archives).

67 Letter from Lee Mullican to Marian Willard Johnson's husband Dan Johnson, November 22, 1955 (Willard Gallery archives).

68 Eugen Herrigel, *Zen in the Art of Archery*, intro. D. T. Suzuki, trans. R. F. C. Hull (New York: Vintage Books, 1999), 77.

69 Mullican, Phillips interview, 120.

70 It is worth noting that New York artist Robert Ryman painted the first of what would become his signature square white paintings in 1957. Like Mullican, Ryman was fascinated by the "mysticism" of white, but he does not seem to have shared Mullican's interest in Zen. See Robert Storr, "Simple Gifts," in *Robert Ryman* (London and New York: Tate Gallery and The Museum of Modern Art, 1993), 16.

71 See Ronald Henry Olsommer, "The Mondo and the Koan," *Look Within*,

http://www.olsommer.com/tsoh/textonly/zmondo-t.html (accessed February 11, 2005).

72 Letter from Mullican to Dan Johnson, November 22, 1955.

73 Mullican, Phillips interview, 136.

74 Rachel Rosenthal in conversation with the author, March 5, 2004.

75 Rosenthal feels that the objects Mullican made at this time were influenced by the Cy Twombly sculptures she had brought with her from New York to Los Angeles.

76 Mullican, Karlstrom interview, January 26, 1993.

77 Mullican chose Croton Falls in upstate New York because the sister of Isamu Noguchi, a close friend of the Mullicans', lived there.

78 See *Lee Mullican: Selected Works, 1948–1980*, exh. cat., essay by Jascha Kessler (Basel and New York: Galerie Schreiner, 1980), n.p.

79 This aspect of Mullican's teaching style was emphasized repeatedly in the author's conversations with Lari Pittman, Tony Berlant, and Matt Mullican. See also Lari Pittman's essay in this catalogue.

80 Tony Berlant in conversation with the author, May 12, 2004.

81 I am grateful to David Rodes and Cindy Burlingham of the Grunwald Center for the Graphic Arts at the Hammer Museum for bringing Mullican's computer prints to my attention.

82 Mullican created his series of raga paintings after attending a performance of sitarist Ravi Shankar around 1962; Mullican inscribed "after Ravi Shankar concert" on the back of *Evening Raga*. (See Sylvia Fink, *The Dynaton: Three Artists with Similar Ideas—Lee Mullican, Gordon Onslow-Ford, Wolfgang Paalen*, [M.A. thesis, Arizona State University, 1973], 118.) A raga is a particular type of ancient traditional melodic pattern in Indian music, including both ascending and descending patterns of a rather limited number of notes. It is worth pointing out that the word "raga" derives from the Sanskrit word for color, and that Mullican's raga paintings involve a limited color palette used in what could be described as ascending and descending visual patterns.

83 *Neo-Tantra: Contemporary Indian Painting Inspired by Tradition*, exh. cat., ed. Edith A. Tonelli (Los Angeles: Frederick S. Wight Art Gallery, UCLA, 1985).

84 Chandra L. Reedy, in *Neo-Tantra*, 12.

85 Reedy, 12.

86 See Mullican's quote at the beginning of this essay.

87 *Visions of Inner Space: Gestural Painting in Modern American Art*, exh. cat., Lee Mullican and Merle Schipper (Los Angeles: Wight Art Gallery, UCLA, 1987). After Los Angeles, the exhibition traveled to the National Museum of Modern Art in New Delhi.

88 Mullican, Karlstrom interview, March 4, 1993.

89 Nitin Kumar, "Tantra—The Art of Philosophy," *Exotic India*, September 2001, http://www.exoticindiaart.com/article/yantra (accessed February 11, 2005).

90 Mullican, Karlstrom interview, March 4, 1993.

91 Quoted in "Landscapes of the Mind," *Time*, November 10, 1952, 74.

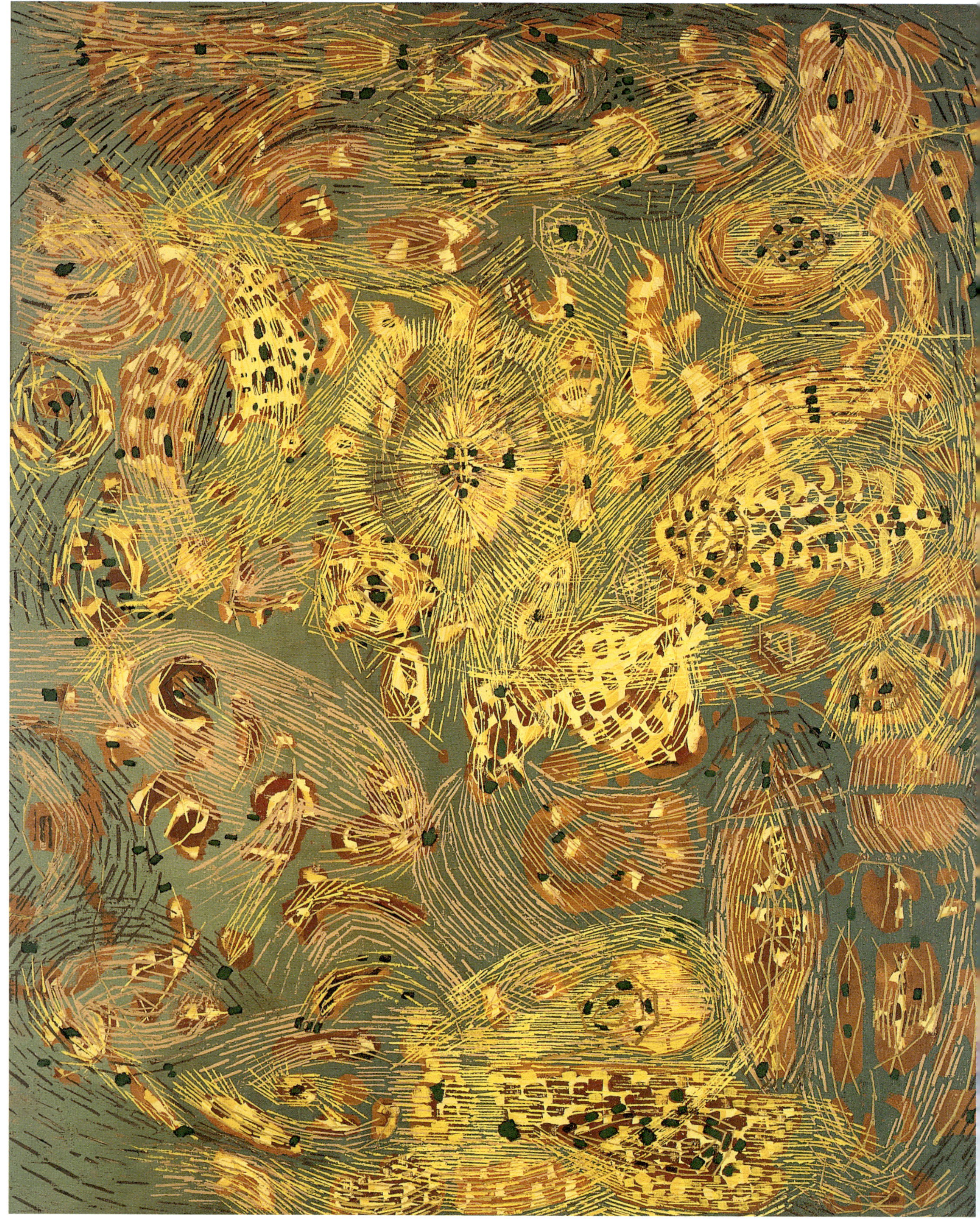

## AMY GERSTLER

# Whither This Golden Glow?

### Chickasha

If you type the name of Lee Mullican's birthplace, *Chickasha, Oklahoma,* into a computer's search engine, you will quickly learn a great deal about real estate prices there. And if you happen to be relocating soon you will be pleased to know that as of this writing, Chickasha's home prices are still quite reasonable. Approximately 7,054 families resided there at last head count, and zero murders occurred in the town in 2002. The median household income in 2000 was $26,369, and the nearest cities in Oklahoma are Ninnekah (a name which sounds partly Native American and partly Old Testament) and Amber. (Amber seems an appropriate name for the burg adjacent to Mullican's natal town, as many of his paintings' surfaces are incised with whirling bursts of amber light. *The Splintering Lions* [fig. 71] is a good example, scored with vortexes of toothpick-sized, palette knife–produced rays, though there are plenty of others.) There's a school for the deaf in Chickasha and the town seems to contain a goodly number of churches, as well as the expected dearth of Buddhist monasteries, synagogues, and mosques, given its current demographics (roughly 77 percent white, 8 percent black, 7 percent Native American, 3.5 percent Hispanic, and 4.5 percent mixed or other races.) Chickasha is the name of a Native American tribe, or one Anglicized corruption of their name.

FIG. 71
*The Splintering Lions,* 1950,
Dean Valentine and Amy Adelson

But none of this information, with the possible exception of the fact that Chickasha has a rich Native American history, provides much of a clue as to how this salt of the earth American town produced Lee Mullican. What, if anything, did Chickasha contribute to the creation of such an omnivorously spiritual, tirelessly reflective artist whose paintings, often populated by scintillating little maelstroms, vortexes, and luminous rain, have such vitality?

This smells like an unanswerable question. How did the little French hamlet of Charleville spawn the great poet Rimbaud? In Mullican's case you might idly theorize that, like a competitive swimmer pushing off the side of a pool when a starting gun is fired, the artist was able to launch himself off Chickasha—not fleeing, exactly, but using its heartland solidity to propel himself in the direction of larger worlds just out of his reach. "It is important to know that I was born in Oklahoma. I mean even today I'm still rather in awe of the fact that where I came from and how I got here today—that I ever really escaped Oklahoma but it was necessary to do so."[1]

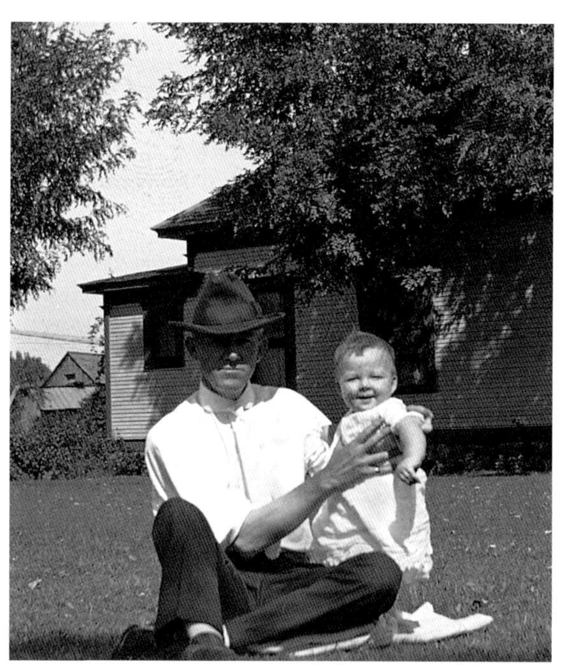

FIG. 72
Lee Mullican with his father, Chickasha, Oklahoma, c. 1920

From beyond the storm cellars, handsome horses, and family farms of Chickasha, future influences on young Mullican's nascent art life were beckoning. They were serenading him like a chorus of seductive, smoky-voiced sirens. And Lee heard them loud and clear. His ears were not stopped with wax. On the contrary, psychically speaking his hearing was phenomenally acute. So he hearkened and, as soon as he was able, lit out looking for all that had been signaling him. This artist was nothing if not attuned. He knew early the virtues of "open-ness," of being a receiver—a specialized kind of seeker who continually makes a beeline for what sets him vibrating on the deepest archetypal and personal levels. I believe it was Henry James who said that an artist or a writer should be someone on whom nothing is lost. Reading about Lee Mullican, he seems to fit this description. About the importance of open-ness to his particular brand of art practice, Mullican said, "I left myself wide open—and still do—and that's why there is such a great range and change in my work from one canvas to the next, and from year to year, and exhibition to exhibition."[2] Gertrude Stein says something in her essay on Picasso that seems to link up with this old, but I think still viable, notion of the artist as one who allows himself to be filled by varying forces, which he then pours into his work: "He is a man who always has need of emptying himself, of completely emptying himself."[3]

As has been well documented elsewhere, Mullican filled himself up with Eastern and Native American religions, Surrealism, Zen, automatism, Dada, writings by the aforementioned Miss Gertrude Stein, William Carlos Williams, jazz, Mexico, African artifacts, Salvador Dali, Paul Klee, Matta, Taos, pre-Columbian art, the I Ching, abstract painting, Henry Miller, Freud and Jung (those feuding spelunkers of the unconscious), and Rachel Rosenthal's Instant Theatre, to name but a few of his formative interests. We might even call these fascinations his muses. All fed dedicated explorations of the micro- and macrocosmic, his study of "degrees of abstraction,"[4] as he put it, as well as "the varieties of religious experience," as explored by Henry James's older brother William in his book of the same title. All fueled what went on every day in his studio—investigations of spiritual cravings and of our endless thirst for manifestations of radiance.

## The aptly named Miss Blue and others

Included among the portents that our hero was destined to become an artist (signs always so recognizable via hindsight) is the fact that Mullican had an elementary school art teacher named Miss Blue. More telling, perhaps, was his strong immediate attraction to images in a catalogue his parents toted back from the 1933 Chicago World's Fair. He would have been about fourteen then, and the catalogue introduced him to works by Picasso and Chagall. The memory of that catalogue with its arresting reproductions was still fresh in his mind sixty years later when he recalled, "Even at that age I was not interested in just setting up a still life of flowers and working from it. I wanted to do more. And all this strangeness intrigued me, something far beyond ... what I had known."[5]

Likewise, because the models in his college art classes in Oklahoma had been clothed, he had his first opportunity to draw from the nude only when he went off to art school in Kansas City. This was a revelation. "Well, it was still an excitement, you see, to go off to a big city like that and into an art school and meet up with other students and go to classes where you could actually draw from the naked woman."[6] Lee was no longer a farm boy. Kansas City had made its small but eye-opening contribution to his artistic development.

Once he graduated from art school, Mullican was drafted into the army. World War II was in hideous progress. He said he "cried most of the way,"[7] as any sensible person in his position would do, during his train ride to basic training. Eventually, Mullican made his way into a "topographical battalion where artists and architects could go and learn how to make maps."[8] The military trained him as an aerial map draftsman. Much has been made—rightly, it seems to me—of the lasting effects on Mullican's visual sensibility of this mapmaking training. Maps seem a Mullicanesque form in several ways. Like some of his paintings, they can hover between representation and abstraction. And the majority of Mullican's paintings that I have seen contain a mapmaker's intense attention to mark making and layering. Many of his paintings resemble slightly the animated continental weather maps shown on TV, with their colorful swirling spirals meant to depict evolving movements of storm fronts and air currents. Mullican's paintings also often have elements that seem as though they could be aerial views of ancient mazes or archaeological sites, or diagrams of same, with their flurries of activated dots and little whirlwinds of broken and wavy lines, which at times suggest both magnificent crumbling temple structures from eons ago viewed from above, and the ghostly nodes of spirit-energy still awhirl within and around them.

Some of Mullican's black and white paintings and drawings remind me of a specific set of aerial photographs I've seen, of geoglyphs called the Nasca Lines—huge, mysterious, ancient drawings on the earth. These gigantic stylized depictions of plant, animal, and human forms engraved on the surface of the Peruvian desert are so vast they can only be properly seen from an airplane. When viewed in aerial photographs, the "presences" in them seem to have more than a little in common with the presences in many of Mullican's pieces whom he referred to as guardians. But I digress.

Even in the military, Mullican continued to follow his aesthetic and philosophical interests. He befriended fellow inductee Jack Stauffacher (the San Francisco designer and typographer) because he first encountered the man sitting on an army latrine reading *The Life of the Buddha*. And after surviving the war, Mullican consistently gravitated towards art and artists. He had tea with Marcel Duchamp and attended early collaborative performances of Merce Cunningham and John Cage. He became pals with James Agee and attended dinner parties with Jean Renoir. Cary Grant visited his studio. He met Martha Graham, Charles and Ray Eames, Christopher Isherwood and Don Bachardy, and Isamu Noguchi, among many other art luminaries. Eventually he connected with his Dynaton buddies Wolfgang Paalen and Gordon Onslow Ford. He married the artist Luchita Hurtado and sired the artist Matt Mullican. (All of the above not necessarily in that order.) And he devoted himself passionately to his art practice.

Because of Mullican's focus on ideas of transcendence and inner vision, it's convenient that in English the word "practice" can mean both an artist's daily labors *and* someone's religious practice, the latter including the practice of those who meditate in one way or another. One gets the idea that these two kinds of practice—artistic and metaphysical/meditative—were very closely related if not fused for Mullican:

> As you are working through this process of painting, the painting's there. You know there's an end to it. I mean the painting is there, but you've gone through this metaphysical process ... more than anything. And it's a meditative act ... the canvas is there before me. And it's this attitude that makes the painting appear. And once it appears, you just put it aside, and for whatever reason, it's there now, and you're not quite sure how it got there.[9]

### "My studio is my refuge, and my paintings are my refuge"

In reading Mullican's discussion of working in the studio, there is a kind of unpretentious reverence, a sense of both continuous surprise and unremitting hard work that I feel comes through in his tone. When asked about the influence of travel on his work, he responded in part, "I guess the real region is in your studio. I think it really comes down to that."[10] Within the studio of his mind and the studio with four walls a great deal of synthesis of influence took place. When you look at Mullican's work and read about his myriad influences, they then make sense, but none stick out like sore thumbs, or seem undigested, or make the work look like pastiche. He noted:

> One thing I've learned as an artist, and that is, whatever that plane is you're on when you're in your studio working, that's where I have always wanted to be and where I have been, and that's where things have happened. And when they're happening, one is not really concerned or doesn't even think to consider what one has really seen before or "Oh, yeah, that was a great Paul Klee exhibition," and so forth. But when I actually begin to work on my canvas, I'm not really thinking about that Paul Klee exhibition or Paul Klee. One is moved and one is put upon by all kinds of different elements, and sometimes they are very direct and sometimes they are very indirect—and sometimes it takes years to really figure out what it was.[11]

This is not to give the impression (and all my impressions in this essay, it should be noted, are gleaned from looking at Mullican's art and reading the Smithsonian's Archives of American Art interview with him as well as critical responses to his work—I never had the pleasure of meeting him) that Mullican had no consciousness of the technical aspects of what he was doing. He recalled, "My techniques, the way I worked, had to do with developing not only on the formal side, layers of paint, but also on the philosophical side, of layers and layers of life or layers of nature, layers of patterning. . . ."[12]

This is something that I love about Mullican's work: that he was an educated painter with serious intellectual and formal concerns about his art practice and that he was also deeply interested in its philosophical, emotional, and spiritual content and effects.

### A WOMAN WHO PAINTS AND A MAN WHO DEEPLY RESPECTS HIS HORSE

Lee was the offspring of a mother who liked to sketch and make oil paintings and a schoolteacher-turned-businessman dad. In an interview, Mullican related an anecdote that could be read as illustrating the provenance of the facet of his sensibility that encompasses both the grounded and the dreamy. This was an incident from his parents' courtship, which he said his mother told him shortly before her death. Mullican's father arrived on horseback one day to pay his respects to his sweetheart and future wife. "He got off his horse and immediately, practically before he said hello to anybody, he began to wipe the horse down and look after it, and my mother's mother said, 'He'll make a good husband. Anyone who treats his horse like that . . .'" he recalled, laughing.[13]

Viewed through the lens of this bit of family lore, it's tempting to peg Mullican as a pure product of an artistically inclined, perhaps romantically minded, mother and a father so rooted in rural life and steeped in sympathy with the natural world that he wouldn't think of pitching woo before his faithful mount was cared for. Whether or not this is an accurate interpretation of Mullican's temperamental heritage, the story does point towards, I think, a wonderful tension in his work. That tension, often cited by writers trying to describe what Mullican did, is the pull between the temporal and the spiritual world(s), the physical and the metaphysical, the devotional and the down-to-earth that seems so key to his vision quest and the magnetic effects it exerts. Many of the paintings resemble stained glass windows in some non-sectarian shrine that pays homage to man's "taste for the infinite" (to quote Baudelaire). These stained glass windows are at once earthy, cosmic, and worshipful in their appearance and mood. There is an ecstatic reaching for the archetypally divine in these pieces, but never at the expense of the loved and valued elements (I could say *sacred elements*) of our green and blue planet: vividness, gusto, light, warmth, biomorphic forms, the hypnotic pleasures of movement and pattern, and the animal, vegetable, and mineral—arguably the raw material for all possible visions.

## "Walks in landscapes that appeared from the depths of the mind"

Now, after having worked on this piece for about two weeks, I have dropped half a tab of good quality acid. Everything I look at—the two-volume shorter Oxford dictionary on my desk, the panting rough-coated dog lying near my feet, the wall calendar with a picture of a buxom Maya maiden on it—appears to be in the same state of humming radiant molecular agitation one sees in Lee Mullican's paintings. (I have not really taken any drugs. I just wanted to see if you were still reading.)

In typewritten notes made in 1980, Mullican writes in reference to his paintings, "I pulled the essence of nature down over my head." He also writes, "there were walks in landscapes that appeared from the depths of the mind," and in the same document, he speaks of making marks on paintings that "excite the surface" and of creating surfaces that seem to "vibrate into being."[14] Now I want to make it abundantly clear at this juncture that I am not at all implying that Lee Mullican was some kind of pinwheel-eyed, high-as-a-kite mystic (though in my universe, "mystic" is not a dirty word, and neither, for that matter, is the practice of getting high something to be looked down upon). Any interest in mind-altering drugs that becomes apparent in this essay must be ascribed to its author and not its subject. As stated earlier, I never met Mr. Mullican and as far as I know he never imbibed anything stronger or more sense-deranging than jasmine tea. However, I am here going to mention Aldous Huxley's *The Doors of Perception* and *Heaven and Hell*, books that deal in part with their author's experiments with mind-expanding chemicals, because there are so many passages in each that constitute uncannily accurate descriptions of perceptual experiences evoked by staring at Mullican's paintings, at least for me. And he did want us to stare at them, saying that "I wanted to set up the possibility of close scrutiny. The surfaces of the canvases were to invite the possibility of close scrutiny. There was an invitation for contemplation."[15]

So here is Huxley coming onto a hit of mescaline as he sits in his study: "Half an hour after swallowing the drug I became aware of a slow dance of golden lights. A little later there were sumptuous red surfaces swelling and expanding from bright nodes of energy that vibrated with a continuously changing patterned life."[16] And later, Huxley observes, "I saw the books, but was not at all concerned with their positions in space. What I noticed, what impressed itself upon my mind was the fact that all of them glowed with living light. . . ."[17] If that doesn't sounds like someone who had entered and was walking around in a Mullican painting, I don't know what does. Huxley also discusses visionary drug experiences in which "heroic figures, of the kind that Blake called 'the Seraphim,' may make their appearance, alone or in multitudes."[18] When reading such passages, the comparison to Mullican's "guardians" is hard to avoid.

In much of *Heaven and Hell* Huxley considers visual art as another possibly viable pathway into alternative worlds. He discusses Monet's *Water Lilies* and Chinese painting with the same rapt enthusiasm and awe he uses to describe the enlightening and life-changing experiences afforded by his experiments with hallucinogens. Here he is talking about staring at the way leaves are painted in a Rousseau jungle: "I peer into the depths of interlacing greenery, and something in me is reminded of those living patterns, so characteristic of the visionary world, of those endless births and proliferations of geometrical forms that turn into objects, of things that are forever being transmuted into other things."[19] I believe this testimony about art that brings us to a more acute consciousness of "those endless births and proliferations of geometrical forms . . . of things that are forever being transmuted into other things" is more articulate and true than anything I can say about Lee Mullican's marvelous paintings.

## The last word

I had originally wanted to end this essay with the above paragraph, to step away from Mullican's work and let the amazing Aldous Huxley have the last word. I think I had that instinct for two reasons. The first is that in some way Huxley and Mullican seem like blood brothers to me: artists who loved wandering around in the archaeology of human consciousness hip-deep in its rich stratified symbology. Both men seem like plumb-ers (not water pipe repairers but sounders of depths) of man's visionary capacities and the infinite legacy of images and ways of seeing that those capacities can offer. The other reason I wanted to let the author of *Brave New World* have the last word here is that I had some hope of mimicking what I thought was a Mullicanesque gesture in stepping aside at the last possible second to let something greater than my personal voice speak. There is a sense of Mullican's doing that in all of his artwork. That may have been true because Mullican wanted to let his artwork itself have the final say. In an interview, Mullican laughingly recalled that his friend Gordon Onslow Ford once said of him, "Well, Lee is the smartest one. He is the one who knows it all and then he just doesn't say a word."[20]

## NOTES

Thanks to Marc Selwyn and Jennifer Pregenzer of Marc Selwyn Fine Art, Carol Eliel, and Trinie Dalton for research help with this piece. Thanks to Sara Cody for her editing efforts.

1 Lee Mullican, interviewed by Paul Karlstrom (May 22, 1992 and January 26, February 11, and March 4, 1993), transcript, Oral History Program, Archives of American Art/Smithsonian Institution. This quote from May 22, 1992.

2 Mullican, Karlstrom interview, February 11, 1993.

3 Gertrude Stein, *Writings: 1932–1946* (New York: The Library of America, 1998), 500.

4 Mullican, Karlstrom interview, May 22, 1992.

5 Mullican, Karlstrom interview, May 22, 1992.

6 Mullican, Karlstrom interview, May 22, 1992.

7 Mullican, Karlstrom interview, May 22, 1992.

8 Mullican, Karlstrom interview, May 22, 1992.

9 Mullican, Karlstrom interview, February 11, 1993.

10 Mullican, Karlstrom interview, February 11, 1993.

11 Mullican, Karlstrom interview, February 11, 1993.

12 Mullican, Karlstrom interview, February 11, 1993.

13 Mullican, Karlstrom interview, May 22, 1992.

14 These quotations are taken from an unpublished, untitled typescript by Lee Mullican, dated July 1980. Carol Eliel kindly provided me with a photocopy of this document, which consists of five pages that appear to have been typed on a manual typewriter. The document contains handwritten corrections and notes, and at the very end is "signed" in typescript: "Lee Mullican, July 1980, Taos."

15 Mullican typescript, n.p.

16 Aldous Huxley, *The Doors of Perception* (1954; repr. with *Heaven and Hell* [1956], New York: Perennial Classics, 2004), 16. All Huxley citations are to the Perennial edition.

17 Huxley, *The Doors of Perception*, 20.

18 Huxley, *Heaven and Hell*, 97.

19 Huxley, *Heaven and Hell*, 128.

20 Mullican, Karlstrom interview, February 11, 1993.

The two Lee Mullican quotes used as subheads in the essay are derived, respectively, from the interview with Paul Karlstrom on February 11, 1993 and the unpublished typescript written by Mullican in 1980.

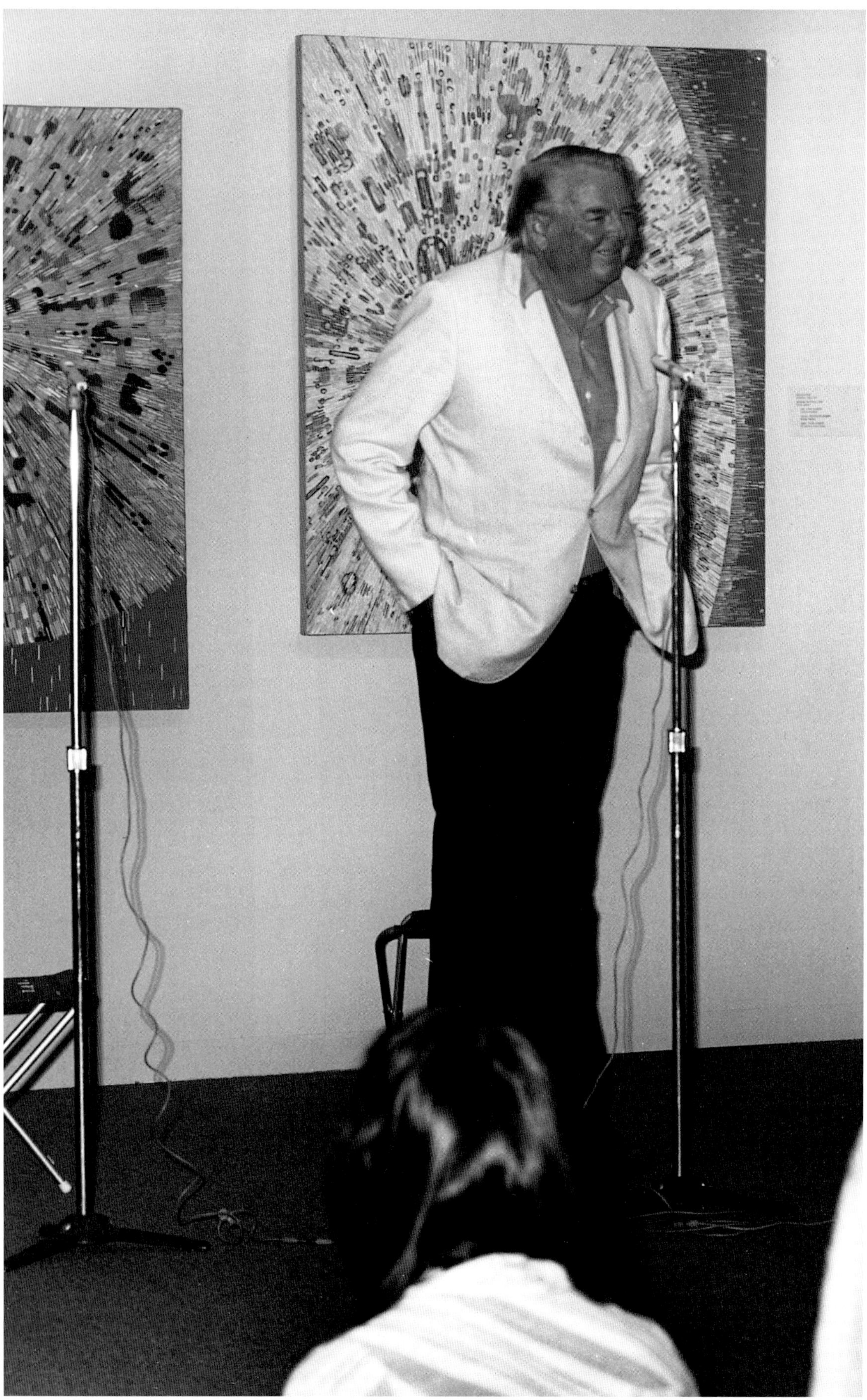

**LARI PITTMAN**

# A Sense of Lee

SUMMER 1998

We had literally just moved into a 1953 Richard Neutra house at the base of the San Gabriel Mountains when we heard of Lee Mullican's death. Frustrated but challenged by the scarcity of usable walls, my companion Roy Dowell and I were fussing over the placement of pieces by both Emerson Woelffer, who was Roy's teacher, and Lee Mullican, who was mine. Emerson's jazz-inspired tempera from 1949, with its highly keyed yellow background and slashes of tomato red and a ghastly teal green would be best on a low white wall. The pale, wan blues butting up against the destabilizing ochres of Lee's late '80s painting would find its place on the deep void of a chocolate brown wall. The décor and the memories were both coming together and unraveling.

Lee's life and death, although exquisite and singular, reverberated more poignantly for me as a historical passing of a world. A slice of history I never knew, only conjectured about, read about, fantasized about, seemed to be coming to an end. This now-abstracted, mid-century bohemian intelligentsia, with its fully "outed" leftist urbanity, once lived in houses we were now timidly trying to occupy. Hoping to inhale the exuberant expansiveness of a more optimistic time, we laughed at the old insinuations that people who lived in flat-roofed houses were invariably Communists and

FIG. 73
Lee Mullican speaking at the Los Angeles County Museum of Art, February 10, 1977, in front of *Third Quarter* (1950)

that the transparency and porosity of such homes congratulated and encouraged nudism. I asked Roy if he remembered the book in which appeared a photograph that I felt encapsulated that life. Pictured is a cavalier and elegantly suited Lee standing behind a stunningly beautiful Luchita Hurtado, dressed in what I would want to be Dior's "New Look," sitting in Wolfgang Paalen's modern living room. Wow! I have often thought of that photograph, in all its perfumed distortion, not knowing or really caring about the actual circumstances surrounding it. I had willfully made it a signifier of a precise moment, of a rarified and refined bohemiana that I envy, that cannot be revisited, that had left forever with Lee.

## Fall 1970

I had anxiously enrolled as an art student at UCLA. For an agitated and closeted gay boy, it was a disaster from the very beginning. The social climate was such that things could still be said openly by professors (to me and about my identity) that, thankfully, would now lead to lawsuits. My older brother, Oscar, had spoken highly of Lee and encouraged me to take his class. On the first day, Mr. Mullican arrived with what appeared to be a cigar box that he carried unusually high on his chest. Teetering on incredibly long legs and in one elegant crane-like swoop, he ceremoniously opened the box and announced that he had brought some of his favorite rocks. Excuse me, a grown man with his "favorite rocks"? Would we like to draw them? His request was utterly guileless. I was floored—no roughness here, no testosterone swagger, only kindness, charm, patience, and delicacy!

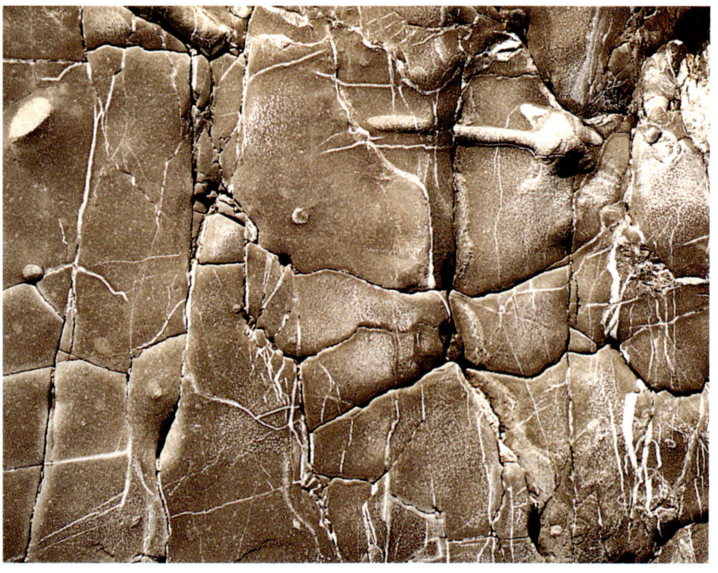

FIG. 74
Photograph taken by Mullican at Point Lobos, California, 1970

Lee offered himself freely and generously—which, as a fussy young man, was precisely what I needed. Sensing my overall discomfort, Lee suggested that I leave UCLA and that perhaps I would find a more sympathetic ambience at CalArts. His son Matt was studying there, and he sensed that "some new things were going on." His natural modesty pointed me in a new direction that forever changed my life. I will always be grateful to Lee Mullican for this intervention. In retrospect, I can only speculate that, like the aristocratic protagonist in Luchino Visconti's *The Leopard*, Lee internalized both the implied poetics and the brutality of imminent cultural change. With an intuitive largesse, he shoved me forward, and I was on my way to becoming an artist and finding an individuated voice.

# Checklist of the Exhibition

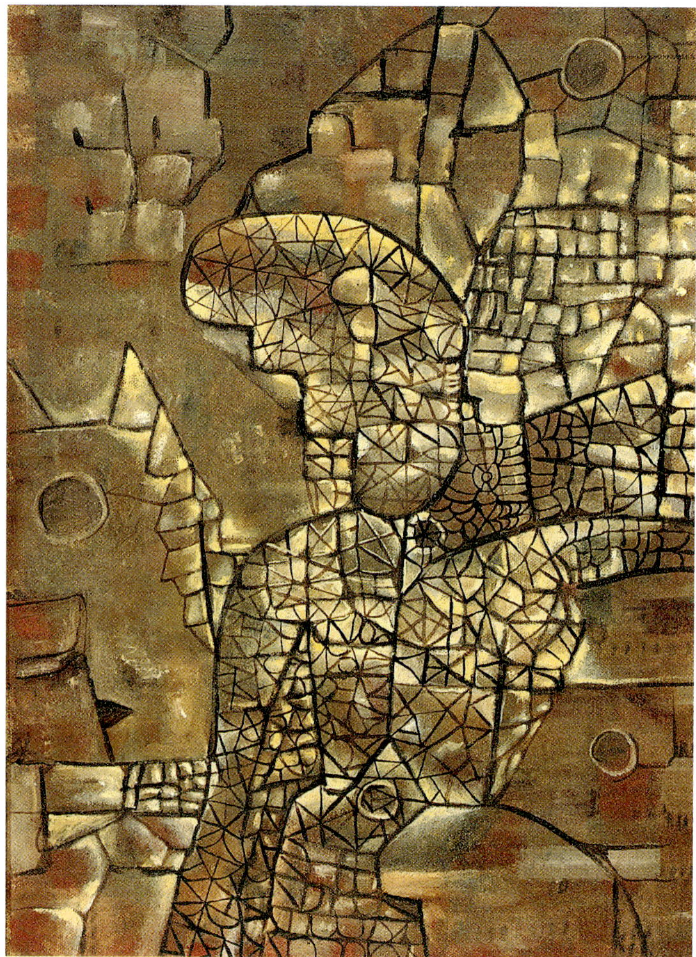

*Untitled*, 1946

## PAINTINGS

**Untitled**, 1946
Oil on canvas
20¼ x 14¼ in. (51.4 x 36.2 cm)
Collection of Luchita Mullican

**The Fossil Swims**, 1948
Oil on canvas
21 x 25 in. (53.3 x 63.5 cm)
Estate of the artist, courtesy Marc Selwyn Fine Art
p. 22

**Luminous Loot**, 1948
Oil on canvas
40 x 50 in. (101.6 x 127 cm)
Thomas Weisel and Emily Carroll
p. 24

**The Playground**, c. 1948–49
Oil on canvas
15 x 18 in. (38.1 x 45.7 cm)
Donna J. Cramer

**The Appointed**, 1949
Oil on canvas
30 x 40 in. (76.2 x 101.6 cm)
Collection of John Lock

**Happily the Chiefs Regard You**, 1949
Oil on canvas
30 x 40 in. (76.2 x 101.6 cm)
Collection of Harold and Gertrud Parker, Tiburon, California
p. 26

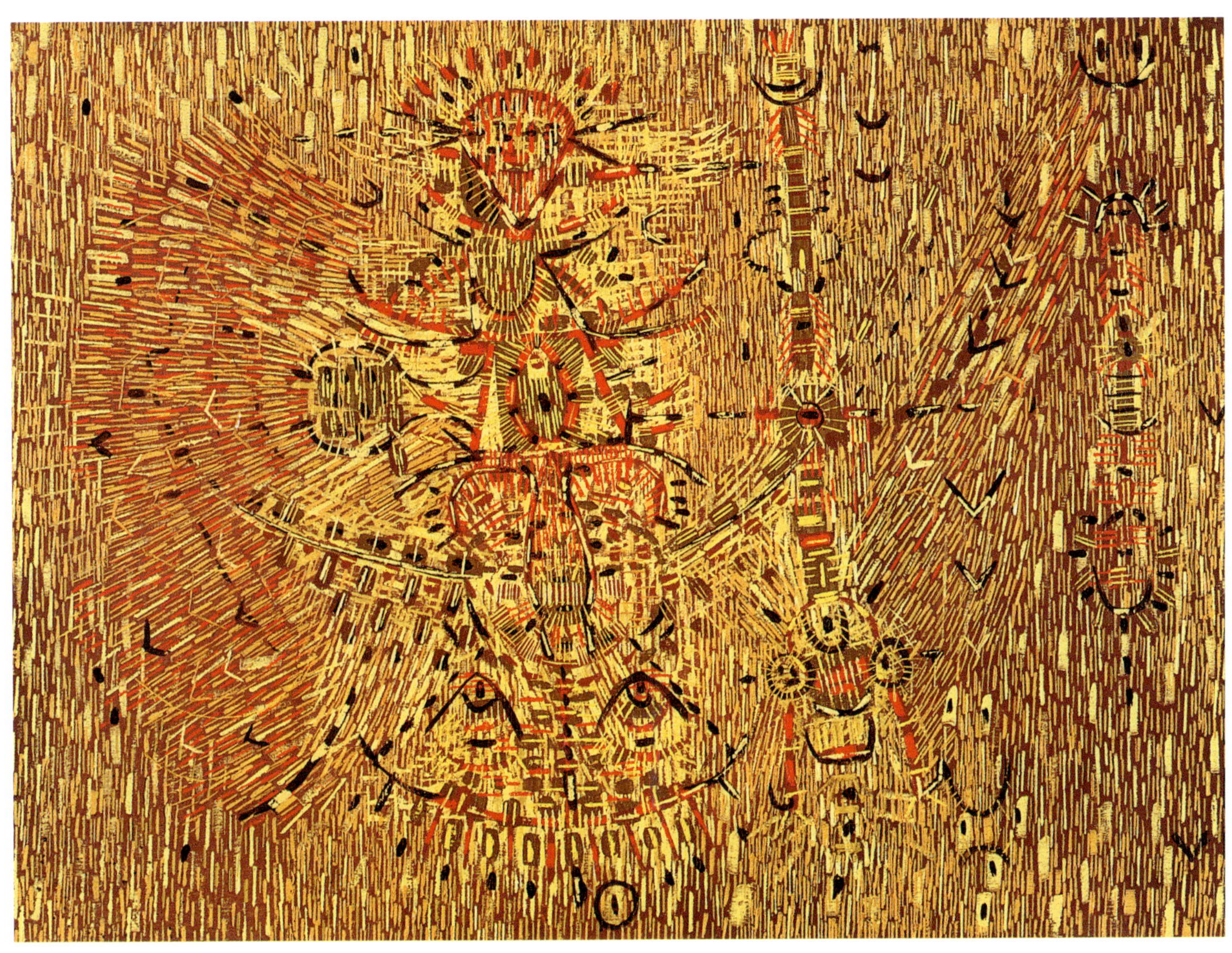

*The Appointed*, 1949

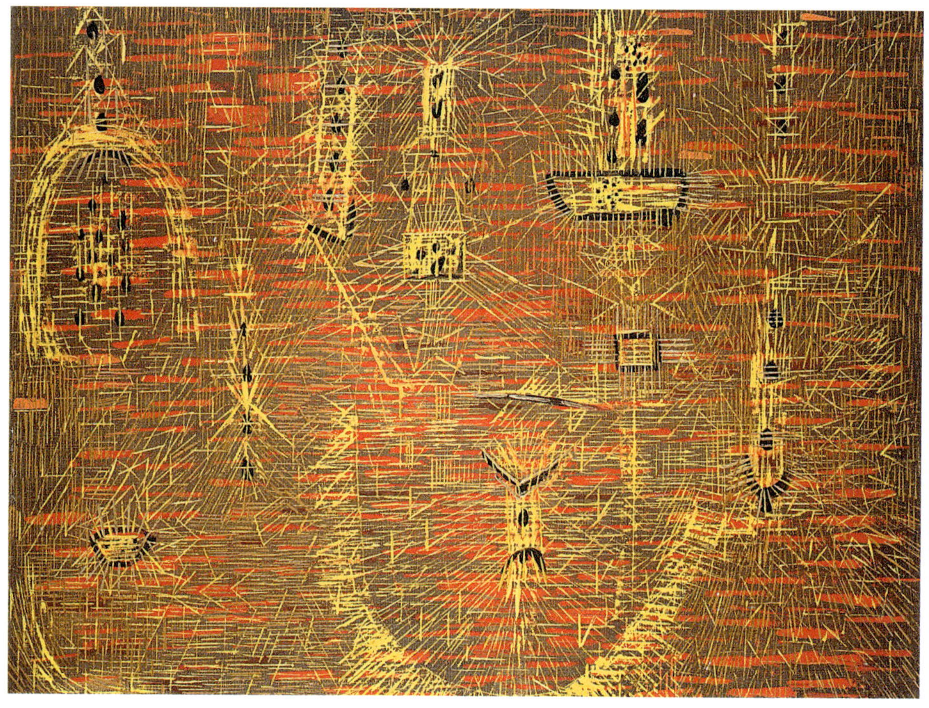

*The Playground*, c. 1948–49

**He-Rain**, 1949
Oil on canvas
20 x 16 in. (50.8 x 40.6 cm)
Estate of the artist, courtesy Marc Selwyn Fine Art
p. 44

**Marin Summer**, 1949
Oil on canvas
20 x 16 in. (50.8 x 40.6 cm)
Estate of the artist, courtesy Marc Selwyn Fine Art

**Premiere Mirage**, 1949
Oil on canvas
20 x 16 in. (50.8 x 40.6 cm)
Kenneth L. Freed Collection

**Untitled**, 1949
Oil on canvas
18 x 24 in. (45.7 x 61 cm)
Nina Anthoine

**Untitled**, c. 1949
Oil on canvas
18¼ x 48 in. (46.4 x 122 cm)
Lucid Art Foundation
p. 16

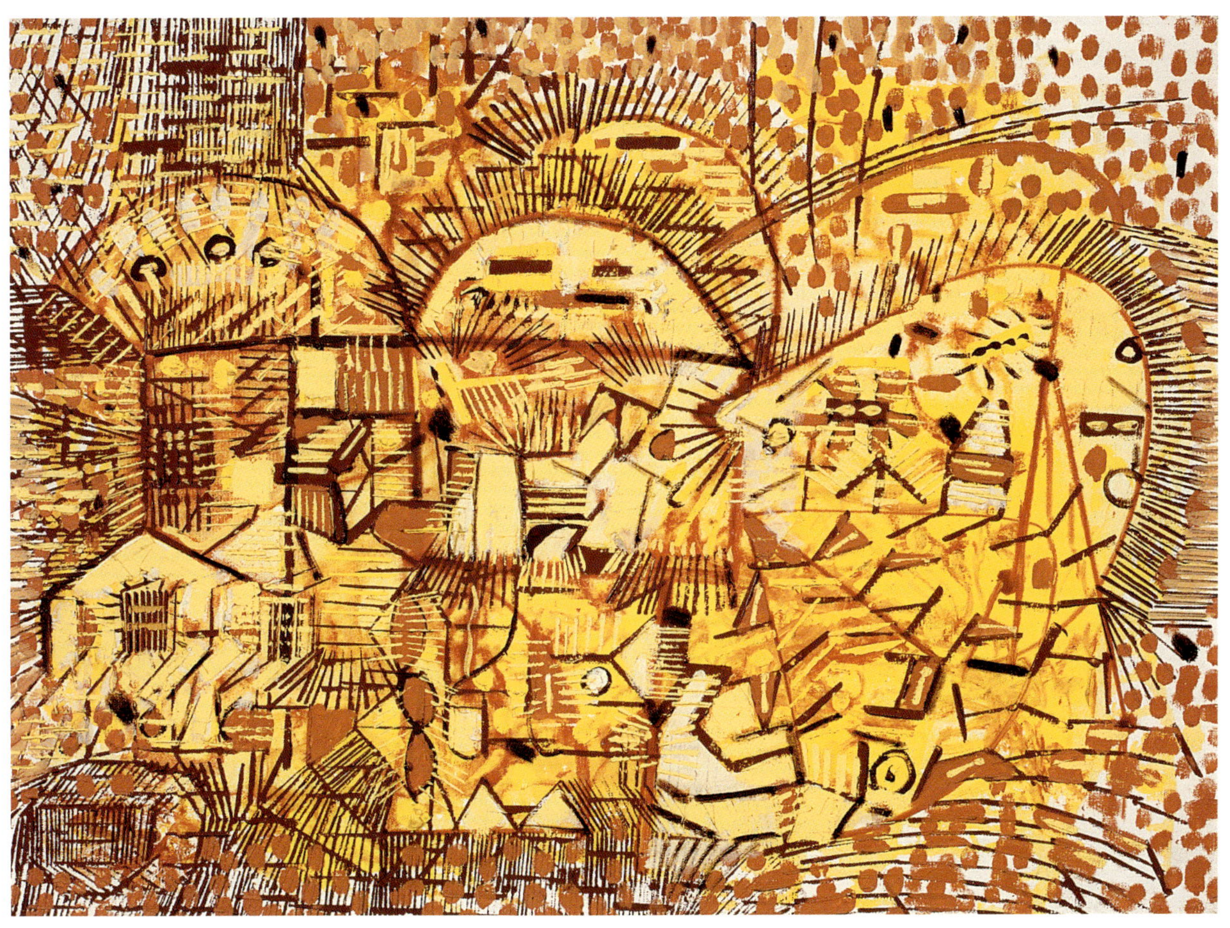

*Untitled*, 1949

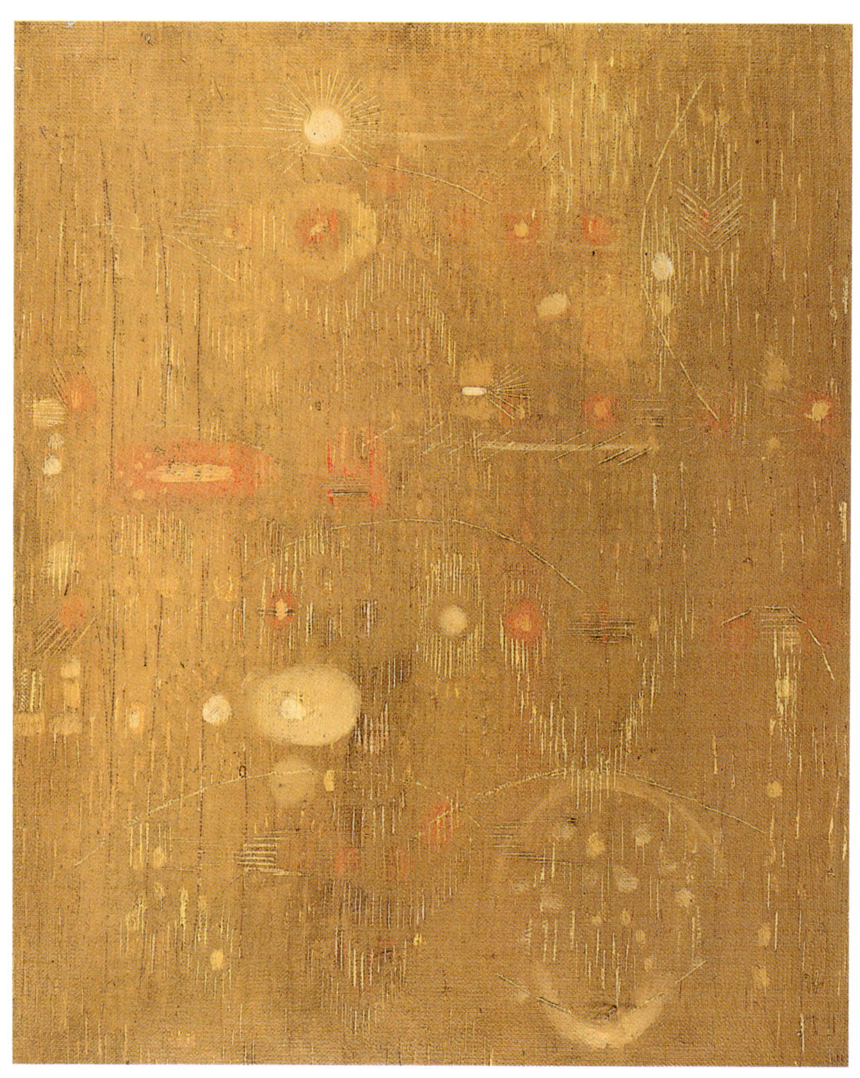

*Marin Summer*, 1949

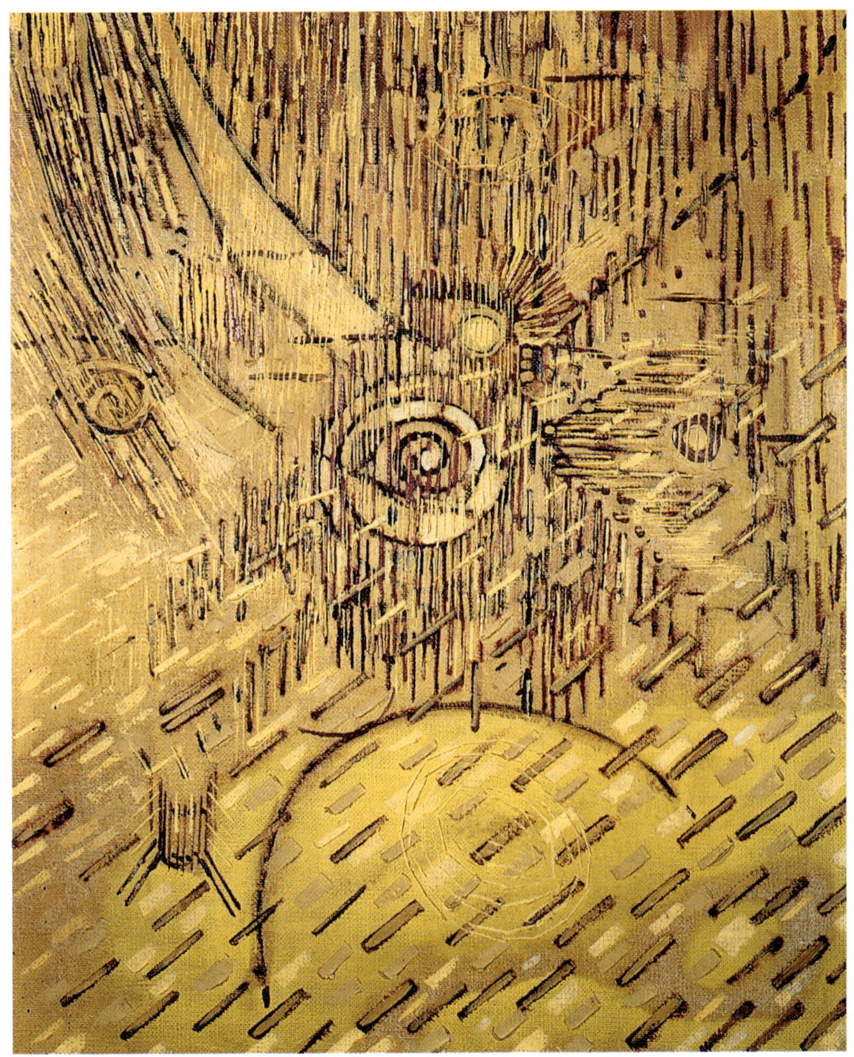

*Premiere Mirage*, 1949

**Agawam (First Quarter)**, 1950
(left section of **Agawam Triptych**)
Oil on canvas
50 x 40 in. (127 x 101.6 cm)
Collection of the Trenton Family Trust
p. 34

**Oblique of Agawam**, 1950 (center section of **Agawam Triptych**)
Oil on canvas
50 x 40 in. (127 x 101.6 cm)
Miani Johnson, Willard Gallery
p. 34

**Third Quarter**, 1950 (right section of **Agawam Triptych**)
Oil on canvas
50 x 40 in. (127 x 101.6 cm)
Harlan and Natasha Levine
p. 35

**The Splintering Lions**, 1950
Oil on canvas
50 x 40 in. (127 x 101.6 cm)
Collection of Dean Valentine and Amy Adelson, Los Angeles
p. 74

**Turning Worlds**, 1950
Oil on canvas
40 x 50 in. (101.6 x 127 cm)
Allan M. Jalon and Mary Tricarico Jalon
p. 36

**Fable**, 1951
Oil on canvas
30 x 40 in. (76.2 x 101.6 cm)
Estate of the artist, courtesy Marc Selwyn Fine Art

**The Measurement**, 1951
Oil on canvas
50 x 30 in. (127 x 76.2 cm)
Collection of Orange County Museum of Art, Newport Beach, California; Museum purchase with support of the Herbert Palmer Gallery
p. 8

**The Ninnekah**, 1951
Oil on linen
50 x 25 in. (127 x 63.5 cm)
Collection Nora Eccles Harrison Museum of Art; Marie Eccles Caine Foundation Gift
p. 38

**Ninnekah Calendar**, 1951
Oil on canvas
30 x 50 in. (76.2 x 101.6 cm)
William Resnick, M.D. and Douglas Cordell, M.D.
p. 37

**Peyote Candle**, 1951
Oil on canvas
50 x 35 in. (127 x 88.9 cm)
Collection of Luchita Mullican
p. 2

**Section from the Burlap Plain**, 1951
Oil on canvas
40 x 50 in. (101.6 x 127 cm)
Collection of Beverly and Mel Rosenthal
p. 17

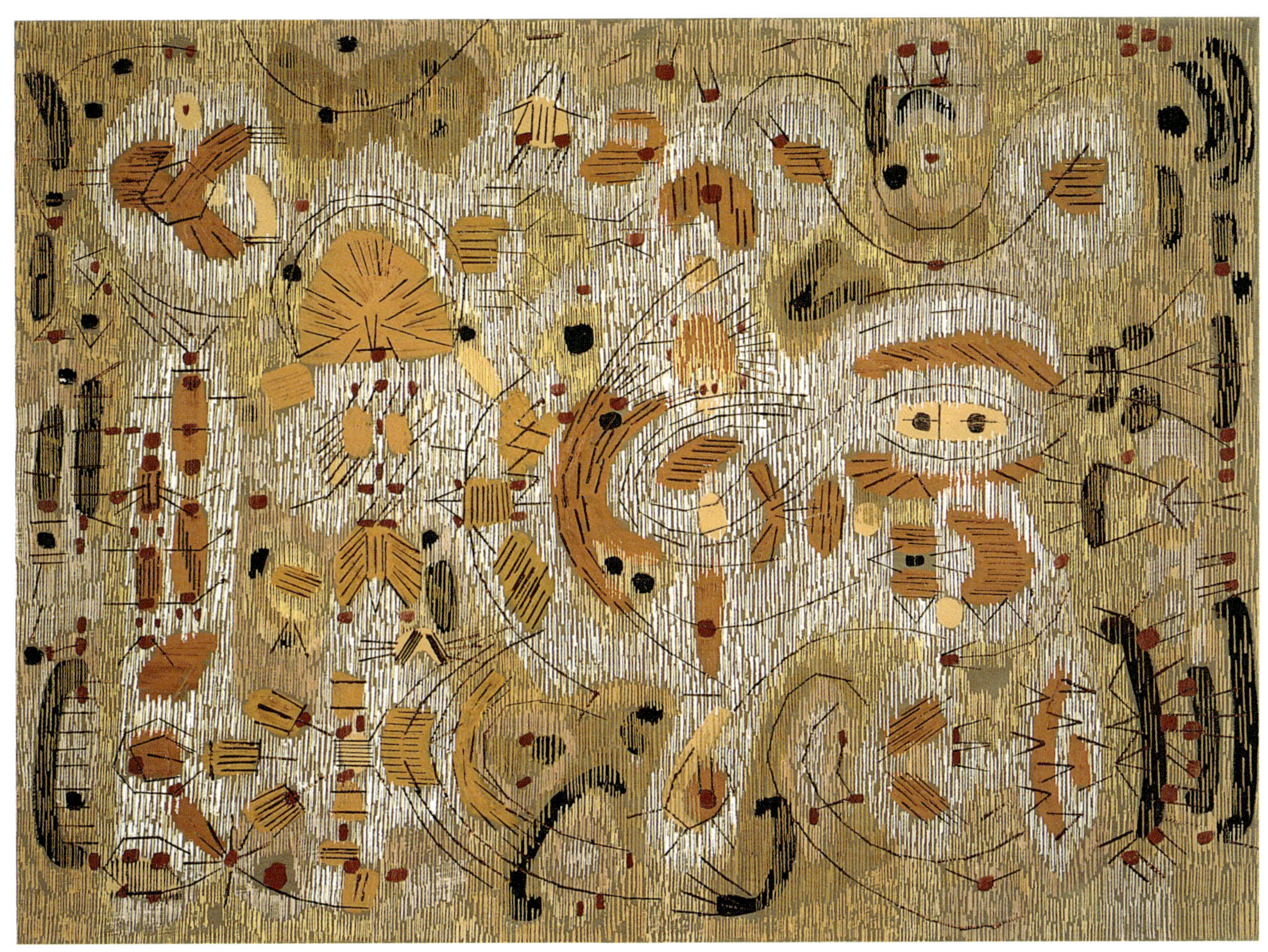

*Fable*, 1951

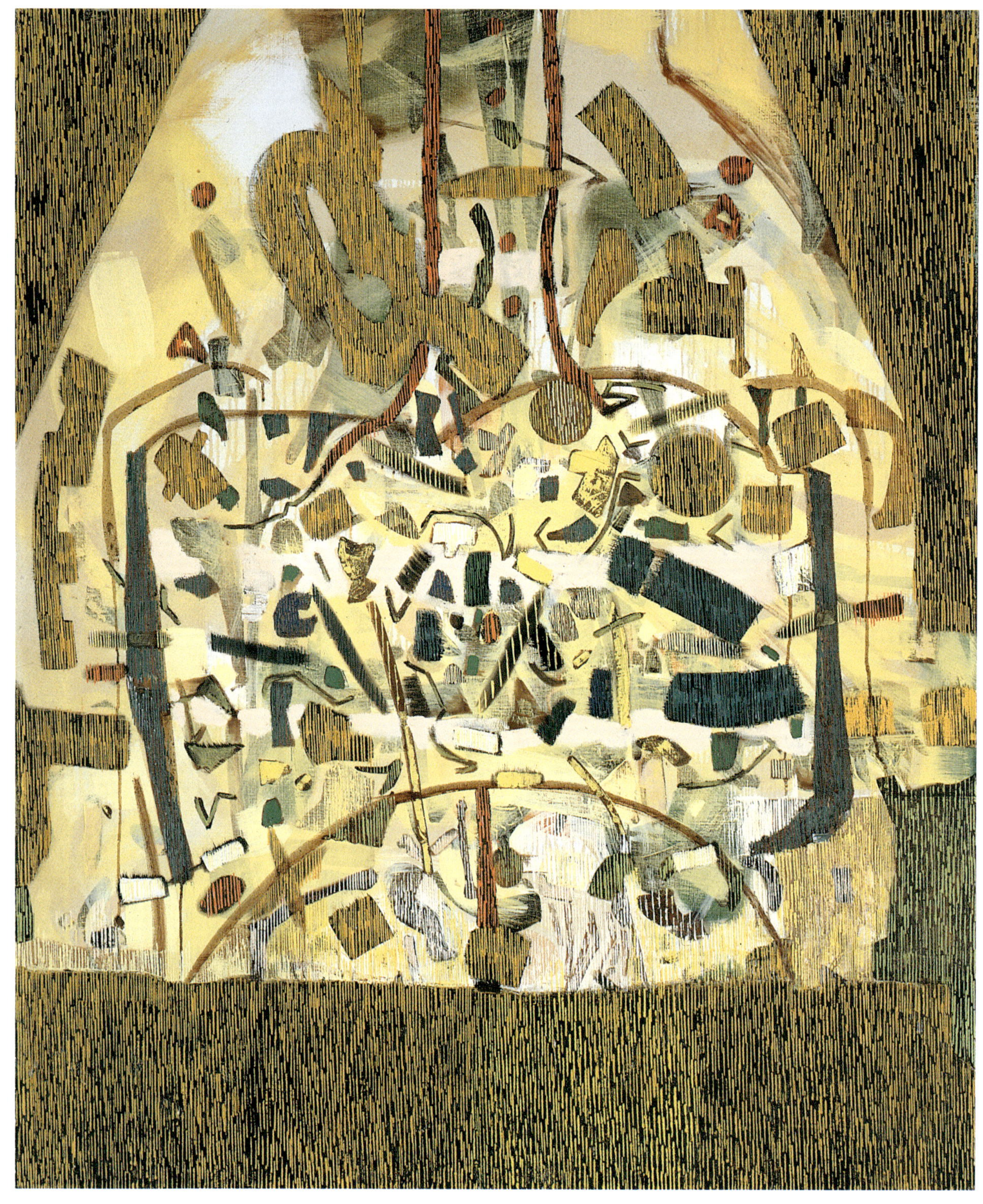

*Asia Minor*, 1953

**Space**, 1951
Oil on canvas
40 x 50 in. (101.6 x 127 cm)
Los Angeles County Museum of Art, gift of Fannie and Alan Leslie
p. 36

**Untitled**, 1951
Oil on canvas
50 x 30 in. (127 x 76.2 cm)
Lent by Orna and Keenan Wolens
p. 39

**Dynaton Triptych**, c. 1952
Oil on board
Three panels, 96 x 144 in. overall (243.8 x 365.8 cm)
Thomas Weisel and Emily Carroll
p. 18

**Asia Minor**, 1953
Oil on canvas
40 x 50 in. (101.6 x 127 cm)
Estate of the artist, courtesy Marc Selwyn Fine Art

**Pendulum Factor**, 1953
Oil on canvas
50 x 40 in. (127 x 101.6 cm)
The Phillips Collection, Washington, D.C.

**Zen Walk**, 1955
Oil on canvas
42 x 14 in. (106.7 x 35.6 cm)
Betye Monell Burton
p. 50

**The Age of the Desert**, 1957
Oil on canvas
40 x 25 in. (101.6 x 63.5 cm)
Collection of Luchita Mullican

**Woman at the Western Window**, 1957
Oil on canvas
44 x 25 in. (111.8 x 63.5 cm)
Collection of Hansen, Jacobson, Teller, Hoberman, Newman, Warren, Sloane & Richman

**California Landscape**, 1958
Oil on canvas
50 x 40 in. (127 x 101.6 cm)
Estate of the artist, courtesy Marc Selwyn Fine Art
p. 56

**The Chalk Garden**, 1958
Oil on canvas
50 x 40 in. (127 x 101.6 cm)
Collection of Aimee Knowlton and Jason Asch
p. 57

**Untitled**, 1958
Oil on Masonite
25 3/8 x 49 5/8 in. (64.5 x 126 cm)
William Resnick, M.D. and Douglas Cordell, M.D.
p. 51

**Untitled**, 1958
Oil on Masonite
24 x 24 in. (61 x 61 cm)
Estate of the artist, courtesy Marc Selwyn Fine Art
p. 52

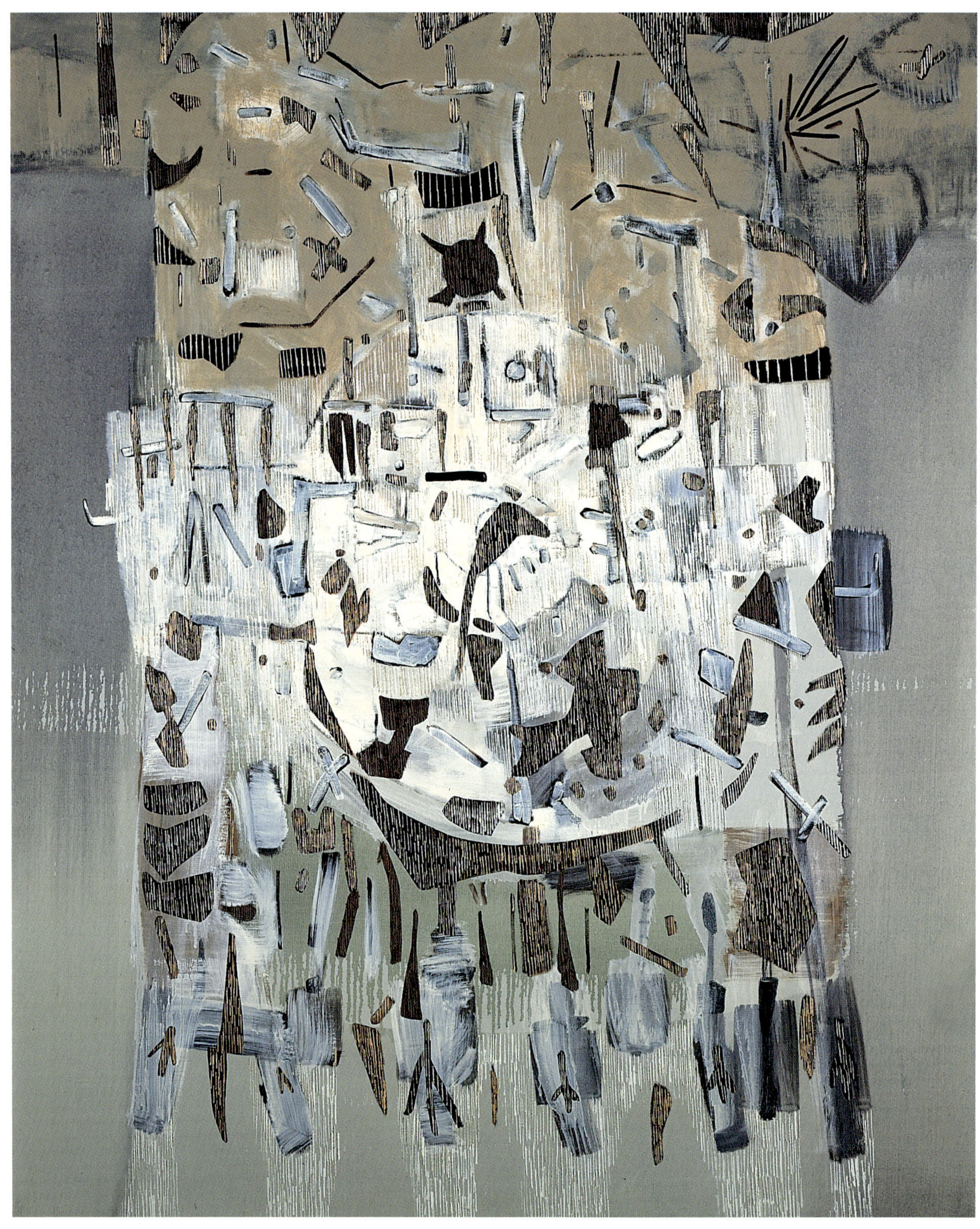

*Pendulum Factor*, 1953

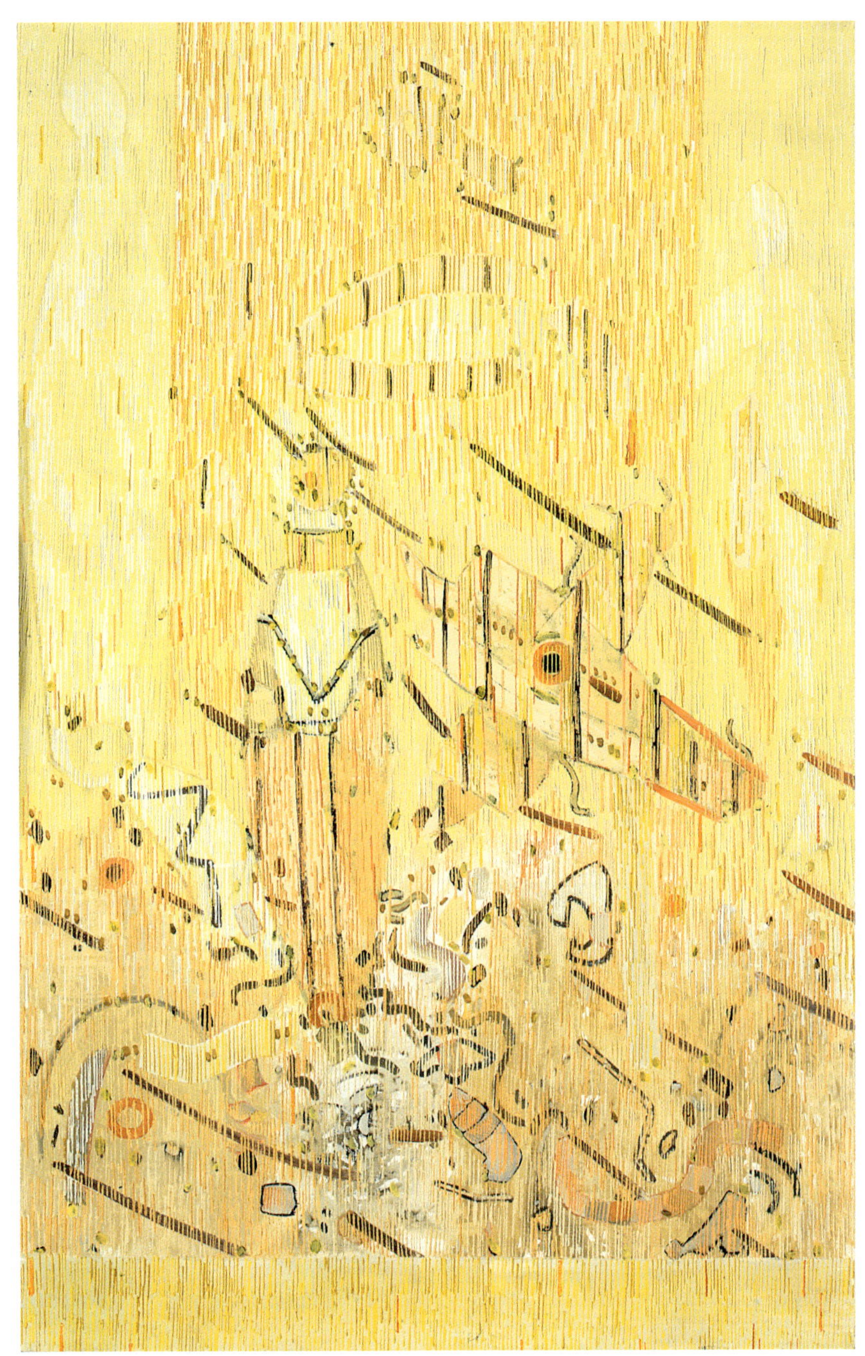

*The Age of the Desert*, 1957

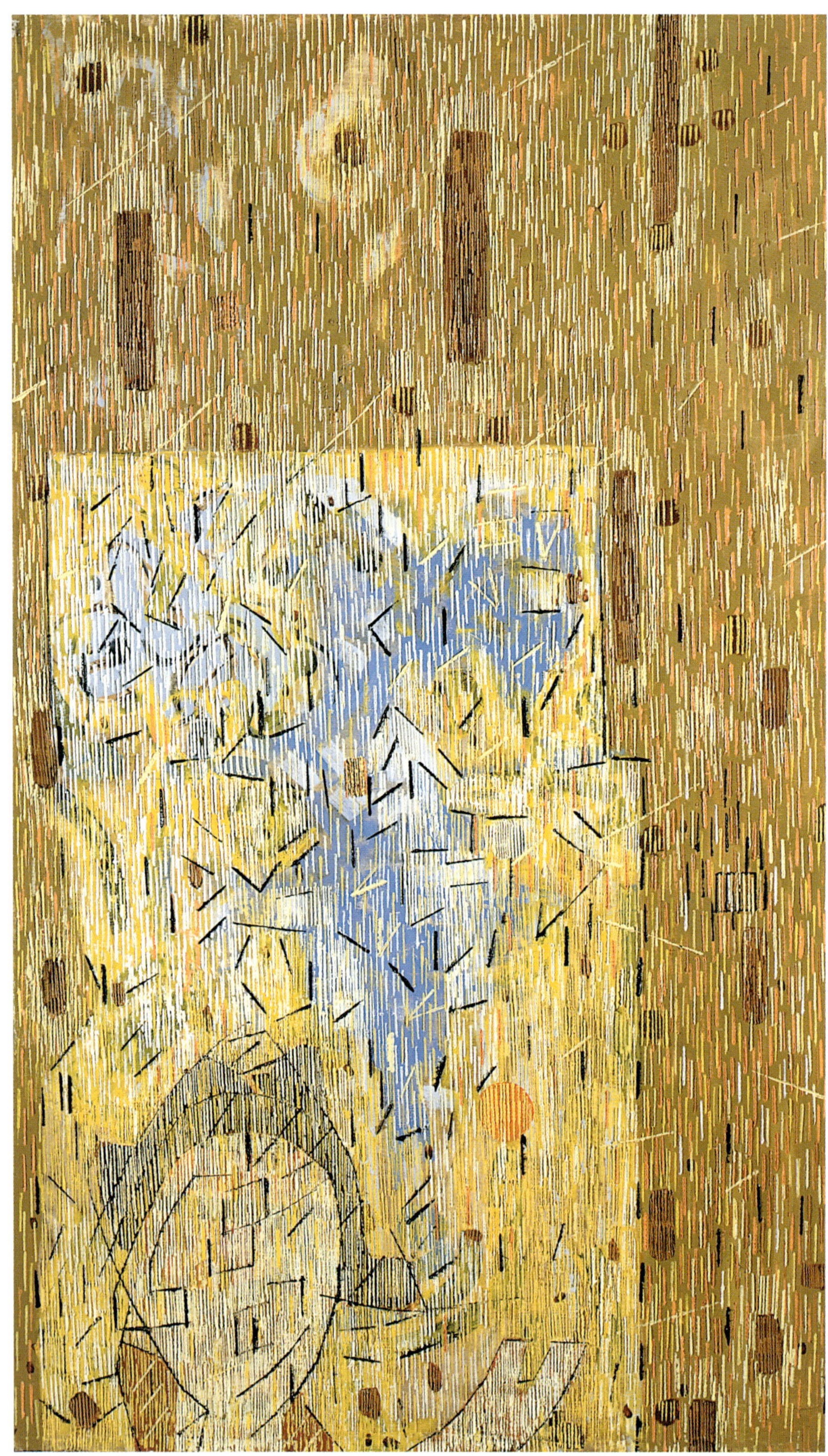

*Woman at the Western Window*, 1957

**Untitled**, 1958
Oil on Masonite
23¾ x 23¾ in. (60.3 x 60.3 cm)
Lucid Art Foundation
p. 53

**Summer Fall**, 1961
Oil on canvas
40 x 50 in. (101.6 x 127 cm)
Estate of the artist, courtesy Marc Selwyn Fine Art
p. 58

**Evening Raga**, 1962
Oil on canvas
40 x 50 in. (101.6 x 127 cm)
Collection of Luchita Mullican
p. 60

**Paradise Gardens: A Walk**, c. 1962
Oil on canvas
75 x 75 in. (190.5 x 190.5 cm)
Collection Dana and Stephen Sigoloff
p. 59

**Untitled** (from the *Raga* series), c. 1962
Oil on canvas
51 x 45 in. (130 x 114 cm)
Donna J. Cramer
p. 61

**Fable**, 1963–64
Oil on canvas
60 x 50 in. (152.4 x 127 cm)
Estate of the artist, courtesy Marc Selwyn Fine Art
p. 62

**Pacific Rhythms**, 1964
Oil on canvas
75 x 35 in. (190.5 x 88.9 cm)
Nina Anthoine
p. 63

**Landscape #5**, 1966
Oil on canvas
36 x 24 in. (91.4 x 60.9 cm)
Collection of Cecilia Dan
p. 63

**Magic Night**, 1966
Oil on canvas
50 x 75 in. (127 x 190.5 cm)
Smith College Museum of Art, Northampton, Massachusetts. Gift of Mr. and Mrs. Robert Anthoine (Edith Frances Hoffman, class of 1945)
p. 43

**Untitled**, 1970
Oil on canvas
30 x 49⅞ in. (76.2 x 126.7 cm)
Santa Barbara Museum of Art, Bequest of Alice Erving to the Donald Bear Memorial Collection
p. 42

**Untitled**, 1972
Oil on canvas
50 x 50 in. (127 x 127 cm)
Collection of Luchita Mullican
p. 41

**Guardian of the Modern**, 1979
Oil on canvas
50 x 40 in. (127 x 101.6 cm)
Los Angeles County Museum of Art, gift of Fannie and Alan Leslie
p. 7

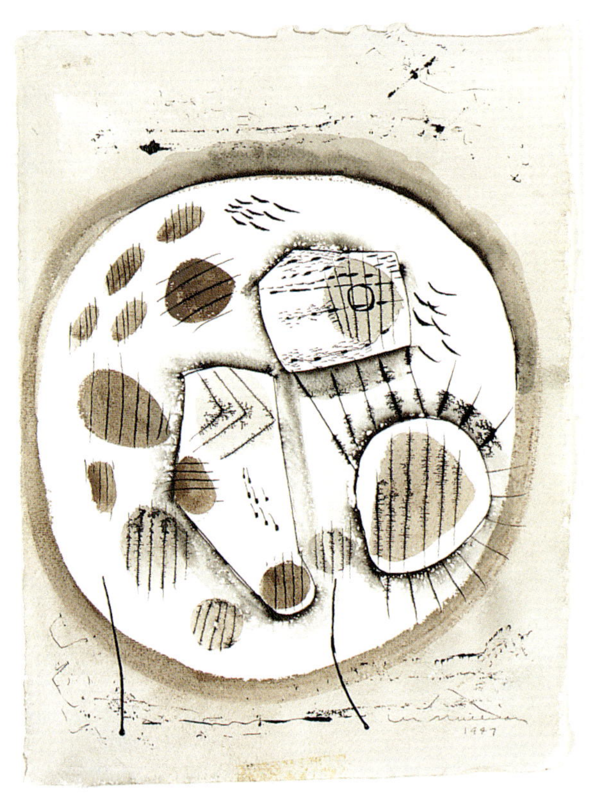

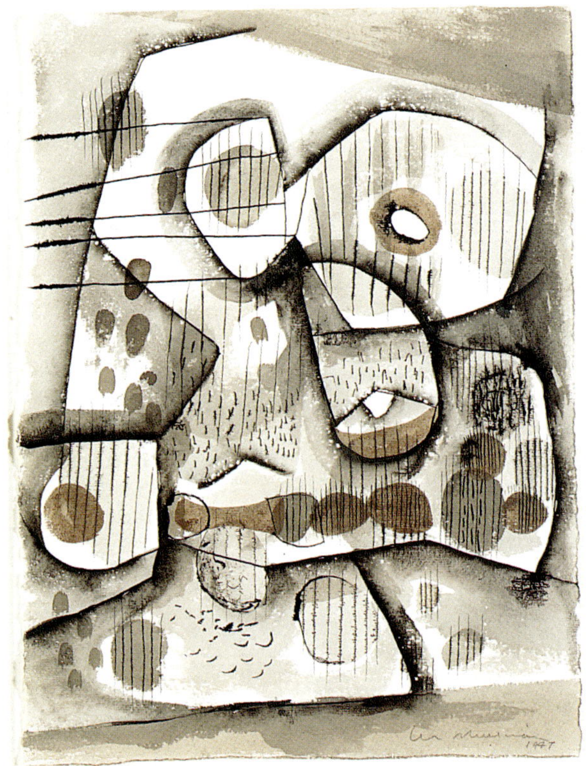

*DYN 21* and *DYN 24*, 1947

## DRAWINGS

**Untitled**, 1945
Ink on paper
14½ x 11½ in. (36.8 x 29.2 cm)
Los Angeles County Museum of Art, purchased with funds provided by Alice and Nahum Lainer through the 2004 Drawings Group
p. 15

**DYN 21** and **DYN 24**, 1947
Watercolor and ink on paper
14⅞ x 10¾ in. and
14¾ x 10¾ in. (37.8 x 27.3 cm and 37.5 x 27.3 cm)
Collection Dana and Stephen Sigoloff

**Personnage**, 1947
Ink and wash on paper
16 x 12½ in. (40.6 x 31.8 cm)
Los Angeles County Museum of Art, purchased with funds provided by Alice and Nahum Lainer through the 2004 Drawings Group
p. 14

**Untitled**, 1947
Ink and wash on paper
10½ x 8 in. (26.7 x 20.3 cm)
The Museum of Modern Art, New York. Purchase 2427.2001

**Untitled**, 1947
Ink on paper
13¼ x 13¼ in. (33.7 x 33.7 cm)
Los Angeles County Museum of Art, purchased with funds provided by Alice and Nahum Lainer through the 2004 Drawings Group
p. 15

**Mineral Collection #3**, 1948
Ink and watercolor wash on paper
14⅝ x 11½ in. (37.1 x 29.2 cm)
Weatherspoon Art Museum, The University of North Carolina at Greensboro, Museum purchase with funds from the Dillard Fund, 2000
p. 13

**Untitled**, 1948
Ink and watercolor on paper
11⅞ x 8⅞ in. (30.2 x 22.5 cm)
Collection of Ron de Salvo

**Untitled**, c. 1948–51
Colored ink on paper
35 x 8¾ in. (88.9 x 22.2 cm)
Hammer Museum, Los Angeles. Gift of Luchita Mullican

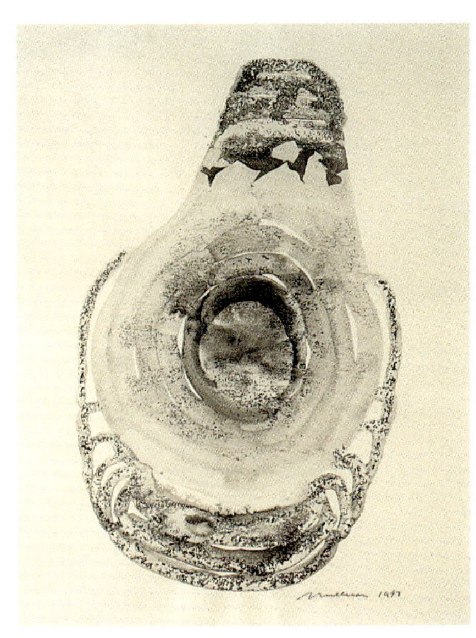

*Untitled*, 1947

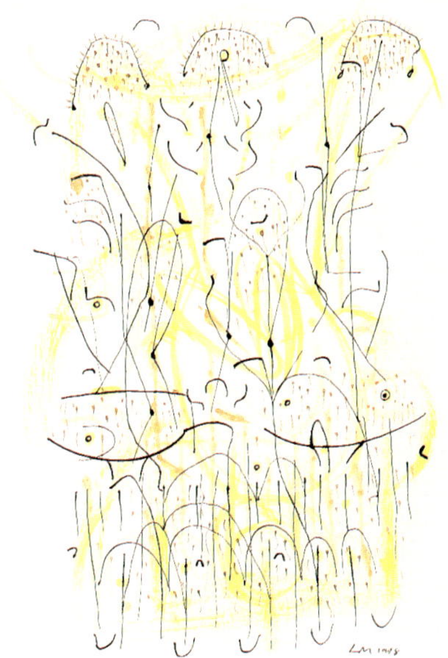

*Untitled*, 1948

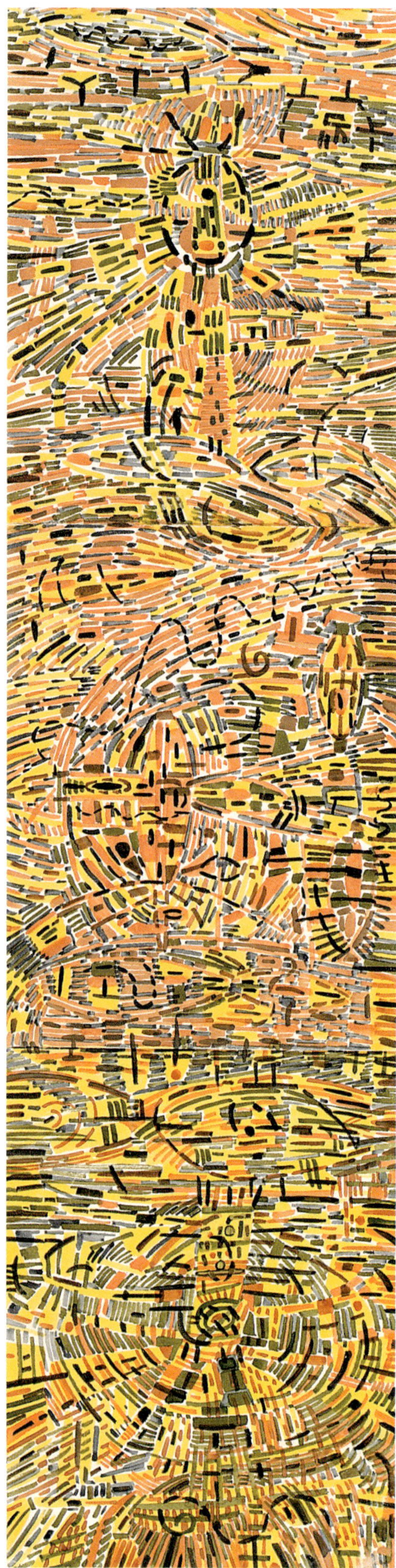

*Untitled*, c. 1948–51

**Drawing 5 Series**, 1949
Ink on paper
14 ½ x 11 ¼ in. (36.8 x 28.6 cm)
Collection of Marc Selwyn

**Untitled**, 1949
Construction paper and ink on paper
18 x 24 in. (45.7 x 61 cm)
Private collection

**Happily I Am Singing**, 1950
Tempera and pencil on paper
11 ⅞ x 8 ⅞ in. (30.2 x 22.5 cm)
The Museum of Modern Art, New York. Purchase 2430.2001

**Quartette of Spider Sounds**, 1950
Ink and charcoal on paper
25 ¼ x 19 in. (64.1 x 48.3 cm)
Laguna Art Museum Collection, Museum purchase with funds provided through prior gift of Lois Outerbridge, 1999.001
p. 33

**Transitory Landscape**, 1950
Ink and charcoal on paper
30 x 22 in. (76.2 x 55.9 cm)
Collection Dana and Stephen Sigoloff

**Untitled (Chamber of the Well)**, 1950
Charcoal on paper
25 x 18 ¾ in. (63.5 x 47.6 cm)
Los Angeles County Museum of Art, gift of Dean Valentine and Amy Adelson and purchased with funds provided by the family and friends of Mr. and Mrs. Howard Gluck in honor of their 50th wedding anniversary

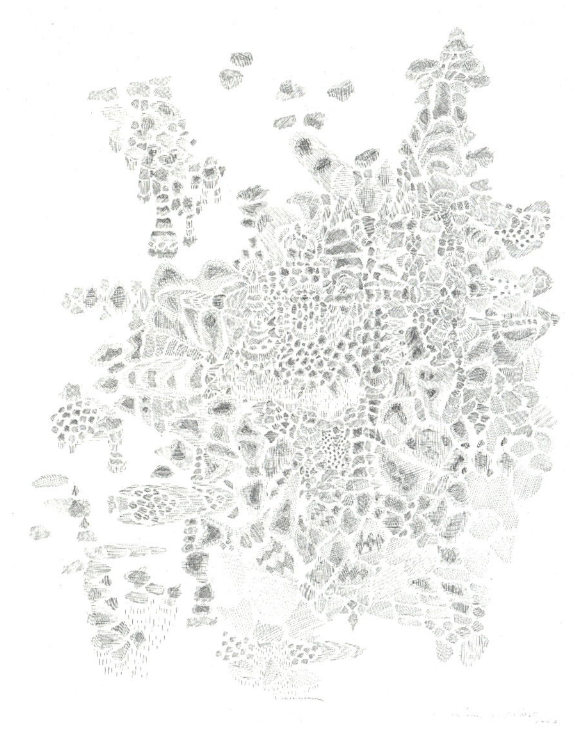

*Drawing 5 Series*, 1949

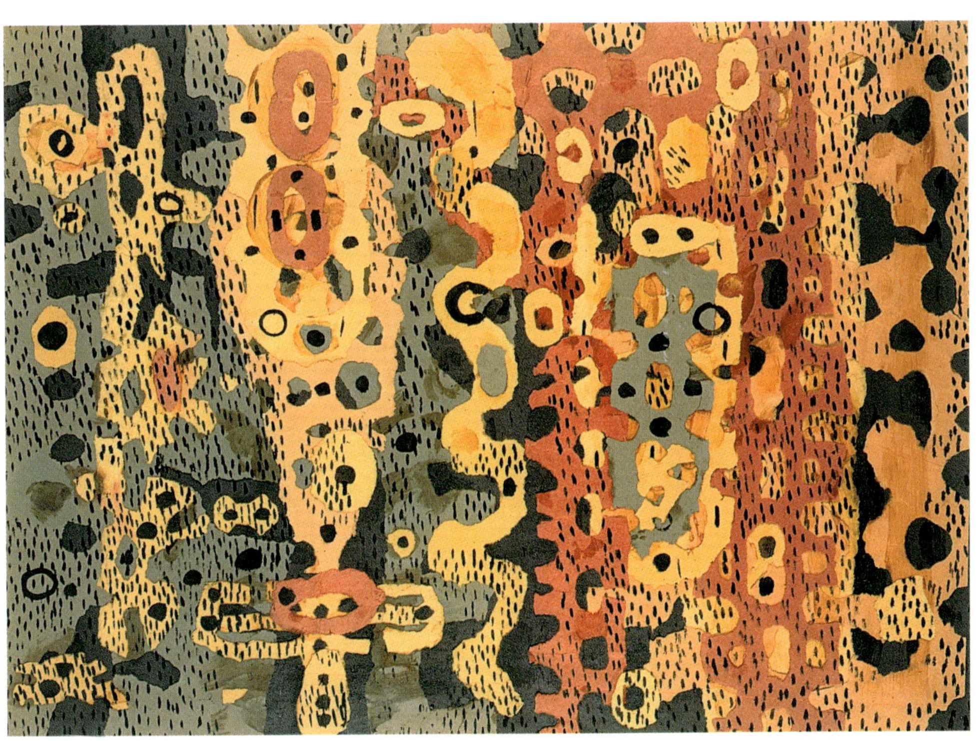

*Untitled*, 1949

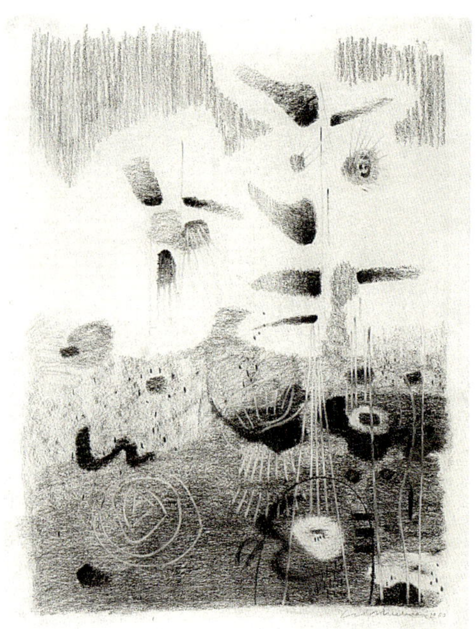

*Untitled (Chamber of the Well)*, 1950

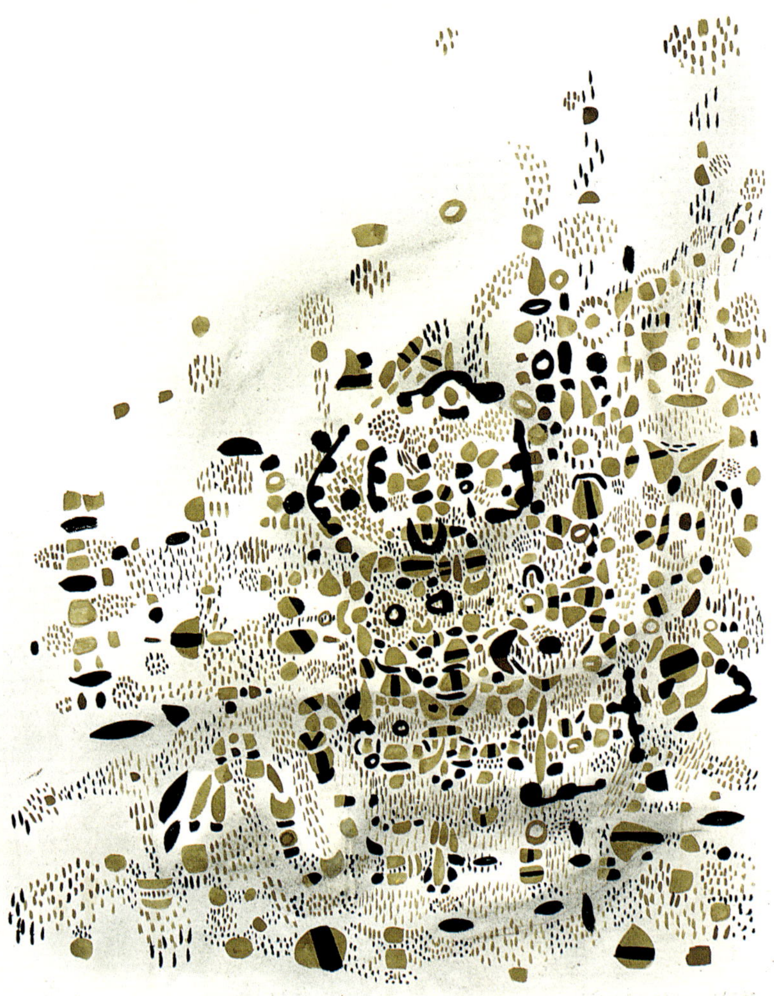

*Transitory Landscape*, 1950

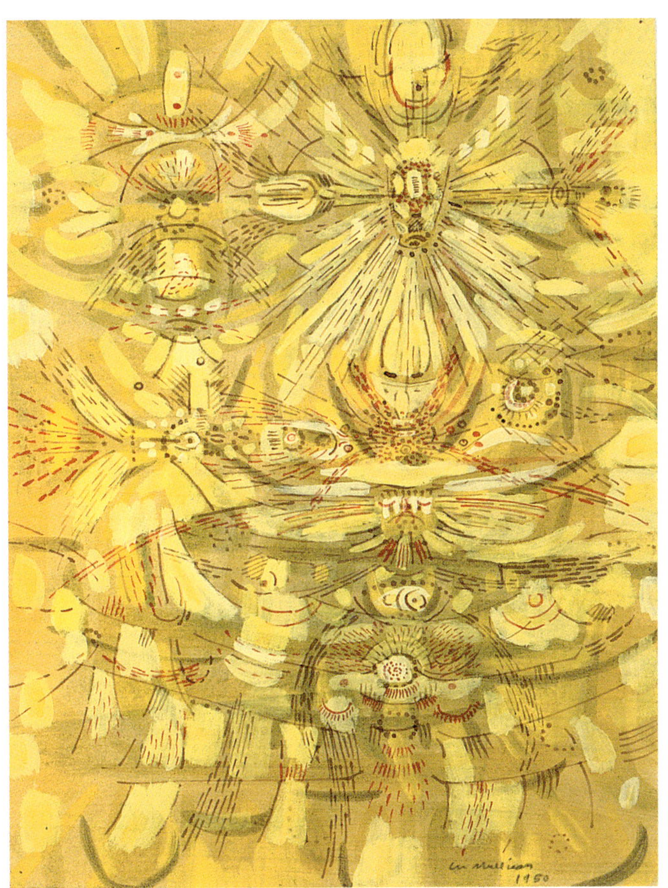

*Happily I Am Singing*, 1950

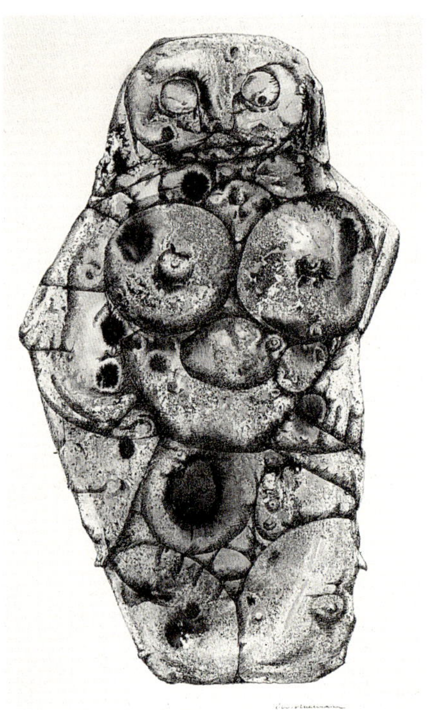

*Untitled (Dyn #7)*, c. 1950

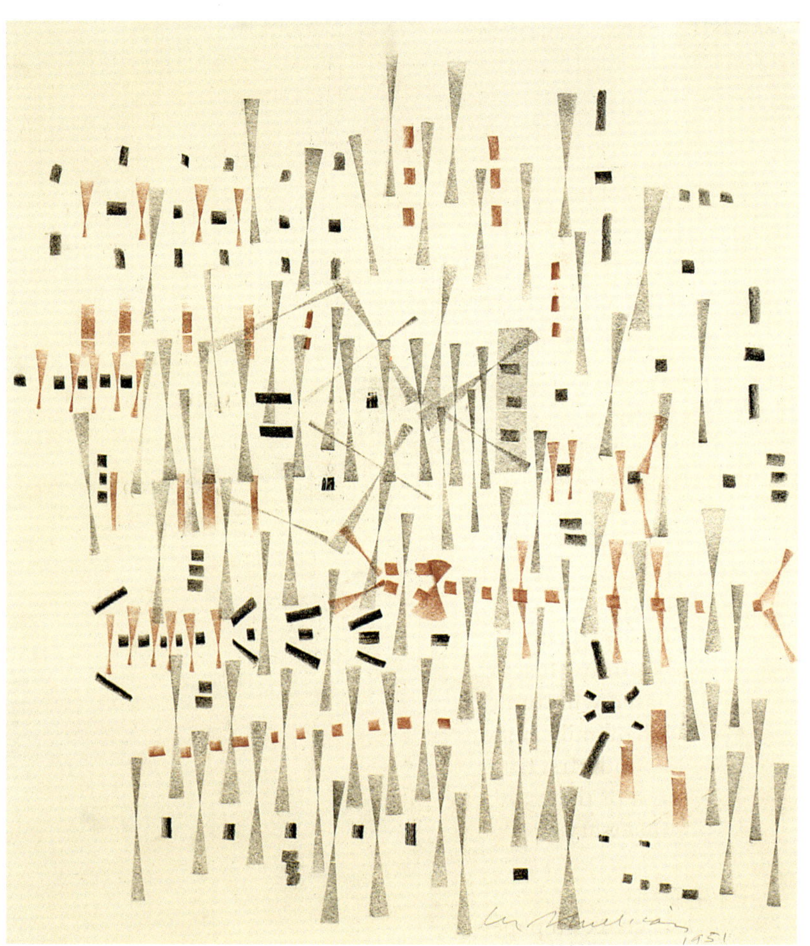

*Untitled*, 1951

**Untitled (Dyn #7)**, c. 1950
Ink on paper
16 x 10½ in. (40.6 x 26.7 cm)
The Museum of Contemporary Art, Los Angeles; purchased with funds provided by Dean Valentine

**Untitled**, 1951
Colored pencil on paper
16¾ x 13⅞ in. (42.5 x 35.2 cm)
Creative Artists Agency, Beverly Hills, California

**Untitled**, 1957
Crayon over gouache on paper
15¾ x 12¾ in. (40 x 32.4 cm)
Vincent Price Gallery & Art Museum, East Los Angeles College

**Shift West**, 1959
Graphite on paper
24 x 19 in. (61 x 48.3 cm)
Los Angeles County Museum of Art, purchased with funds provided by the family and friends of Mr. and Mrs. Howard Gluck in honor of their 50th wedding anniversary

**Untitled**, 1964
Gouache and chalk on paper
23½ x 17¾ in. (59.7 x 45.1 cm)
Estate of the artist, courtesy Marc Selwyn Fine Art

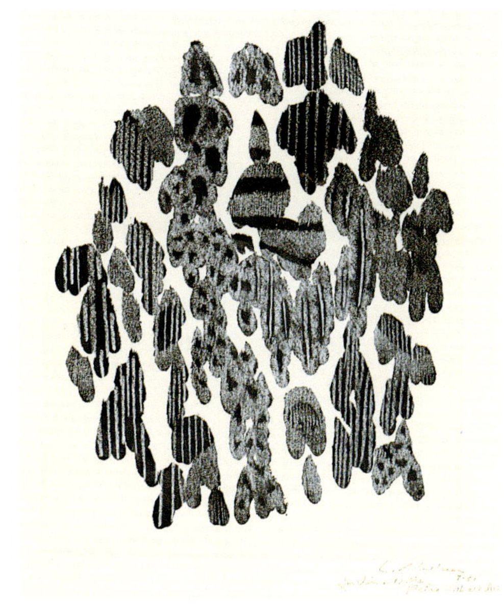

*Untitled*, 1957

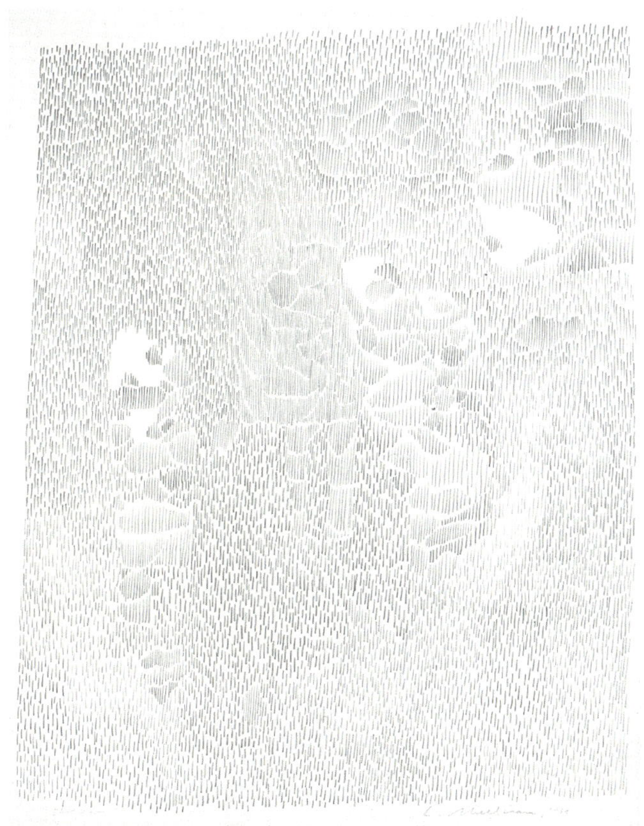

*Shift West*, 1959

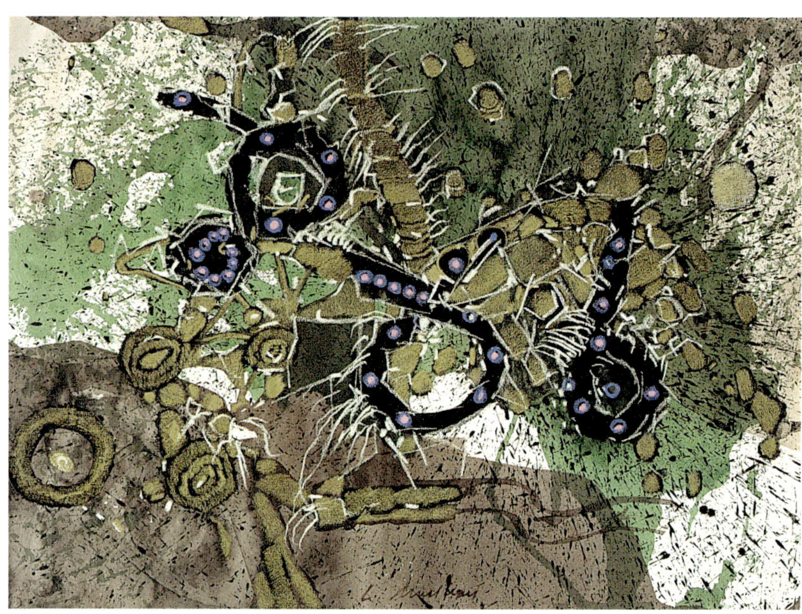

*Untitled*, 1964

**Passage in Thin Air**, 1965
Pencil and watercolor on paper
29¼ x 23¼ in. (74.3 x 59.1 cm)
Collection of Orange County Museum of Art, Newport Beach, California; Gift of the Betty Parsons Foundation

**Mondo Interior**, c. 1970
Oil pastel on paper
24 x 18 in. (61 x 45.7 cm)
Estate of the artist, courtesy Marc Selwyn Fine Art
p. 54

**Chickasha to Ninnekah**, 1979
Pencil on paper
22 x 14 in. (55.9 x 35.6 cm)
Herbert Palmer Gallery

**Sage Series Five**, 1979
Pencil on paper
14 x 11 in. (35.6 x 28 cm)
Herbert Palmer Gallery

**Untitled**, 1985
Pastel on paper
15½ x 12 in. (39.4 x 30.5 cm)
Ed Wortz and Karen Comegys-Wortz

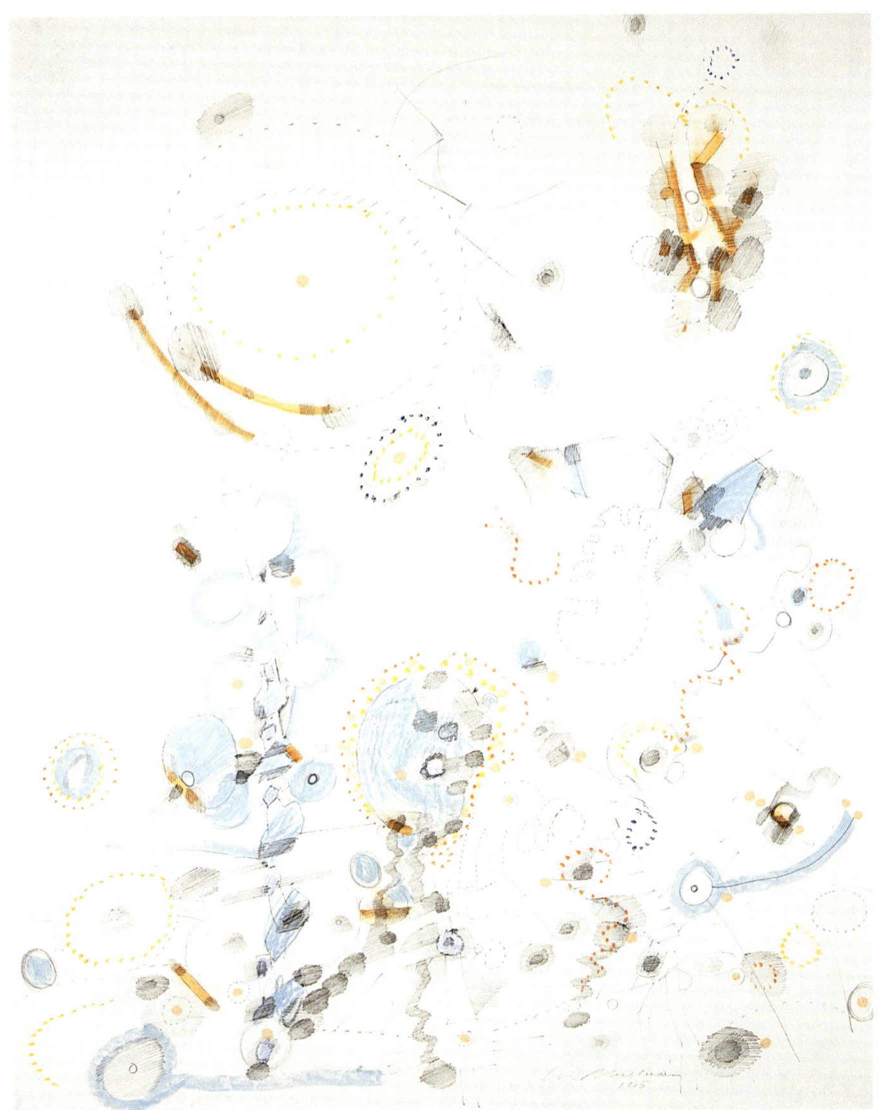

*Passage in Thin Air*, 1965

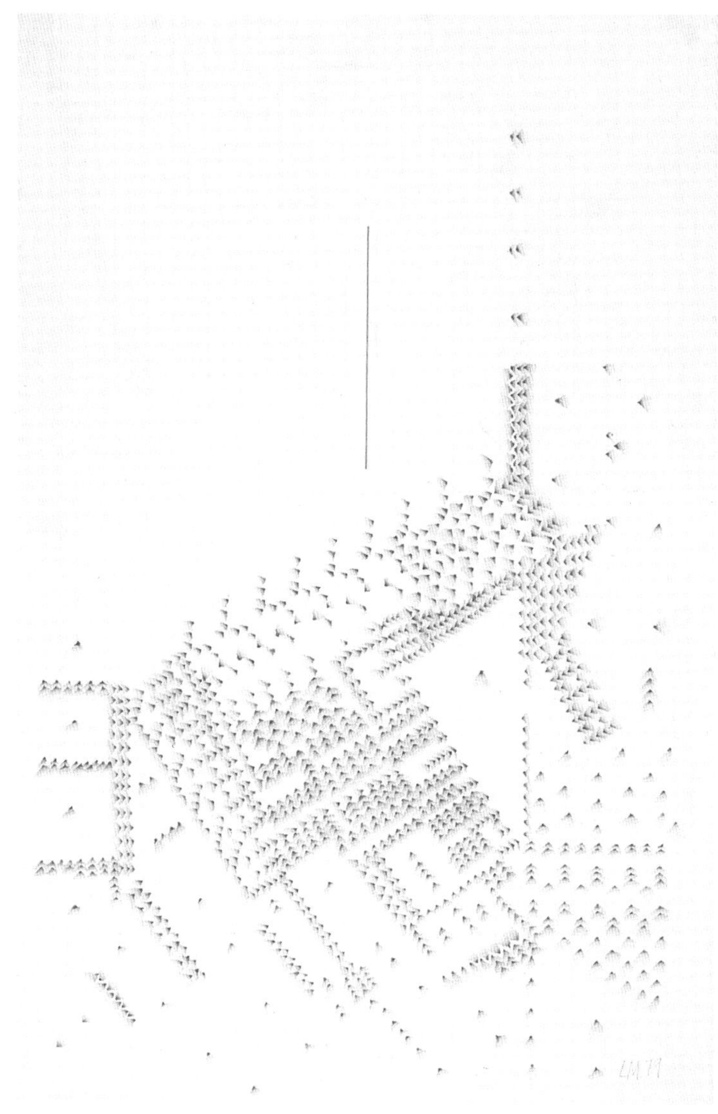

*Chickasha to Ninnekah*, 1979

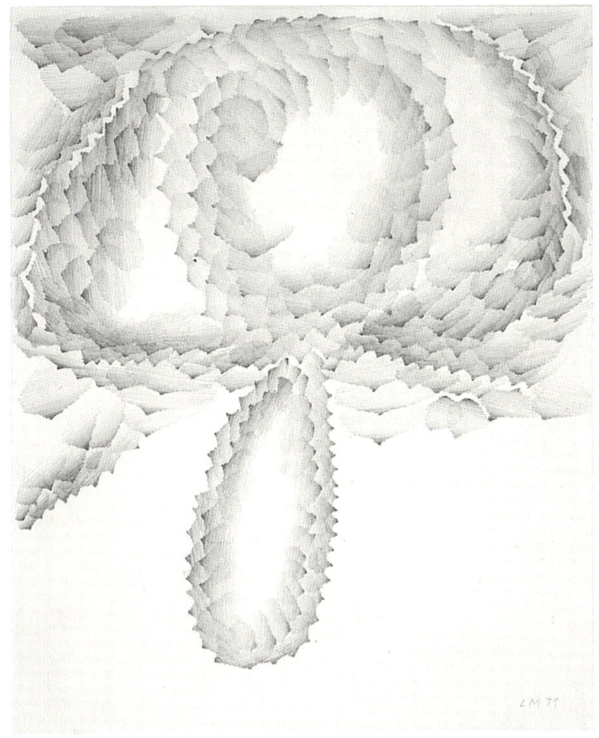

*Sage Series Five*, 1979

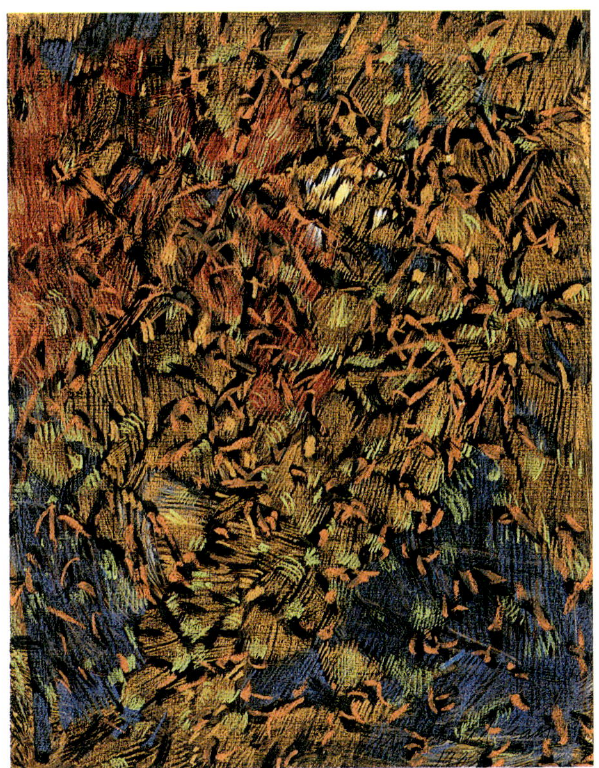

*Untitled*, 1985

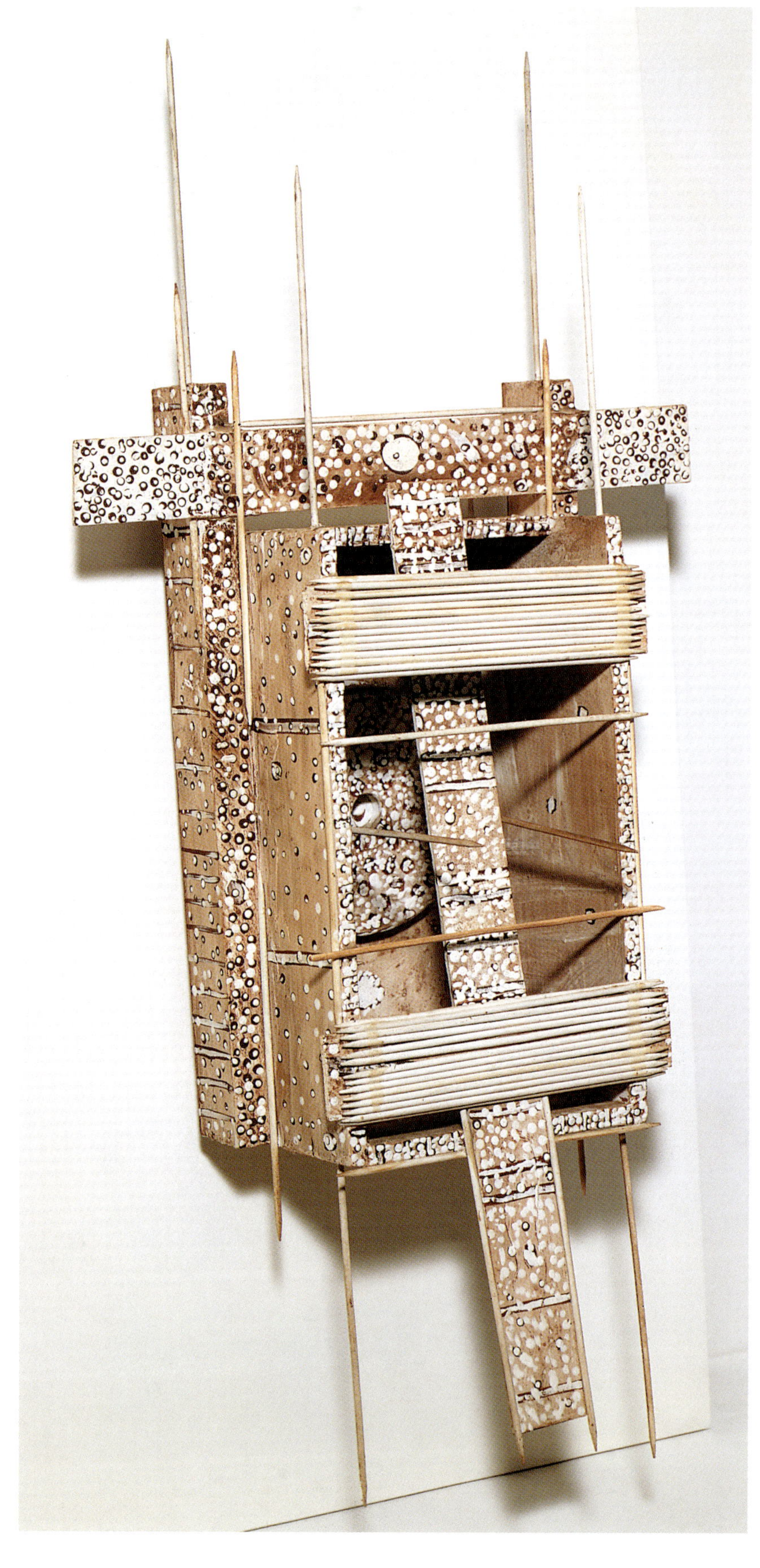

*Mask (Head)—A Tactile Ecstatic*, 1954

## SCULPTURE

**Mask (Head)—A Tactile Ecstatic**, 1954
Painted wood and string
28½ x 13¾ x 8½ in.
(72.4 x 34.9 x 21.6 cm)
Collection Nora Eccles Harrison Museum of Art; Marie Eccles Caine Foundation Gift

**Presence**, 1955
Painted wood
36⅛ x 17⅜ x 1¼ in.
(91.8 x 44.1 x 3.2 cm)
The Museum of Modern Art, New York, Mr. and Mrs. Roy R. Neuberger Fund, 1956
p. 47

**Untitled**, c. 1950–55
Painted wood and string
45 x 10 x 8 in.
(114.3 x 25.4 x 20.3 cm)
Los Angeles County Museum of Art, promised gift of Mr. and Mrs. Gifford Phillips
p. 45 (left)

**Untitled**, c. 1950–55
Painted wood and feathers
24 x 1½ x 2 in. (61 x 3.8 x 5.1 cm)
Los Angeles County Museum of Art, promised gift of Mr. and Mrs. Gifford Phillips
p. 45 (right)

**Untitled**, c. 1950–55
Twigs, string, and feathers
56¾ x 19 x 2 in.
(144.1 x 48.3 x 5.1 cm)
Collection of Luchita Mullican
p. 46 (left)

**Untitled**, c. 1950–55
Painted wood, string, and feathers
42 x 5½ x 3 in.
(106.7 x 14 x 7.6 cm)
Donna J. Cramer
p. 46 (right)

**Untitled** (Power Wand), 1950s
Painted wood, string, and feathers
40 x 2¾ x 2 in.
(101.6 x 7 x 5.1 cm)
Collection of Luchita Mullican

**Untitled**, 1950s
Painted wood
20¼ x 6½ x 2½ in.
(51.4 x 16.5 x 6.4 cm)
Collection of Luchita Mullican

**Untitled**, 1950s
Painted wood
18½ x 6 x 2½ in.
(47 x 15.2 x 6.4 cm)
Collection of Luchita Mullican
back jacket

**Untitled (Tactile Ecstatic)**, 1960
Painted wood, string, and feather
44 x 30 x ¾ in.
(111.8 x 76.2 x 2 cm)
Collection of Susan and Bill Ehrlich

## PERIODICALS

**DYN**, volumes 1–6, April/May 1942–November 1944
Periodical, published by Wolfgang Paalen
11 x 8½ in. each (28 x 21.6 cm) (closed dimensions)
Research Library, The Getty Research Institute, Los Angeles
p. 20

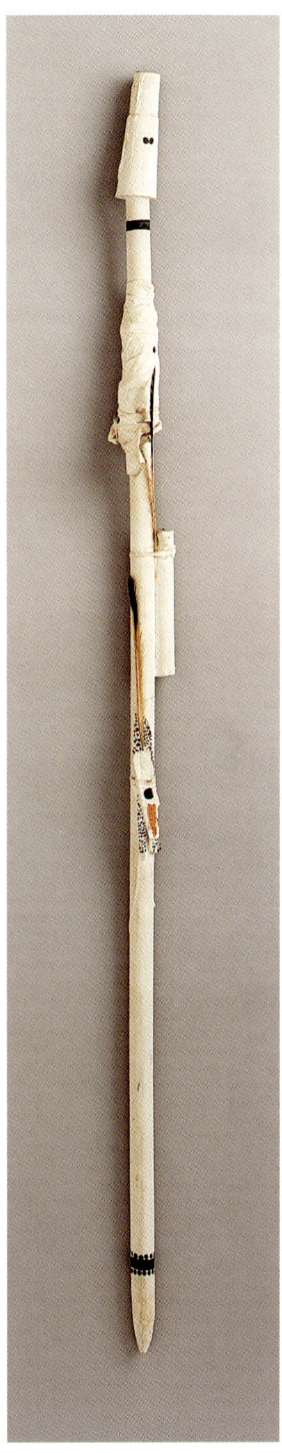

*Untitled* (Power Wand), 1950s

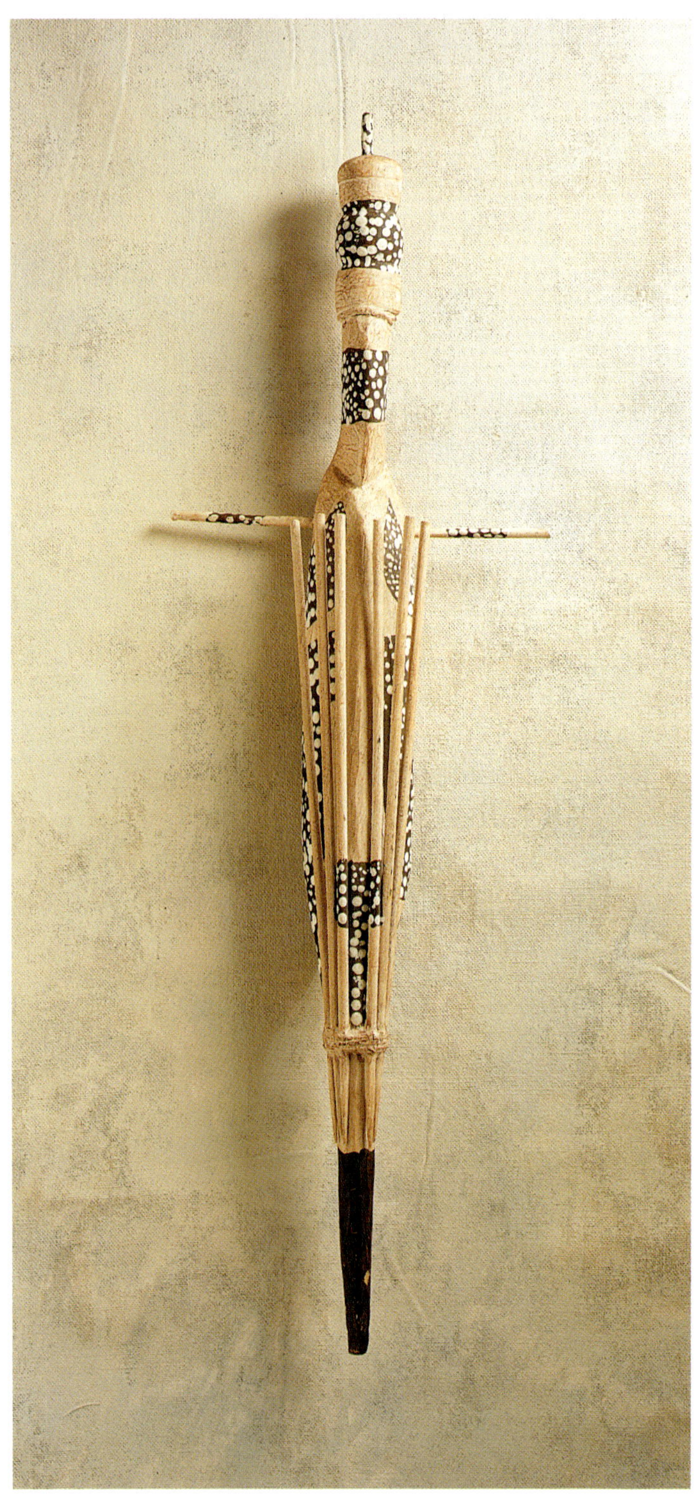

*Untitled*, 1950s

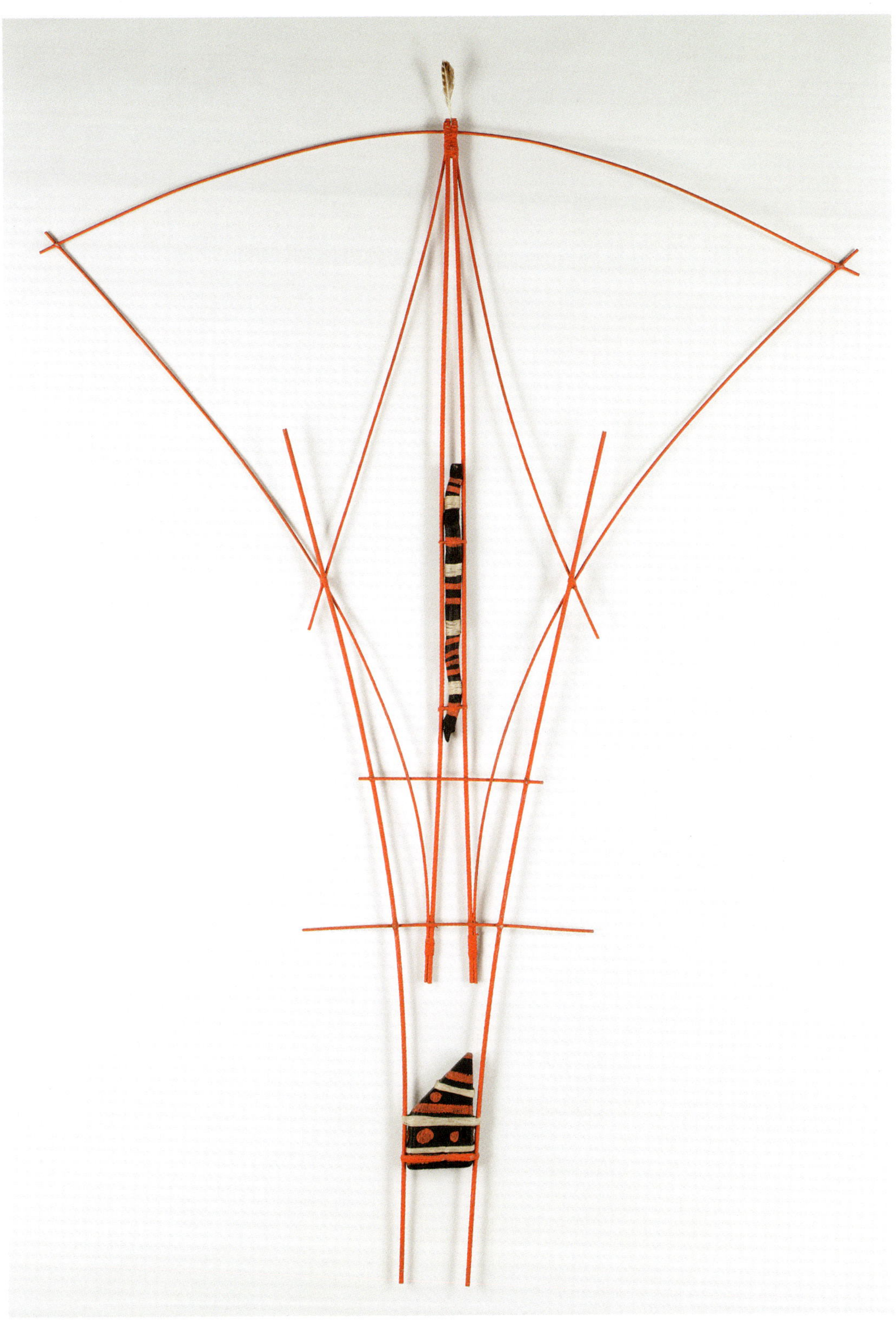

*Untitled (Tactile Ecstatic)*, 1960

# Chronology

*(Compiled with the assistance of Roz Leader)*

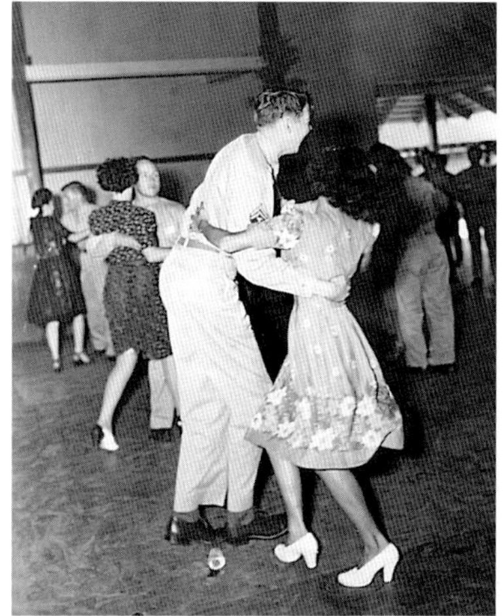

Mullican at army dance, Hawaii, c. 1944

**1919**
Born December 2, Chickasha, Oklahoma

**1937–39**
Studies at Abilene Christian College, Abilene, Texas

**1939**
Transfers to the University of Oklahoma

**1941–42**
Transfers to and graduates from the Kansas City Art Institute

**1942**
Joins the U.S. Army; assigned to the Corps of Engineers. Attends topographic school, Fort Belvoir, Virginia

**1942–46**
Stationed in California, Hawaii, and Guam, drawing topographic maps based on aerial photographs. Discovers *DYN* magazine and the work of Wolfgang Paalen

**1946**
Travels to Japan. Discharged from the army

**1947**
Moves to San Francisco and meets Gordon Onslow Ford

**1948**
Meets Paalen and Luchita Hurtado

**1949**
Solo exhibition with catalogue at The San Francisco Museum of Art (text by Paalen)

**1950**
First of six solo exhibitions (also 1952, 1953, 1959, 1961, and 1967) at the Willard Gallery, New York

**1951**
*Dynaton* exhibition with catalogue at The San Francisco Museum of Art with Paalen and Onslow Ford. Birth of son Matthew (Matt) with Luchita Hurtado

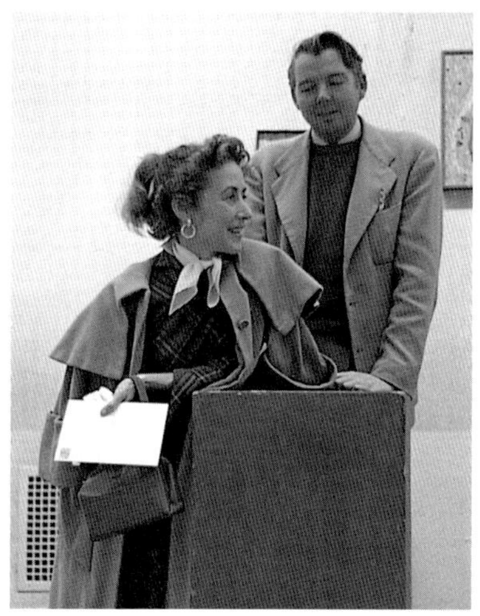

Mullican with Jacqueline Johnson at the *Dynaton* exhibition, San Francisco, 1951

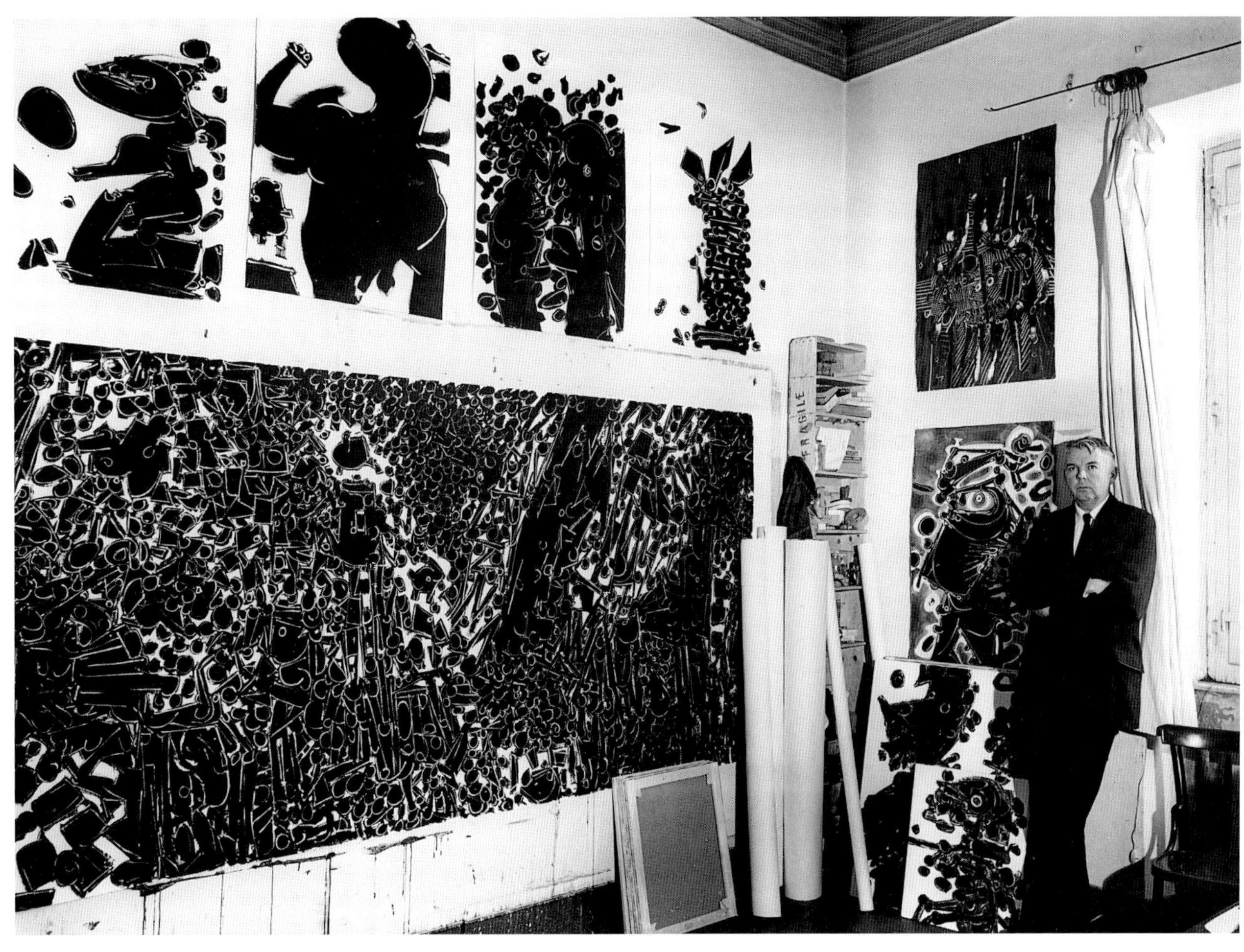

Mullican in his studio in Rome, 1960

**1952**
Settles in Santa Monica with family

**1957**
Marries Luchita Hurtado

**1959–60**
Teaches at UCLA Extension. In Rome on a Guggenheim Fellowship

**1961**
Returns to Southern California. Joins the UCLA Art Department

**1962**
Birth of son John

**1968**
On UCLA exchange program with the University of Chile, Santiago

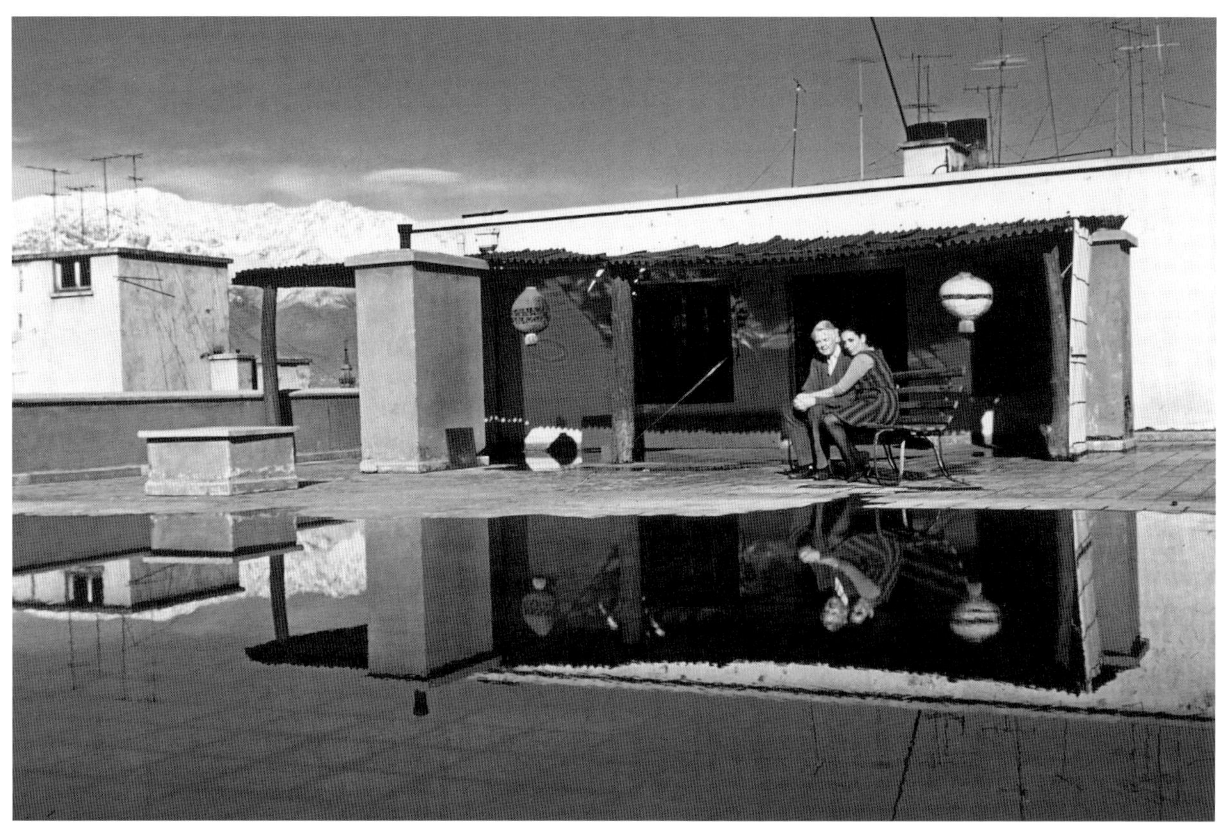

Lee and Luchita Mullican outside his studio in Santiago, Chile, 1968

1980
First of several trips to India

1985
Coorganizes *Neo-Tantra: Contemporary Indian Painting Inspired by Tradition* for the Wight Art Gallery, UCLA

1986
Coorganizes *Visions of Inner Space: Gestural Painting in Modern American Art* for the Wight Art Gallery, UCLA as part of a cultural exchange program between India and the U.S.

1998
Dies July 7, Santa Monica, California

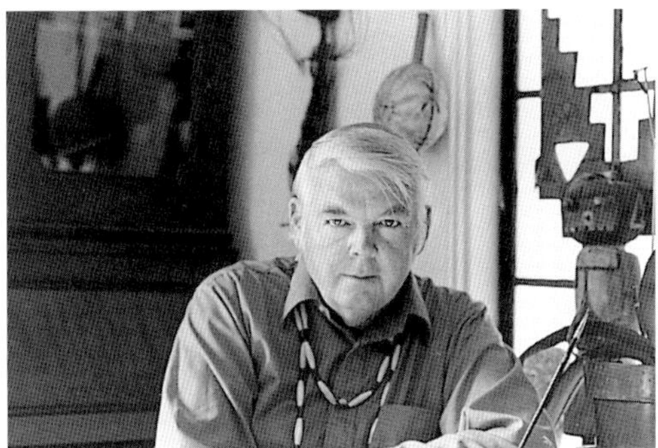

Mullican, c. 1970

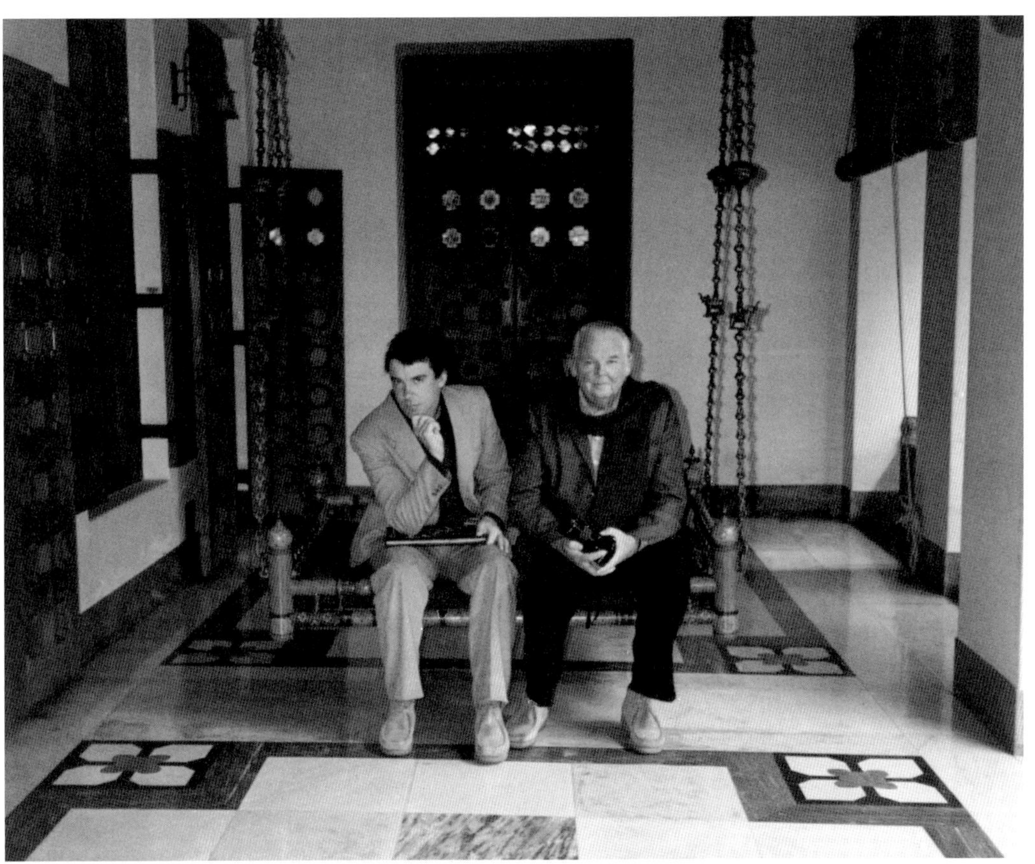

Matt and Lee Mullican in Ahmedabad, India, at the home of Gautam Sarabhai (founding family of the Calico Museum of Textiles), 1982

# Lenders to the Exhibition

Nina Anthoine
Betye Monell Burton
Donna J. Cramer
Cecilia Dan
Ron de Salvo
Susan and Bill Ehrlich
Kenneth L. Freed
Allan M. Jalon and Mary Tricarico Jalon
Miani Johnson, Willard Gallery
Aimee Knowlton and Jason Asch
Harlan and Natasha Levine
John Lock
Luchita Mullican
Harold and Gertrud Parker
Mr. and Mrs. Gifford Phillips
William Resnick, M.D. and Douglas Cordell, M.D.
Beverly and Mel Rosenthal
Marc Selwyn
Dana and Stephen Sigoloff
Trenton Family Trust
Dean Valentine and Amy Adelson
Thomas Weisel and Emily Carroll
Orna and Keenan Wolens
Ed Wortz and Karen Comegys-Wortz
and a private collector who wishes to remain anonymous

Creative Artists Agency, Beverly Hills, California
Getty Research Institute, Los Angeles
Hammer Museum, Los Angeles
Hansen, Jacobson, Teller, Hoberman, Newman, Warren, Sloane & Richman
Herbert Palmer Gallery
Laguna Art Museum
Los Angeles County Museum of Art
Lucid Art Foundation
Estate of Lee Mullican, courtesy Marc Selwyn Fine Art
The Museum of Contemporary Art, Los Angeles
The Museum of Modern Art, New York
Nora Eccles Harrison Museum of Art
Orange County Museum of Art, Newport Beach, California
The Phillips Collection, Washington, D.C.
Santa Barbara Museum of Art
Smith College Museum of Art, Northampton, Massachusetts
Vincent Price Gallery & Art Museum, East Los Angeles College
Weatherspoon Art Museum, The University of North Carolina at Greensboro

# Acknowledgments

Very rarely in a curator's career do all the parts of an exhibition fall neatly into place. This was the case with *Lee Mullican: An Abundant Harvest of Sun*, which is due not only to the timeliness of the project but also, and in no small measure, to the extraordinary support and enthusiasm of colleagues and friends in Southern California and across the country. The exhibition would never have been possible without the warm and loving support of Luchita Hurtado Mullican and her sons Matt and John Mullican and Daniel del Solar. My friendship with Luchita is one of the unexpected but delightful side products of the show, and for that alone I am grateful. Equally important from the very beginning have been the energy and enthusiasm of Marc Selwyn and his staff at Marc Selwyn Fine Art (first Lexi Brown and now Jennifer Pregenzer). Without Marc, this show would never have come to fruition. Numerous scholars have been extremely generous in sharing information about Lee and his Dynaton colleagues, including Fariba Bogzaran, Nora Halpern, Michel Oren, Amy Winter, and David L. Witt. Likewise, various dealers willingly shared their expertise; my thanks go to Joni Gordon (Newspace Gallery, Los Angeles), Miani Johnson (Willard Gallery, New York), James Kelly (James Kelly Gallery, Santa Fe), Tobey Moss (Tobey C. Moss Gallery, Los Angeles), Herbert Palmer and Susan M. Becker (Herbert Palmer Gallery, Los Angeles), and Rose Rabow (formerly Rose Rabow Gallery, San Francisco). I am also grateful to Rachel Rosenthal, with whom Lee collaborated in the mid-1950s, for sharing her recollections and her photographs. Others who kindly gave of their time and assistance include Rochelle Caper, Judy Fiskin, Morelle Levine, Michael Rubel (Creative Artists Agency), Richard Smith (Cartographic Section, National Archives), Hank Saxe and Cynthia Patterson (Saxe-Patterson Ceramics for Art and Architecture), Steven Wolf (Steven Wolf Fine Arts), and Lee's former students and fellow artists Tony Berlant and Michael McMillen. I also want to acknowledge the indispensable assistance of the staff at the Research Library at the Getty Research Institute and of Marian Kovinick at the West Coast Research Center of the Archives of American Art/Smithsonian Institution.

Many LACMA colleagues were very helpful to me in organizing this exhibition. I am grateful to Irene Martin, Beverley Sabo, Kristin Fredricks, Janelle Aieta, and Elaine Peterson of Exhibition Programs, who make everything happen; to Cristin McKnight and Michele Urton of the department of Modern and Contemporary Art for their flawless, graceful, and thoughtful administrative support; to Roz Leader, volunteer *extraordinaire*, for her help with numerous aspects of the project; to Nancy Sutherland in the research library for procuring innumerable books and obscure articles via inter-library loan; to Stephanie Emerson and Sara Cody in the Publications department for so ably shepherding and editing this book; to freelance designer Sandy Bell for creating such an elegant publication; to Piper Wynn Severance in Rights and Reproductions and Steve Oliver in Photo Services for procuring existing photography and shooting new images; to Elma O'Donoghue in Paintings Conservation for her deft and sensitive work; to associate registrar Sandy Davis and Tessa Gonzalez for coordinating all the shipping; to Bernard Kester, a longtime colleague and friend of Lee's, for his sensitive exhibition design; to Jeff Haskin and the staff of Art Preparation and Installation for their careful handling of the art; and to Tobey Tannenbaum in Museum Education for her able assistance on related programs. (I would also like to thank Andrew Perchuk and Rani Singh of the Getty Research Institute for their collaborative efforts.) In addition, I would particularly like to acknowledge Kevin Salatino, curator of Prints and Drawings; thanks to Kevin's love of Lee's work, LACMA now boasts one of the world's best holdings of his drawings. Kevin was never too busy to look at and discuss Mullican's work with me and to offer his astute comments and advice. I am also grateful to my curatorial colleagues in Modern and Contemporary Art, Stephanie Barron, Howard Fox, Lynn Zelevansky, and Ilona Katzew, who have been there with and for me all along the way.

Special thanks are due to Lynn Gumpert, director of the Grey Art Gallery, New York University, for courageously agreeing to host an exhibition of an artist whose work has been largely ignored in New York for the past forty years. I also wish to thank Amy Gerstler and Lari Pittman for contributing their unique and wonderful voices to this book. Of course no exhibition or catalogue is possible without financial support, and I am grateful to The Warhol Foundation, the Herta and Paul Amir Foundation, The Judith Rothschild Foundation, and the Pasadena Art Alliance for their generosity. Lenders are at least as critical to an exhibition's success, and I want to thank all the individuals and institutions (listed on p. 124) for their willingness to part with works from their collections for an extended period. Staff members at various institutional lenders were particularly helpful, including Janet Blake (Laguna Art Museum), Cindy Burlingham and David Rodes (Hammer Museum), Tom Callas (Orange County Museum of Art), Diana du Pont (Santa Barbara Museum of Art), Gary Garrels and Cora Rosevear (The Museum of Modern Art), Robert Hollister (The Museum of Contemporary Art, Los Angeles), and Wim de Wit (Getty Research Institute).

Lastly I would like to acknowledge four individuals who each played a critical role in this project. I am grateful to Emily Braun for being my sounding board and a constant source of moral support and sage advice. The ongoing support and encouragement of my husband Tom Muller in a myriad of ways have been invaluable to me during this project and every aspect of my life. Finally, I would like to dedicate this catalogue to Fannie and Alan Leslie, who first opened my eyes to Lee Mullican's work. Without them and without the inspiration of Lee's exquisitely beautiful 1951 painting *Space* (which they gave to LACMA), there would be no exhibition.

Carol S. Eliel
*Curator of Modern and Contemporary Art*

# Selected Bibliography


Arb, Renee. "Lee Mullican [Willard Gallery]." *Art News* 48, no. 10 (Feb. 1950): 48.

*The Artist as Collector: Selections from Four California Collections of the Arts of Africa, Oceania, the Amerindians and the Santeros of New Mexico.* Exh. cat. Edited by James B. Byrne. Newport Beach, CA: Newport Harbor Art Museum, 1975.

Bogzaran, Fariba. *Images of the Lucid Mind: A Phenomenological Study of Lucid Dreaming and Modern Painting.* Ph.D. diss., California Institute of Integral Studies, 1994.

Brown, John. *Ciphers.* Rome: Rome-New York Art Foundation, 1960.

*The California Connection: Sixteen Paintings from the Gifford and Joann Phillips Collection.* Exh. cat. Essay by Anne Carnegie Edgerton. Santa Fe: Museum of New Mexico Press, 1983.

*California: 5 Footnotes to Modern Art History.* Exh. cat. Edited by Stephanie Barron. Los Angeles: Los Angeles County Museum of Art, 1977.

"Diebenkorn, Woelffer, Mullican: A Discussion." *Artforum* 1, no. 10 (April 1963): 24–28.

Duncan, Michael. "Dynaton: Before & Beyond." *Art Issues* 27 (March/April 1993): 44.

*DYN* 1–6. April/May 1942–November 1944. Facsimile edited by Christian Kloyber. Vienna and New York: Springer, c. 2000.

*Dynaton*. Exh. cat. Essays by Jacqueline Johnson and Wolfgang Paalen. San Francisco: The San Francisco Museum of Art, 1951.

*DYNATON, Before & Beyond*. Exh. cat. Edited by Nora Halpern. Malibu, CA: Frederick R. Weisman Museum of Art, Pepperdine University, 1992.

*Dynaton Re-Viewed*. Exh. cat. Essay by Lee Mullican. San Francisco: Gallery Paule Anglim, 1977.

*Fifteen Profiles: Distinguished California Modernists*. Exh. cat. Essay by Daphne Lane Beneke. Fresno, CA: Fresno Art Museum, 1995.

Fink, Sylvia. *The Dynaton: Three Artists with Similar Ideas—Lee Mullican, Gordon Onslow Ford, Wolfgang Paalen*. M.A. thesis, Arizona State University, 1973.

*Flight Patterns*. Exh. cat. Essays by Cornelia H. Butler, Lee Weng Choy, and Francis Pound. Los Angeles: The Museum of Contemporary Art, 2000.

Gibson, Ann Eden. *Issues in Abstract Expressionism: The Artist-Run Periodicals*. Ann Arbor, MI: UMI Research Press, 1990.

*The Gifford and Joann Phillips Collection*. Exh. cat. Introduction by Frederick S. Wight. Los Angeles: UCLA Art Galleries, 1962.

Goodnough, Robert. "Lee Mullican [Willard Gallery]." *Art News* 51, no. 1 (Mar. 1952): 54.

*Gordon Onslow-Ford: Retrospective Exhibition*. Exh. cat. Oakland, CA: Oakland Museum, 1980.

Greenberg, Clement. "Cubist, Abstract, Surrealist Art." *The Nation* 156 (Jan. 30, 1943): 177.

——. "Surrealist Painting." In *The Collected Essays and Criticism*, vol. 1, *Perceptions and Judgments, 1939–1944*. Edited by John O'Brian. Chicago and London: The University of Chicago Press, 1986.

Greenstein, Jane. "A View of India's Modern Tantric Art." *Los Angeles Times*, December 25, 1985, section VI, p. 2.

Guest, Barbara. "Lee Mullican [Willard Gallery]." *Art News* 52, no. 7 (Nov. 1953): 42.

*Hommage to Wolfgang Paalen*. Exh. cat. Essays by Wolfgang Paalen, Jacqueline Johnson, André Breton, José Emilio Pacheco, and Gordon Onslow-Ford. Mexico City: Museo de Arte Moderno, 1967.

Hopkins, Henry. "Visionaries." *Antiques & Fine Arts* (March/April 1992): 74–81.

Hurtado, Luchita. Interview by Amy Winter. Transcript. May 1, 1994. Oral History Program, Archives of American Art/Smithsonian Institution.

———. Interview by Paul Karlstrom. Transcript. April 13, 1995. Oral History Program, Archives of American Art/Smithsonian Institution.

Knight, Christopher. "Taking the Long View." *Los Angeles Times*, July 21, 1999, section F.

"Landscapes of the Mind: Show in Los Angeles." *Time* (Nov. 10, 1952): 74.

Langsner, Jules. "Lee Mullican [Kantor Gallery]." *Art News* 51, no. 6 (Oct. 1952): 63–64.

———. "Mullican Paints a Picture." *Art News* 52, no. 6 (Oct. 1953): 34–37, 66–67.

———. "Mullican Moves On." *Art News* 53, no. 9 (Jan. 1955): 53.

*Lee Mullican*. Exh. cat. Essay by Wolfgang Paalen. San Francisco: The San Francisco Museum of Art, 1949.

*Lee Mullican*. Exh. cat. Essay by Wolfgang Paalen. New York: Willard Gallery, 1950.

*Lee Mullican*. Exh. brochure. Essay by Robert M. Church. Tulsa, OK: Philbrook Art Center, 1951.

*Lee Mullican*. Exh. cat. Essay by Jack Hirschman. San Francisco: The San Francisco Museum of Art, 1965.

*Lee Mullican: Paintings, 1965–1969*. Exh. cat. Introduction by Gordon Onslow Ford. Los Angeles: UCLA Art Galleries, 1969.

*Lee Mullican: Selected Drawings, 1945–1980*. Exh. cat. Introduction by Claudine Isé, essay by Allan McCollum. Los Angeles: UCLA Hammer Museum of Art and Cultural Center, 1999.

*Lee Mullican: Selected Works, 1948–1980*. Exh. cat. Essay by Jascha Kessler. Basel and New York: Galerie Schreiner, 1980. Published in conjunction with the Los Angeles Municipal Art Gallery.

Leopold, Michael. "Los Angeles Letter." *Art International* XVIII/1 (Jan. 20, 1974): 26–28.

*Moderns in Mind: Gerome Kamrowski, Lee Mullican, Gordon Onslow-Ford*. Exh. cat. Essay on Lee Mullican by Susan Larsen. New York: Artists Space, 1986.

Muchnic, Suzanne. "A Spiritual Expression from India." *Los Angeles Times*, January 13, 1986, section VI, 1, 3.

———. "Still Cosmic after All These Years." *Los Angeles Times*, January 3, 1993, Calendar section, 7.

Mullican, Lee. Interview by Joann Phillips. *Los Angeles Art Community: Group Portrait: Lee Mullican*. Los Angeles: Oral History Program, UCLA, 1977.

———. Interview by Paul Karlstrom. Transcript. May 22, 1992 and January 26, February 11, and March 4, 1993. Oral History Program, Archives of American Art/Smithsonian Institution.

———. Vertical file. Library of The Museum of Modern Art, New York.

*Mullican + Mullican*. Exh. cat. Essay by Kim Bradley. Albuquerque: Jonson Gallery of the University Art Museum, 1989.

"Mullican Collection." Los Angeles: The Egg and The Eye, Inc.: 1969.

*Neo-Tantra: Contemporary Indian Painting Inspired by Tradition*. Exh. cat. Edited by Edith A. Tonelli. Los Angeles: Frederick S. Wight Art Gallery, UCLA, 1985.

Neufert, Andreas. *Wolfgang Paalen 1905–1959: Denker und Visionär im Medium der Malerei/The Painter as Thinker and Visionary*. Translated by Thomas J. Minnes. Dresden: Galerie Döbele, 2001.

———. *Wolfgang Paalen Im Inneren des Wals: Monografie–Schriften–Oeuvrekatalog*. Vienna and New York: Springer, 1999.

*1965 Annual Exhibition of Contemporary American Sculpture, Watercolors and Drawings*. Exh. cat. New York: Whitney Museum of American Art, 1965.

Onslow-Ford, Gordon. *Towards a New Subject in Painting*. San Francisco: The San Francisco Museum of Art, 1948.

———. *Painting in the Instant*. New York: Harry N. Abrams, 1964.

———. *Création*. Basel: Galerie Schreiner, 1978.

———. Interview by Ted Lindberg. Transcript. March 26, 1984. Oral History Program, Archives of American Art/Smithsonian Institution.

Paalen, Wolfgang. *Form and Sense*. Problems of Contemporary Art, no. 1. New York: Wittenborn and Co., 1945.

*Pacific Dreams: Currents of Surrealism and Fantasy in California Art, 1934–1957*. Exh. cat. Edited by Susan Ehrlich. Los Angeles: UCLA at the Armand Hammer Museum of Art and Cultural Center, 1995.

Plagens, Peter. "Los Angeles." *Artforum* VIII, no. 4 (Dec. 1969): 74–75.

*Pursuit of the Marvelous: Stanley William Hayter, Charles Howard, Gordon Onslow Ford*. Exh. cat. Essay by Susan M. Anderson. Laguna Beach, CA: Laguna Art Museum, 1990.

*Realizing the Possible: The Art of Lee Mullican*. Exh. brochure. Essay by David L. Witt. Taos: Harwood Foundation Museum, University of New Mexico, 1990.

Reed, Judith Kaye. "Mullican's War Paint [Willard Gallery]," *Art Digest* 24, no. 10 (Feb. 15, 1950): 20.

Regler, Gustav. *Wolfgang Paalen*. New York: Nierendorf Editions, 1946.

Rushing, W. Jackson. *Native American Art and the New York Avant-Garde: A History of Cultural Primitivism.* Austin: University of Texas Press, 1995.

Sandler, Irving. "Lee Mullican [Willard Gallery]." *Art News* 60, no. 3 (May 1961): 12.

Sawin, Martica. *Surrealism in Exile and the Beginning of the New York School.* Cambridge, MA and London: The MIT Press, 1995.

Schipper, Merle. "Lee Mullican." *Art News* 86, no. 3 (March 1987): 32.

Seldis, Henry J. "Art Trends of the West Coast." *Art in America* 42, no. 4 (Dec. 1954): 296–301.

———. "Mullican Spiritual Brother." *Los Angeles Times,* August, 1973.

*Selected Artists—'67.* Exh. cat. Des Moines, IA: Des Moines Art Center, 1967.

*The Spiritual in Art: Abstract Painting, 1890–1985.* Exh. cat. Essays by Maurice Tuchman et al. Los Angeles: Los Angeles County Museum of Art and New York: Abbeville, 1986.

Stauffacher, Jack. Interview by Paul Karlstrom. Transcript. February 8, 1993. Oral History Program, Archives of American Art/ Smithsonian Institution.

Tillim, Sidney. "Lee Mullican [Willard Gallery]." *Arts* 33, no. 6 (March 1959): 60–61.

Tobey, Mark. "Japanese Traditions and American Art." *College Art Journal* XVIII, no. 1 (Fall 1958): 20–24.

*Turning the Tide: Early Los Angeles Modernists 1920–1956.* Exh. cat. Edited by Paul J. Karlstrom and Susan Ehrlich. Santa Barbara, CA: Santa Barbara Museum of Art, 1990.

*Visions of Inner Space: Gestural Painting in Modern American Art.* Exh. cat. Text by Lee Mullican and Merle Schipper. Los Angeles: Wight Art Gallery, UCLA, 1987.

Wilson, William. "The Stick-to-itiveness of Artist Lee Mullican." *Los Angeles Times*, November 9, 1980, Calendar section, p. 86.

Winter, Amy. *Wolfgang Paalen: Artist and Theorist of the Avant-Garde*. Westport, CT and London: Praeger, 2003.

Winter, Amy. "The Germanic Reception of Native American Art: Wolfgang Paalen as Collector, Scholar, and Artist." *European Review of Native American Studies* 6, no. 1 (1992): 17–26.

Witt, David L. *Modernists in Taos from Dasburg to Martin*. Santa Fe, NM: Red Crane Books, 2002.

*Wolfgang Paalen, Zwischen Surrealismus und Abstraktion*. Exh. cat. Includes essay by Lee Mullican. Klagenfurt, Austria: Ritter, 1993. Published in conjunction with Museum Moderner Kunst Stiftung Ludwig, Vienna.

Wortz, Melinda. "'Five Footnotes to Modern Art History.'" *Art News* 76, no. 1 (Jan. 1977): 73–75.

# Photography Credits

Works by Lee Mullican illustrated in the catalogue are licensed and copyright protected under © Estate of Lee Mullican. Other works of art illustrated in the catalogue are licensed and copyright protected by the artist listed.

Most photographs are reproduced courtesy of the creators and lenders of the material depicted. For certain artworks and documentary photographs we have been unable to trace copyright holders. We would appreciate notification of additional credits for acknowledgment in future editions.

Front cover, pp. 2, 7, 14 bottom, 15, 17, 22, 25 bottom, 34 left, 35, 36 bottom, 37, 41, 44, 46 left, 51, 52, 54, 57, 58, 59, 60, 62, 90, 94, 101, 104, 105 bottom, 107 top, 108 top, 111 bottom, 112, 114, 115, 117, 118, back cover: © 2005 Museum Associates/LACMA; pp. 34 right, 63 left, 93: © 2005 Museum Associates/LACMA, Danny Bright; p. 86: © 1977 Museum Associates /LACMA
pp. 1, 27, 31, 49, 76, 88, 120, 122, 123: courtesy the Estate of Lee Mullican
pp. 8, 113: © 2004 Orange County Museum of Art, Chris Bliss
p. 10: © 2004 Fred Jones Museum of Art, Konrad Eek
p. 12: © The Phillips Collection, Edward Owen
pp. 13 bottom: © Weatherspoon Art Museum
pp. 16, 30 top, 53: © Lucid Art Foundation
pp. 18 top, 19 left, 24, 33 top, 36 top, 38, 39, 50, 56, 63 right, 74, 91, 92, 97, 98, 102, 107 bottom, 108 bottom, 109, 116: courtesy of Marc Selwyn Fine Art
p. 19 right: courtesy of Matt Mullican
p. 20: © The Research Library, The Getty Research Institute, Los Angeles
p. 21: © 1996 The Art Institute of Chicago
p. 25 top: I. Serisawa
p. 26, 30 bottom: © Ben Blackwell
p. 28: © The Walter J. Mann Company
pp. 32, 33 bottom: courtesy of the Wolfgang Paalen-Archiv, Berlin
p. 42 top: © 2005 Santa Barbara Museum of Art, Scott McClaine
p. 43: © Smith College of Art
p. 45: © 2004 Wendy McEahern
pp. 46 right, 61: © 2004 Dan Kramer
p. 47: © Museum of Modern Art, New York, courtesy of Art Resource
p. 55: © Rachel Rosenthal
pp. 64, 106: © UCLA Hammer Museum, Robert Wedemeyer
pp. 66, 69: © The Museum of Contemporary Art, Los Angeles
p. 95: © Alison Carroll
p. 100: © The Phillips Collection
p. 105 top: courtesy of The Museum of Modern Art, New York
p. 110 left: © The Museum of Contemporary Art, Los Angeles, Brian Forrest
p. 110 right: © Tony Cuhna
p. 111 top: © Artworks
p. 119: © Q Siebenthal
p. 121: © Oscar Savio